AN ANTHOLOGY
OF IRISH
LITERATURE

AN ANTHOLOGY OF IRISH LITERATURE

EDITED, WITH AN INTRODUCTION, BY

David H. Greene, NEW YORK UNIVERSITY

VOLUME I

New York University Press
New York

Library of Congress Catalog Card Number: 70-164022
ISBN: 0-8147-2953-3 (cloth)
ISBN: 0-8147-2954-1 (paper)
Manufactured in the United States of America

CONTENTS

Part II: Myth, Saga, and Romance

TRANSLATIONS FROM THE GAELIC

Part III: The Bardic Tradition

COURT POETRY TRANSLATED FROM THE GAELIC

Contents

ix

Contents

INTRODUCTION

I

IRELAND today is an independent republic with little but her independence to compensate her for centuries of agitation. She is dollar poor. Her population is shrinking because of emigration and the lowest marriage rate in Europe. The only influence she wields in the society of nations is through the millions of Irishmen who are citizens of other countries. But she helps feed other nations with her beef and potatoes, clothe them with her homespuns and make them happy with Jameson's Irish whiskey and Guinness' beer. She also continues to produce writers who display an attitude to their craft which can only be explained by the fact that an ancient poetic tradition is still alive.

The Celtic poet of old practiced his art according to rules which had been formulated as early as the eighth century and continued to be enunciated as late as the sixteenth century. His people considered him a vital part of their society and awarded him a privileged position, which he managed to retain among the country people at least until modern times. His power for satire made him so formidable a foe that nobody dare cross him. He once became the center of a fierce controversy in which he was accused of having too much power and threatened with banishment, but one of the greatest of Irish saints (St. Columkille) intervened in his behalf. Like the priest he eventually became the target of oppressive legislation directed at him by the English who conquered his people. Even today the title of poet has a meaning in Celtic countries which it does not have anywhere else in western Europe.

The modern Irish poet cannot fail to be aware of this. Neither exile—the customary fate of Irish writers—nor the fact that he writes in English, which his ancient predecessors consider'd the language of a foreign enemy, makes him any less conscious of the heritage. The greatest of modern Irish poets, who knew scarcely a word of Gaelic, wrote at the very threshold of his career, "Can we not build up . . . a national literature which shall be none the less Irish in spirit from being English in language?" Yeats knew that a literary movement taking its inspiration from the Gaelic past as the Irish Literary Revival did must avoid mere antiquarianism. "Can we not keep the continuity of the nation's life," he wrote, "by translating or retelling in English which shall have an indefinable Irish quality of rhythm and style, all that is best of the ancient literature? Can we not write and persuade others to write histories and romances of the great Gaelic men of the past, from the son of Nessa to Owen Roe, until there has been made a golden bridge between the old and the new?" The golden bridge between the old and the new was to be built by listening to the country people upon whose lips the tales of the Fiana were still alive, and who spoke English with that "indefinable Irish quality of rhythm and style." Irish writers, Synge wrote in the preface to one of his plays, "start with a chance that is not given to writers in places where the springtime of the local life has been forgotten, and the harvest is a memory only, and the straw has been turned into bricks."

II

LOOKING back to the earliest point in history where the tradition can be observed, we find that the poet of ancient Ireland, called a *fili*, was a professional who had gone through many years of training so that he could discharge the official duties of composing in verse the laws and genealogies, and listing the kings, festivals and traditions of his people. Much of what he wrote should probably be described as state papers, put into verse because they could more easily be memorized and recited by the bards, who were strictly performers, not composers, and who came to be the walking repositories of the national traditions. Many of the Irish manuscripts which have survived—there are, for example, more than thirteen hundred in the Royal Irish Academy alone—are treatises on ecclesiastical, historical and learned subjects having only a subsidiary interest for the student of imaginative literature. But the body

of narrative tales and poems of warfare, romance and adventure
—of deities or mortals, or of both—is impressive in bulk and
imaginative power and is probably older than the vernacular
literature of any other western European people.

The story of how this literature of the ancient Celt has
come down to us largely centers about the scribe, that consum-
mate artist who copied, illustrated and annotated the great
stories of his people and treasured up the lifeblood of long-
dead master spirits in great folio vellum manuscripts—each
one of them a whole library in itself. *The Book of the Dun
Cow*, the work of a scribe who died in 1106, gives us many of
the Ulster sagas and some Fenian pieces. *The Book of Leinster*,
written before 1160, gives us history, genealogy, imaginative
stories of place names, poetry and some of the same stories
found in *The Book of the Dun Cow*. *The Great Book of Lecan*,
The Book of Hy Many, *The Book of Ballymote*, *The Speckled
Book of MacEgan*, *The Book of Lismore* and *The Book of
Fermoy*, all written in the fourteenth and fifteenth centuries,
are some of the other important manuscripts.

Since none of these compilations was made before the
twelfth century, the language of the tales they give us is largely
Middle Irish. The stories themselves, however, are not of the
Middle Irish period but are for the most part Old Irish texts
modernized by the scribe, who altered the language so as to
bring it into some agreement with that of his own day. It
has been possible to determine on the basis of the Old Irish
word forms and inflectional marks which still remain in a
twelfth-century text that the story it tells has gone through
several such modernizations since it was first committed to
writing some three or four hundred years earlier.

For our knowledge of Old Irish we are chiefly indebted not
to the scribe who compiled the great Middle Irish vellums of
the twelfth and succeeding centuries but to his predecessor
of the ninth century, particularly the scribe in the Irish monas-
teries on the continent who in transcribing a text of St. Paul or
Priscian was given to providing his reader with marginal para-
phrases or amplifications of the text, not in Latin but in his
native language. It was these Old Irish glosses which supplied

modern philologists with the key to the language of ancient
Ireland. In addition to glossing his text—and this appears to
have been characteristic of only Irish scribes at this time—the
Irish scribe also used the margins for recording personal ob-
servations, prayers to his favorite saint and snatches of poetry
from his native land. Thus we find in a manuscript of Priscian
in the monastery of St. Gall, Switzerland, a short poem on
the enjoyment a scribe has working in the open air after a long
winter indoors ("The Scribe," p. 10) and a quatrain com-
menting on the fact that although bad weather is uncomfort-
able it discourages Viking raids ("The Viking Terror," p. 3).
In a codex of St. Paul in the monastery of St. Paul in Carinthia,
Austria, we find a poem in praise of a Leinster chieftain named
Aed ("In Praise of Aed," p. 9) and the celebrated poem about
a scholar and his favorite cat ("Pangur Ban," p. 11).

These brief lyrics—originally the work of hermit poet and
fili of the seventh, eighth and ninth centuries—are the earliest
examples we have in manuscript of the imaginative literature
of the medieval Celt. Not all of them are preserved in conti-
nental manuscripts. For example, *The Martyrology of Angus
the Culdee*, from which a charming poem about St. Ita (p. 13)
who nurses the baby Jesus in a vision is taken, is a ninth- or
tenth-century festology or calendar of saints' days, composed
in Ireland by a monk named Angus. (*Culdee* in Old Irish
means *fellow of God* and was apparently used to describe an
ascetic monk.) Angus was patriotic. In recording the festivals
of saints he was partial to Irish saints, particularly if they also
had some claim to literary eminence. His glosses and notes are
extensive. They give us, for example, a personal description of
St. Columkille and tell a story about the subject of the poem
"On a Dead Scholar" (p. 14) who was "master in theology,
in history, in Brehon law and in poetry" and who greedily hid
his books so that St. Columkille, who was visiting him, could
not borrow them. "So Columkille left a curse on the books,"
writes Angus. " 'May that which thou grudgest be useless after
thee,' said he. And so it was, for the books abide still, but no
man can read them."

Turning from these glosses to the longer pieces preserved in

the great vellum manuscripts of the Middle Irish peiiod, we
find the bulk of early Irish imaginative literature classified into
types. The most famous group of stories is the Ulster cycle.
Cuchulain, about whom Yeats wrote no fewer than five plays,
is the central hero. The stories deal with the ancient kingdom
of Ulster, its king Conchubor MacNessa and the warriors of
the Red Branch House. Modern scholarship and tradition agree
in assigning a date of the first century before Christ to the
heroes and events. But the stories did not assume literary form
until the seventh century, and they have come down to us in
recensions made no earlier than the eighth century.

The Cattle Raid of Cooley, the great epic of the Ulster
cycle, which tells the story of how Maeve, queen of Connaught, stole a prize bull and fought a war over it with Cuchulain and the men of Ulster, is preserved in *The Book of the
Dun Cow* and also in *The Book of Leinster.* Cuchulain had to
fight Maeve's army single-handed because the men of Ulster
were all stricken with birth pangs as the result of an ancient
curse levelled against them for an indignity they once admin-
istered to a pregnant goddess. Among Cuchulain's feats was
the defeat of Ferdiad, his boyhood friend and sworn brother,
who with other Ulster warriors had gone over to the enemy
after the betrayal of the sons of Usnech by Conchubor, the
king of Ulster. The lamentation (p. 66) which the hero
utters over the body of his friend is one of the most moving
passages in Irish literature.

"The Tragic Death of Connla" (p. 61), preserved in *The
Yellow Book of Lecan,* is an Irish equivalent of the story of
Sohrab and Rustum. When Cuchulain was in Scotland he defeated and seduced an amazon named Aife, who gave birth to
his son. When the boy Connla came to Ireland he was forced
into a fight to the death with his own father because he had
been instructed never to refuse combat and never to divulge
his identity on demand. Such injunctions, by which many Irish
heroes, including Cuchulain, were bound, were called *geasa.*
Modern readers are familiar with the story through Yeats's
poem "Cuchulain's Fight With the Sea" (p. 428) and his play
On Baile's Strand, in which the hero is deluded by a Druid's

spell into taking his anger out on the waves of the sea, a modern addition to the story.

But heroes must die, and the story of Cuchulain's death is told in "The Death of Cuchulain" (p. 68), from *The Book of Leinster*. The story has survived in a fragment, however, and we must go to later versions to learn that Cuchulain's old enemy Maeve assembles another army, supplemented this time by the sons of men whom Cuchulain had killed. She once more times her attack so that he has to fight singlehanded, this time knowing that he is doomed because he has violated one of his *geasa*. Help from the men of Ulster does not arrive until Cuchulain has died against a stone pillar to which he had lashed himself with his belt so that he might meet death on his feet.

The most famous single story from the Ulster cycle, however, does not deal with Cuchulain but with Deirdre. "The Story of Deirdre" (p. 76), from *The Book of Leinster*, has furnished many modern Irish writers, including Yeats, Synge (p. 451), AE and James Stephens, with a theme for tragedy, epic or romance. In its essentials—the destruction of Deirdre and her lover Naisi by Deirdre's betrothed, Conchubor— it resembles the story of Tristan and Iseult and also the great romance of the Fenian cycle, "The Pursuit of Diarmait and Grania."

The next great collection of stories is the Fenian cycle, which deals with bands of semi-nomadic warriors known as the *fiana*. The most important of the leaders of the *fiana* was Finn MacCumail, whose *fian*, it appears, was composed of two clans, one commanded by himself, the other by Goll MacMorna, who had slain Finn's father at the battle of Cnucha. Though Finn is at first reconciled to Goll, warfare ultimately breaks out between the two clans and Goll is destroyed. Other heroes associated with Finn are his son Oisin, Oscar son of Oisin, Cailte son of Ronan and Diarmait, who elopes with Grania, Finn's betrothed. In modern times Oisin's fame eclipsed his father's when the eighteenth-century Scottish poet James Macpherson published "An Ancient Epic Poem in Six Books" purporting to be a translation of a third-century Fenian poem written by

Oisin. Macpherson's *Fingal* took the public by storm, and
before the fraud was exposed the Fenian hero had become
famous throughout Europe, then in the grip of the romantic
movement, as an example of "the noble savage."

Finn and his companions are generally believed to have lived
in the third century, three hundred years later than Cuchulain.
There are other differences between the two cycles. The action
of the Ulster cycle is located mainly in Connaught and Ulster,
the north of Ireland, the texts are mostly of the Old Irish or
early Middle Irish periods and the tales are heroic in temper.
They give the impression of having been the property of an
aristocratic people who were preserving the record of their own
past. The action of the Fenian cycle is confined mainly to
Leinster and Munster, the south of Ireland, the texts are
mostly of the late Middle Irish period and the tales and poems
are romantic in temper, their most characteristic form being
the ballad. They give the impression of having been the property of a subject race. Finally the *Fiana*, with their strange
initiation rites, are a feature of the Fenian tradition for which
there is no parallel in the older cycle. The warrior had to pass
prescribed physical ordeals, excel in the twelve traditional forms
of poetry and renounce family life within the tribe for a life
outside it ("The Fianna," p. 95).

"The Colloquy of the Old Men" (p. 81), preserved in two
fifteenth-century manuscripts and in a manuscript of the
seventeenth century, is a formless compilation of Fenian
stories from many sources, some of them clearly inconsistent
with others. The narrative tells how a handful of warriors,
including Oisin and Cailte, not only survived the disastrous
defeat of Finn and his *fian* at the Battle of Ventry but also
managed to live for a century and a half after the battle so that
they could meet St. Patrick and regale him with stories of the
heroic past. After visiting Finn's old governess, who has also
defied the ravages of time, Oisin disappears forever into a fairy
mound, but Cailte and his companions go south to Tara. The
meeting with St. Patrick results in the conversion of the
Fenians to Christianity. The stories which Cailte tells of the
mighty Finn enthrall the saint and his clerics so much that

Patrick has a guilty conscience. Finally his two guardian angels assure him that it is not only proper for him to listen to pagan tales but necessary so that he might be the agent of the preservation for posterity. The pleasant synthesis of Fenian paganism and Patrician Christianity contrasts sharply with a later ballad on the same theme in which St. Patrick denounces the Fenians as sinful pagans and is defiantly told that it is better to be in Hell with Finn than in heaven with flimsy angels.

"The Colloquy of the Old Men" bears an obvious relationship to "Oisin in the Land of Youth" (p. 105), a poem written by an eighteenth-century poet named Michael Comyn, in which Oisin's longevity is explained by his having been in _Tir na n-Og_, a kind of Celtic Shangrila. Comyn's poem is one of the great achievements of later Gaelic poetry. Published with translation for the first time in 1859 in _The Transactions of the Ossianic Society_, it provided Yeats with the material for his narrative poem "The Wanderings of Oisin."

The other great collection of Fenian stories is "The Poem Book of Finn," a seventeenth-century manuscript with an interesting history of its own. Characteristic of the stories in this collection are "The Headless Phantoms" (p. 96), in which Finn and his companions fight a desperate hand-to-hand encounter in a darkened house with headless apparitions; "The Bathing of Oisin's Head" (p. 100), in which the aged warrior on his deathbed laments the passing of "the fair hair that all men saw on my head; it has left me for good and all, till I am a disease-smitten grey-face"; and "Goll's Parting With His Wife" (p. 103), in which Finn's rival, cornered by his enemy on a crag, urges his wife to leave him before he is slain.

Not all, or necessarily the best, of early Irish literature belongs to these two heroic cycles. The mythological cycle, for example, which is made up of tales dealing with exploits of supernatural beings from the Celtic pantheon, contains some of the best stories in Irish literature. "The Dream of Oenghus" (p. 39), which gave Yeats the material for one of his poems, tells the story of Angus Og the master of love, who pined for a girl he had seen in a dream only to discover when he found her in the flesh, after long searching, that it was swan's flesh

How he became a swan in order to "paddle in the cold companionable streams or climb the air" with her provides an interesting contrast to the classical myth in which Zeus became a swan in order to effect a union with a mortal.

The ancient Celt was apparently fond of tall tales and adventures, if one can judge by the texts which have come down to us. The early scribes distinguished between a Voyage (*Imram*), which was merely a traveller's tale, and an Adventure (*Echtrae*), which was an account of a visit to the other world. Only three Voyages have survived, the most interesting being "The Voyage of Maelduin," which apparently influenced the author of the famous medieval story of the voyage of St. Brendan the Navigator. *The Voyage of Bran* (p. 131) is perhaps the best known of the Adventures. It is preserved in seven different manuscripts, the oldest of which, from *The Book of the Dun Cow*, is unfortunately a fragment. Kuno Meyer, who published an edition of the text in 1895, was able to reconstruct the entire poem from later copies belonging to the fourteenth, fifteenth and sixteenth centuries.

The Frenzy of Suibhne ("Mad Sweeney" p. 143), a Middle Irish romance, belongs to the Historical cycle, or the "Cycles of the Kings" as these tales are frequently referred to. Although the action in these stories, unlike that in the Ulster, Fenian or Mythological cycles, the Adventures or the Voyages, revolves around historical personages, the blending of history and legend is frequently so complete as to make it impossible for the modern reader to distinguish fact form fiction. Certainly the author of *The Frenzy of Suibhne* found the historical framework of his story no deterrent in utilizing legendary material or in exercising his imagination. The madness which came upon Sweeney, ruler of a petty kingdom in southern Antrim and County Down, was the result of a curse laid upon him by St. Ronan. Sweeney had interrupted the saint in the act of pacing off boundaries for a new church by throwing the saint's psalter into the lake and laying hands on him. The saint was saved by the arrival of a messenger summoning Sweeney to the battle of Mag Rath, an actual battle fought in 637 between the king of Ireland and the king of Dal Riada,

an Irish kingdom in Scotland which included a small part of
Ulster. Sweeney's wits went astray at the height of the battle,
and he fled thenceforth to wander naked through Ireland,
flitting from tree to tree like a bird. Whether or not the remarkable poetry which Sweeney utters was part of the meta-
morphosis which the saint prophesied is not made clear. But
Sweeney mad achieved a fame which Sweeney sane could only
have envied. George Moore believed that the story of Sweeney's
madness was one of the world's great stories. Flann O'Brien is
indebted to it for the motif—and large parts of the text—of his
satire *At Swim-Two-Birds*. William Saroyan is indebted to it
for the title of his play *Sweeney in the Trees*. Although *The
Frenzy of Suibhne* survives in three relatively late manuscripts,
the most important having been written between 1671 and
1674 in County Sligo, the story is older than the twelfth century. In fact a poem called "The Ivy Crest" (p. 19) is attributed to Sweeney the Mad in a ninth-century manuscript.

III

AFTER THE Norman invasion of Ireland in 1170 the rule of the
fili, who composed poetry, blended with that of the bard, who
recited it. The word *bard* is Celtic and during the Middle Irish
period, between the twelfth and seventeenth centuries, was
applied to a professional poet attached to the household of a
chieftain whose achievements he recorded and recited in verse.
The bardic poet belonged to a privileged, hereditary class and
practiced a profession in which membership was carefully re-
stricted on a family basis. The poetry he wrote was dominated
by formal conventions. The tricks of the trade were passed on
only to those who were eligible and willing to study for six or
seven years in a school presided over by a master bard.

A trustworthy account of life in the Irish bardic schools,
written before 1722 in Tipperary where the tradition lingered,
tells us that the neophyte attended regular classes during a
school term which ran from November to March, lived in a
cubicle and did homework which consisted of composing a
poem on an assigned theme while he lay in darkness upon his
bed. In the morning he recited his poem to the teacher who

criticized it. Although the core of the curriculum was obviously metrics—bardic poetry was written in complicated meters and was characterized by an elaborate system of rhyme, assonance, consonance and alliteration—the student had also to acquire a knowledge of the legends and history of his people and become an educated man generally.

Edmund Spenser was almost certainly describing bardic poems of the formal kind when he wrote in *A View of the Present State of Ireland,*

> I have caused divers of them to be translated unto me, that I might understand them; and surely they savoured of sweet wit and good invention, but skilled not of the goodly ornaments of poetry; yet were they sprinkled with some pretty flowers of their natural device which gave good grace and comeliness unto them, the which it is great pity to see so abused, to the gracing of wickedness and vice, which with good usage would serve to adorn and beautify virtue. This evil custom therefore needeth reformation.

It hardly needs to be pointed out that Spenser was an enemy and that he held an altogether different view of the nature and function of poetry. His judgment upon this "evil custom" was prompted more by political than aesthetic considerations, for the Irish bardic poet exercised a political influence which made him dangerous. Had not The Statute of Kilkenny in the fourteenth century forbade under penalty of heavy fine the harboring or encouraging of Irish minstrels, rhymers or taletellers?

The influence of the bard was not entirely secular. There is evidence which indicates that bardic schools were sometimes affiliated with monastic schools so that the training of both bard and cleric could be mutually enriched. We have a large body of religious poetry written within the bardic tradition. But mostly the bard depended for his existence upon a society composed of powerful clans and ruled over by affluent chieftains. After the Williamite War of the seventeenth century, when the Gaelic order had been destroyed and the last of the chieftains had fled to the continent, the bard fell on evil days.

Looking through the volumes of bardic poetry which have

been published by the Irish Texts Society, one wonders why
Irish poetry allowed itself to get sidetracked for nearly four
hundred years. The bard was a professional and seldom put
his pen to any use for which he was not paid. And since he was
paid chiefly to compose only formal verse which glorified his
patron we can thank him for little of the personal or popular
poetry written in Ireland during the period. With few exceptions, therefore, the bardic poems do not appeal to modern
taste any more than they did to Spenser's. In fact the only
good one can see in a system which left the writing of personal
verse largely to amateurs, discouraged originality of thought
or expression, and made writing poetry a mystery into which
only the elite could be initiated was that it helped to save the
language, preserved the tradition and gave Irish writers of a
later period the historical sense so indispensable, as T. S. Eliot
says, to a literature that would achieve maturity.

The most famous of the court poets would appear to have
been Tadhg Dall O'Huiginn. Of the forty poems ascribed to
him which survive in manuscript copies none are in the author's hand and only two could have been copied in his life-
time. According to the popular traditions about him which
flourished as late as the eighteenth century, he was born about
1550 and brought up in Donegal, was attached to the household of the chieftain O'Connor Sligo, was blind for all or
most of his life—his middle name means *blind*—and was murdered in 1593 by members of the O'Hara clan whom he had
satirized in one of his poems. Tradition has apparently been
more faithful in preserving biographical facts about him than
it has the texts of his poems, for his editor Eleanor Knott be-
lieves that the surviving poems represent only a small part of
his entire work.

Six years after their defeat at Kinsale in 1601, the earls of
Tyrone (Hugh O'Neill) and Tyrconnell (Rory O'Donnell,
the brother of Red Hugh O'Donnell) fled to the continent
with the surviving members of their clans. What remained of
the Gaelic aristocracy was either destroyed or driven into exile
during the Williamite War of 1690-91. The bardic poet was
then left high and dry, without patron or audience and sur-

rounded by a people who, even if they had a taste for his for-
malized and sophisticated verse, had not the means to sub-
sidize it. Complains one poet,

> Her chiefs are gone. There's none to bear
> Her cross or lift her from despair;
> The grieving lords take ship. With these
> Our very souls pass overseas. (p. 199)

And another,

> Ask but a lodging for the night
> And all men turn you from the door. (p. 197)

The bardic poet who achieved the greatest influence, though
not because of his verse, was Geoffrey Keating, the Irish
Herodotus, who was born about 1570 in Tipperary of Anglo-
Norman stock. Keating is the bridge between ancient and
modern Ireland, for his *History of Ireland* marks the beginning
of modern Irish literature and at the same time is one of our
most important sources of information about medieval Ireland. It was Keating who during the darkest days kept alive
in the people a feeling for their own past. Educated for the
priesthood on the continent, he returned to Tipperary about
1610 and lived the life of a parish priest until he was forced
to take to the hills as a fugitive because an influential woman
parishioner whom he had publicly reprimanded for loose
morals brought the soldiers of the crown after him. The *History of Ireland* was apparently written before 1640, during the
years when he was either hiding in the glens or, as tradition
has it, travelling in disguise throughout the country. Eventually he was able to come out of hiding and return to his
parish, where he died about 1650. The *History of Ireland*
seems to have been the most popular book ever written in
Irish. Literally hundreds of transcripts of it were made and
continued to be made over one hundred years after it had been
printed in an English translation in 1723. In fact it was probably the last important book in western Europe to circulate in
manuscript.

IV

NATURALLY not all Irish poetry written between the twelfth
and the seventeenth centuries was the work of professional
poets. Gifted amateurs like Gerald Fitzgerald, the Earl of
Desmond, in the fourteenth century, Manus O'Donnell in
the sixteenth century, or semi-professionals like Pierce Ferriter
in the seventeenth century were writing lyric poetry that was
more popular than the set pieces which were the bardic poet's
stock in trade. A collection of love lyrics written during this
period has been edited by T. F. O'Rahilly (*Danta Gradha*,
Cork, 1926) and a good many of them have been translated
by Robin Flower, Frank O'Connor and the Earl of Longford.
Flower claimed that the Irish love lyric developed out of a
French original imported from Europe by the Normans but
that it took "a very different form, extremely characteristic of
the Irish situation." In translation, however, most of these
lyrics are little different in either theme or manner from the
English love lyric of the same period. Desmond's "Against
Blame of Women" (p. 219) and Pierce Ferriter's "He Charges
Her to Lay Aside Her Weapons" (p. 235), for example, could
easily have been written by English poets. One novel adapta-
tion of the form which was distinctly Irish, however, may be
seen in the kind of poem of which "Dark Rosaleen" (p. 226)
is the most celebrated example—the love lyric in praise of a
woman who is Ireland. The usual explanation of this phe-
nomenon is that the singing of patriotic songs was illegal, like
the wearing of the green, and patriotic verse had to assume an
erotic disguise.

Readers of Daniel Corkery's *The Hidden Ireland* know that
Gaelic poetry of distinction was written throughout the darkest
days of the eighteenth century. In fact three poems written in
this period—Michael Comyn's "Oisin in the Land of Youth"
(p. 105), Eileen O'Leary's "The Lament for Art O'Leary" (p.
241), and Brian Merriman's "The Midnight Court" (p. 252)
—are as remarkable as anything in Irish literature. Eileen
O'Leary was the aunt of Daniel O'Connell, the great nineteenth-century patriot. When her husband was murdered in

1773 by soldiers in the employ of an enemy she composed a lament modelled upon a traditional kind of utterance called a keen. The practice of keening, which Edmund Spenser described as "lamentations at their burials with dispairful outcries and immoderate wailings," is a primitive custom which had the significance of ritual in the early history of the race. The custom was peculiar to Ireland to the extent only that it survived almost to our own day. J. M. Synge saw women keening in the Aran Islands as recently as 1898 and described the scene in a notable passage. "Each old woman, as she took her turn in the leading recitative, seemed possessed for the moment with a profound ecstasy of grief swaying to and fro, and bending her forehead to the stone before her, while she called out to the dead with a perpetually recurring chant of sobs."

Out of this primitive custom developed a form of literary composition which F. B. Gummere, who saw keening in the Isle of Man, described as "never-ending, intricate, genealogical verses." A nineteenth-century collector named Thomas Crofton Croker translated and published a number of these compositions in *The Keen of the South of Ireland* (London, 1844). "The Lament for Art O'Leary," which its translator Frank O'Connor describes as "first and foremost a ritual over the dead, with its dramatised characters, its story-telling, its chorus of cloaked weepers who keep up a continuous humming and break in at some moment of excitement with shrill cries," is not so far removed from the "dispairful outcries and immoderate wailings" which Spenser described. When one considers the associations with the racial past which such a poem suggests it does not seem so strange that it should exist only in two modern texts both of which had to be assembled entirely from oral sources.

Not much is known about the author or the composition of "The Midnight Court," that strange masterpiece of Gaelic mockery. Brian Merriman's brief obituary in a Limerick newspaper gives us the only solid facts we have about him—that he was a teacher of mathematics and that he died in that city on July 27, 1805. If one can conclude anything from the evidence of the poem, he was a native of Clare, well-educated and a Protestant—though it has been argued from the same evidence that he was a Roman Catholic. "The Midnight Court" is a vision poem and to that extent belongs to a native genre. But it is written in the idiom of Merriman's own day and not in the formal language of the bardic schools. Moreover, as Frank O'Connor points out, the poem is classical in temper and has a closer kinship with English poetry of Merriman's day than with native literary tradition. Whatever the major influences on Merriman may have been, one thing is clear. His poem deals with an Irish problem which is even more acute today than it was in Merriman's day—the lack of enthusiasm which Irishmen demonstrate for matrimony. According to the census figures of 1946 more than 80 percent of the men between twenty-five and thirty years of age, and 63 percent of the men between thirty and thirty-five, are unmarried. Many writers have called attention to these figures, and some have even seen in the population decline which is obviously explained by it the eventual disappearance of the Irish people. Is it any wonder that the young girl in Merriman's poem should complain,

> For here I am at the place I started,
> And this is the cause of all my tears,
> I am fast in the rope of the rushing years
> With age and want in lessening span
> And death at the end and no hopes of a man.

V

THE READER who finds it a paradox that so much of Ireland's literature should be written in English, some of it indeed at a time when Irish was still spoken by a majority of the people who lived there, need only think of the ironic fact that Ireland was a colony and at the same time a mother country. Up to the time of Elizabeth I, when a new wave of English conquest and colonization began, Ireland had been able to absorb and even Hibernicize her invaders. But the colonists who flocked into Ireland in 1586 with the plantation of Munster—they

included Sir Walter Raleigh and Edmund Spenser—were not
to be absorbed as their Anglo-Norman predecessors had been.
They settled down on their newly acquired lands, survived the
rebellion led by Hugh O'Neill and Hugh O'Donnell at the
end of the sixteenth century, the Ulster rebellion of 1641 and
the Cromwellian and Williamite wars of the seventeenth century. During these two troublous centuries they maintained
their link with the crown, their language, their religion and
their culture. By the beginning of the eighteenth century the
country was in their hands and the native Gael was groaning
under the infamous penal laws which were designed to sub-
due him by destroying his culture, his language and his priests.

One need only turn to Lecky's *History of Ireland in the
Eighteenth Century*, to the accounts of European travellers
in Ireland, or to Swift's great satire "A Modest Proposal" (p
299), for an indication of how life in the hovel differed from
life in the big house. "It is a melancholy object to those who
walk through this great town [Dublin] or travel in the country
when they see the streets, the roads and cabin doors crowded
with beggars of the female sex, followed by three, four, or six
children, all in rags and importuning every passenger for an
alms."

Needless to say the penal laws did not wholly succeed. The
priest and the schoolmaster took to the hills and the hedges,
the old traditions survived—even if it seemed that the people
would not—and throughout the eighteenth century at least
native poets continued to compose in Gaelic for the people
outside the cities and the Pale who could still understand and
appreciate them.

But if the period which began with the Treaty of Limerick
in 1691 saw the complete ascendancy of the Anglo-Irish, it
also witnessed the gradual rift between the Anglo-Irish and
the crown. It is one of the ironies of Irish history that the descendants of those Elizabethan, Stuart, Cromwellians and
Williamite settlers who had resisted absorption by the native
Irish, now began to resist domination by the crown. No longer
in fact English but Anglo-Irish, they had begun to erect the
big houses, develop a distinctive culture of their own and

build up industries which placed them into direct competition
with England. It was no longer the impoverished and dis-
franchised Celts who provided rich pickings for the royal
treasury but the landowning Anglo-Irish capitalists who were
building breweries, manufacturing silk, glass and pottery, and
establishing a linen and a cotton industry. When the mother
country systematically destroyed their industries and by the
Act of Union in 1800 abolished their parliament, the gap between English and Anglo-Irish was nearly as great as that between Irish and Anglo-Irish. It was not a Celt but an Anglo-
Irishman who wrote in *The Drapier's Letters*, "Am I a freeman
in England, and do I become a slave in six hours by crossing
the Channel?" Henceforth the great rebel leaders for a whole
century from Wolfe Tone to Parnell were to be, with few exceptions, Anglo-Irishmen. One final irony is to be seen in the
fact that when at the end of the nineteenth century Ireland
began to reconstruct a picture of her ancient past, the chief
figures in the movement known as the Irish Literary Revival
were, at first, men whose ancestors were not Celts but Saxons.
Today the Anglo-Irish, who are mostly Episcopalians and members of the Church of Ireland, comprise only 6 percent of the
population of the Republic of Ireland. Unlike the Scottish
Presbyterians on the other side of the border in northeast
Ulster, they have lost their political influence, seen their big
houses go up in flames during the troubles or be taken over
by a Free State government and even yielded their leader-
ship in the arts.

One might then ask how many of Ireland's writers who wrote
in English had any awareness of Gaelic Ireland. Or to put it
more directly, how many of the writers represented in Part
V of this book had any knowledge of the literature represented
in Parts I through IV. With few exceptions the literature in
English written before the nineteenth century—while the
Gaelic tradition was still intact—was the work of Anglo-Irish,
Protestant writers. Of the first four selections in Part V, the
only one which can with certainty be ascribed to an author
resident in Ireland complains about fraternization and the evil
that will result if the garrison continues to adopt native customs

and speak the language of the natives ("An Anglo-Irishman's Complaint," p. 298). With the next two selections we jump over a vast territory but a bleak one to the eighteenth century and to Swift and Goldsmith, who were born and educated in Ireland but are better known for their contributions to the literature of England.

For the nineteenth century the story is the same. Of the nine writers represented who predate the Literary Revival—which began in the nineties—six were educated at Trinity College, the fountainhead of Ascendancy culture (Moore, Lever, Ferguson, DeVere, Todhunter and Larminie). Only one of the nine came from Irish peasant stock and had heard Gaelic spoken in his youth (Carleton). One was a serious student of Gaelic antiquity (Ferguson). One is credited with being successful in capturing an authentic note in his adaptations of Gaelic poems, though he knew no Gaelic and was forced to work from English translations (Mangan). Thomas Moore, the most famous of the nine and known throughout the English-speaking world as the national poet of Ireland, has been treated harshly by some Irish writers of the twentieth century and described as "an old shopkeeper who had dealt in the marrowbone of his neighbors"[1] and as "a Firbolg in the borrowed cloak of a Milesian."[2]

By 1890, the picture begins to change. The story of the Irish Literary Revival which produced Synge, O'Casey, Yeats and Joyce, to mention only the Titans, is well known and does not need repeating here. Yeats, Lady Gregory, George Moore and Synge founded their movement upon the rediscovery of Gaelic Ireland and the common people, whom AE once described as the descendants of Oscar and Cuchulain. Lady Gregory retold the ancient stories of the heroic past, Yeats wrote

---

[1] Patrick Kavanagh, "A Wreath for Tom Moore's Statue," *A Soul for Sale* (London, 1947), p. 29.

[2] James Joyce, *A Portrait of the Artist as a Young Man* (New York, The Modern Library), p. 209. The Firbolgs were one of the pre-Gaelic peoples of Ireland, described in the legends as small, dark and evil. The Milesians were the last invaders of ancient Ireland and the legendary founders of the Celtic aristocracy.

"The Wanderings of Oisin" and "Cathleen Ni Houlihan," and Synge went to the Aran Islands to study the peasant and, in Yeats's words, "to express a life that has never found expression." But the fact is that the native Celt had never really lost the ability to express his own life. He needed only the new Ireland, with its language revival, its national theatre, and its new burst of revolutionary zeal to give him his opportunity. Yeats, Lady Gregory, George Moore and Synge gave him his new models. Only twenty-five years separate Synge's visit to Aran and the arrival upon the literary scene of one of those Aran peasants—Liam O'Flaherty.

Perhaps these facts explain why the literature of modern Ireland, unlike the literature of ancient Ireland, is largely in English. The term Anglo-Irish cannot accurately be applied to all the literature in English any more than the term Irish can be exclusively reserved for the literature in Gaelic. It would be just as absurd to assume that all the literature in English was written by Anglo-Irishmen as it would be to claim that all Irishmen write in Gaelic. The fact is that the literature of the last two centuries and a half is bilingual, and one is forced to describe all of it as Irish.

DAVID H. GREENE

ACKNOWLEDGMENTS

I am indebted to the following people for their suggestions, criticism, and help on textual matters: Russell Alspach, John Fisher, Devin Garrity, John Kelleher, David McDowell, Vivian Mercier, Frank O'Connor, Karl Pfeiffer, Horace Reynolds, my wife Catherine Greene and my editors Leonore Crary and Jess Stein.

Acknowledgments are also due to the following publishers and individuals who have granted permission for the inclusion of material in this book:

George Allen & Unwin Ltd. and Random House, Inc., for the excerpt from *Deirdre of the Sorrows* by J. M. Synge. Copyright renewed 1937, by the executors of the estate of John M. Synge .

Ernest Benn Ltd.:

> For "The Brow of Nephin," "My Grief on the Sea," "Ringletted Youth of My Love," and "I Shall Not Die for Thee," from Douglas Hyde's *Love Songs of Connaught*. By permission also of Dr. Hyde's executors, The Royal Bank of Ireland.
>
> For "The Croppy Boy" from Donagh MacDonagh's *Literature in Ireland*.
>
> For "Cuchulain's Lament for Ferdiad" from George Sigerson's *Bards of the Gael and the Gall*.

Daniel Binchy and R. J. Best, as executors of the estate of Osborn Bergin, for "On the Breaking-Up of a School," translated by Osborn Bergin.

The Henry Bradshaw Society for the version of "The Vision of Ita" by Whitley Stokes.

Cambridge University Press, for "Cokaygne," "The Irish Dancer," "A Rhyme-beginning Fragment," and "An Anglo-Irishman's Complaint" from St. John Seymour's *Anglo-Irish Literature*.

Simon Campbell, for the following poems by Joseph Campbell: "The Old Age Pensioner," "The Unfrocked Priest," "I Am the Mountainy Singer," "I Am the Gilly of Christ," "As I Came Over the Grey, Grey Hills," "The Herb Leech," and "I Will Go with My Father A-Ploughing."

The Clarendon Press, Oxford, and Dr. Robin Flower, for the following poems from *The Irish Tradition*: "Pangur Ban," "In Praise of Aed," "The Ivy Crest," "On a Dead Scholar," "He That Never Read a Line,"

"A Storm at Sea," "Death's Warning to Beauty," "Of Women No More Evil," "No Sufferer for her Love," "He Praises His Wife When She Has Left Him," "The Good Tradition," "On the Flight of the Earls," and "Were Not the Gael Fallen."

Constable & Co. Ltd., for the following translations from Kuno Meyer's *Selections from Ancient Irish Poetry*: "The Deer's Cry," "To Crinog," "A Song of Winter," "St. Columcille the Scribe," "The Scribe," "The Blackbird," "The Pilgrim at Rome," "The Church Bell in the Night."

The Devin-Adair Company:

> For "A Drover" and "A Poor Scholar of the 'Forties" by Padraic Colum.
>
> For "Night and Morning," "Tenebrae," and "The Straying Student" by Austin Clarke.
>
> For "The Crab Tree," "Ringsend," "Exorcism," "To the Liffey with the Swans," "Per Iter Tenebricosum," "Verse," "To the Maids not to Walk in the Wind," "To W. B. Yeats, who says that his Castle of Ballylee is his Monument," and "Leda and the Swan" by Oliver St. John Gogarty.

Doubleday and Company, Inc., for "A Difficult Question" from *The Land of Spices* by Kate O'Brien. Copyright 1941 by Kate O'Brien. Reprinted by permission of Doubleday & Company, Inc.

John Farquharson, London, for "Poisson d'Avril" from *Further Experiences of an Irish R.M.* by E. Œ. Somerville and Martin Ross.

Farrar, Straus and Young, Inc., for "Lent," "Christ Walking on the Water," "The Net," and "Spring" from *Europa and the Bull*, Copyright 1952 by W. R. Rodgers, Farrar, Straus and Young, Inc., publishers.

M. H. Gill & Son Ltd., for "Dark Rosaleen," "The Woman of Three Cows," "Lamentation of Mac Liag for Kincora," "The Geraldine's Daughter," "A Vision of Connaught in the Thirteenth Century," and "To My Native Land" from *Poems* by James Clarence Mangan.

Harcourt, Brace and Company, Inc. and Martin Secker & Warburg Ltd., for "The Raider" from *Awake! and Other Wartime Poems* by W. R. Rodgers. Reprinted by permission of Harcourt, Brace and Company, Inc.

Harvard University Press and Routledge and Kegan Paul Ltd.:

> For "The Story of Deirdre," "The Dream of Oenghus," "Reconciliation," "Do Not Torment Me, Woman," "Winter has Come," "The Praises of God," "Civil Irish and Wild Irish," "Egan

O'Rahilly and the Minister," "Who Will Buy a Poem," "St. Columba's Island Heritage," "The Wish of Manchin of Liath," "I Should Like to Have a Great Pool of Ale" from Kenneth Jackson, A Celtic Miscellany; and "The Convict of Clonmel" from Geoffrey Taylor, editor, Irish Poets of the 19th Century (The Muses' Library). Cambridge, Mass.: Harvard University Press, 1951.

Hodges, Figgis & Co. Ltd. and the Earl of Longford, for "Against Blame of Women," "He Praises Her Hair," and "He Charges Her to Lay Aside Her Weapons," from Poems from the Irish; and "The First Vision" and "The Second Vision" from Dove in the Castle.

The Irish Texts Society, for "The Headless Phantoms," "The Bathing of Oisin's Head," "Goll's Parting With His Wife," from Duanaire Finn; "Maelmora MacSweeney" from The Bardic Poems of Tadhg Dall O'Huiginn; "Sweeney the Mad" from The Adventures of Suibhne Geilt; and all the selections from The History of Ireland by Geoffrey Keating.

The Irish Times, Dublin, for "If Ever You Go To Dublin Town," by Patrick Kavanagh.

The Macmillan Company:

For "Cuchulain's Fight with the Sea," "The Folly of Being Comforted," "To a Shade," "In Memory of Robert Gregory," "Sailing to Byzantium," "Leda and the Swan," "Among School Children," "The Wild Old Wicked Man," and "The Statues" from The Collected Poems of W. B. Yeats, Copyright 1951 by The Macmillan Company and used with their permission and that of The Macmillan Co. of Canada, A. P. Watt & Son, and Mrs. W. B. Yeats.

For "The Wind," "The College of Surgeons," "The Crest Jewel," and "Check" from Collected Poems by James Stephens, Copyright 1944 by The Macmillan Company and used with their permission and that of Macmillan and Co., Ltd. And for "I Am Raftery" and "The County Mayo" from Reincarnations by James Stephens, Copyright 1944 by The Macmillan Company.

For "The Raid" from Inishfallen, Fare Thee Well by Sean O'Casey, Copyright 1949 by Sean O'Casey and used with the permission of The Macmillan Company and of Macmillan and Co., Ltd.

For "Song for the Clatter-Bones" from The Gap of Brightness by

AN ANTHOLOGY
OF IRISH
LITERATURE

PART I

Early Irish Lyrics

TRANSLATIONS FROM THE GAELIC

The Viking Terror

Fierce is the wind tonight.
It ploughs up the white hair of the sea.
I have no fear that the Viking hosts
Will come over the water to me.

7TH OR 8TH CENTURY.
Translator F. N. Robinson.

A Pet Crane

My dear little crane
Is the glory of my goodly home.
I have not found so good a friend.
Though he is a servant he is a gentleman.

7TH OR 8TH CENTURY.
Translator Myles Dillon.

The Son of the King of Moy

The son of the king of Moy in midsummer
Found a girl in the greenwood.
She gave him black fruit from thornbushes.
She gave an armful of strawberries on rushes.

7TH OR 8TH CENTURY.
Translator Myles Dillon.

The Wife of Aed mac Ainmirech, King of Ireland, Laments Her Husband

Dear to me were the three sides
Which I hope not to visit again:
The side of Tara,[1] the side of Teltown[2]
And the side of Aed son of Ainmire.

7TH OR 8TH CENTURY.
Translator Myles Dillon.

---

[1] A dwelling place of the ancient High Kings of Ireland.
[2] Teltown (in County Meath) is the anglicized form of Tailltiu, dwelling place of a number of ancient High Kings of Ireland.

A Love Song

He is a heart,
An acorn from the oakwood.
He is young.
A kiss for him!

7TH OR 8TH CENTURY.
Translator Myles Dillon.

The Drowning of Conaing

The shining waters rise and swell
And break across the shining strand,
And Conaing gazes at the land,
Swung high in his frail coracle.

Then she with the white hair of foam,
The blinding hair that Conaing grips,
Rises, to turn triumphant lips,
On all the gods that guard his home.

8TH CENTURY.
Translator Frank O'Connor.

The Deer's Cry[1]

I arise to-day
Through a mighty strength, the invocation of the Trinity,
Through belief in the threeness,
Through confession of the oneness
Of the Creator of Creation.

I arise to-day
Through the strength of Christ's birth with His baptism,
Through the strength of His crucifixion with His burial,
Through the strength of His resurrection with His ascension,
Through the strength of His descent for the judgement of
    Doom.

I arise to-day
Through the strength of the love of Cherubim,
In obedience of angels,
In the service of archangels,
In hope of resurrection to meet with reward,
In prayers of patriarchs,
In predictions of prophets,
In preachings of apostles,
In faiths of confessors,
In innocence of holy virgins,
In deeds of righteous men.

---

[1] Saint Patrick is supposed to have composed this hymn and sung it to deceive assassins, lying in wait for him, into thinking that he and his companions were a herd of deer passing.

I arise to-day
Through the strength of heaven:
Light of sun,
Radiance of moon,
Splendor of fire,
Speed of lightning,
Swiftness of wind,
Depth of sea,
Stability of earth,
Firmness of rock.

I arise to-day
Through God's strength to pilot me:
God's might to uphold me,
God's wisdom to guide me,
God's eye to look before me,
God's ear to hear me,
God's word to speak for me,
God's hand to guard me,
God's way to lie before me,
God's shield to protect me,
God's host to save me
From snares of devils,
From temptations of vices,
From every one who shall wish me ill,
Afar and anear,
Alone and in multitude.

I summon to-day all these powers between me and those evils,
Against every cruel merciless power that may oppose my body
     and soul,
Against incantations of false prophets,
Against black laws of pagandom,
Against false laws of heretics,
Against craft of idolatry,
Against spells of women and smiths and wizards,
Against every knowledge that corrupts man's body and soul.

Christ to shield me to-day
Against poison, against burning,
Against drowning, against wounding,
So that there may come to me abundance of reward.
Christ with me, Christ before me, Christ behind me,
Christ in me, Christ beneath me, Christ above me,
Christ on my right, Christ on my left,
Christ when I lie down, Christ when I sit down,
     Christ when I arise.
Christ in the heart of every man who thinks of me,
Christ in the mouth of every one who speaks of me,
Christ in every eye that sees me,
Christ in every ear that hears me.

I arise to-day
Through a mighty strength, the invocation of the Trinity,
Through belief in the threeness,
Through confession of the oneness
Of the Creator of Creation.

8TH CENTURY.
Translators Whitley Stokes, John Strachan, and Kuno Meyer.

In Praise of Aed[1]

Kindler of glory's embers,
Aed, goodly hand of giving;
Comeliest that song remembers
By pastoral Roeriu living.

A mighty shaft and loyal
Whom glory overarches;
Of all men else most royal
In grassy Maistiu's marches.

My love—if such his pleasure—
To Dermot's son I bring it;
My song—more worth than treasure—
To his high praise I sing it.

Dear name! renowned in story,
Aed! no man may decry him;
Where Liffey flows in glory
Fame's voice shall ne'er bely him.

Grandchild of that fierce fighter
Muireach, a cliff of splendours,
Honour—no fame is brighter—
To his race Cualu renders.

A stately tree, a glowing
Jewel whom strife embolden;
A silver sapling growing
From soil of princes olden.

---

[1] A chief of north Leinster.

Songs at the alefeast ringing,
Scales climbed of comely measures,
Bards with their heady singing
Acclaim Aed and his pleasures.

8TH CENTURY.
Translator Robin Flower.

The Scribe

A hedge of trees surrounds me.
A blackbird's lay sings to me.
Above my lined booklet
The trilling birds chant to me.

In a grey mantle from the top of bushes
The cuckoo sings.
Verily—may the Lord shield me!—
Well do I write under the greenwood.

8TH OR 9TH CENTURY.
Translator Kuno Meyer.

A Miserly Patron

I have heard
He does not bestow horses for poems;
He gives what fits his kind,
A cow!

9TH CENTURY.
Translator Myles Dillon.

Pangur Ban

I and Pangur Ban my cat,
'Tis a like task we are at:
Hunting mice is his delight,
Hunting words I sit all night.

Better far than praise of men
'Tis to sit with book and pen;
Pangur bears me no ill will,
He too plies his simple skill.

'Tis a merry thing to see
At our tasks how glad are we,
When at home we sit and find
Entertainment to our mind.

Oftentimes a mouse will stray
In the hero Pangur's way;
Oftentimes my keen thought set
Takes a meaning in its net.

'Gainst the wall he sets his eye
Full and fierce and sharp and sly;
'Gainst the wall of knowledge I
All my little wisdom try.

When a mouse darts from its den
O how glad is Pangur then!
O what gladness do I prove
When I solve the doubts I love!

So in peace our tasks we ply,
Pangur Ban, my cat and I;
In our arts we find our bliss,
I have mine and he has his.

Practice every day has made
Pangur perfect in his trade;
I get wisdom day and night
Turning darkness into light.

9TH CENTURY.
Translator Robin Flower.

The Vision of Ita

Jesukin, nursed by me in my little hermitage!
Though it be a cleric with treasures—
All is a lie save Jesukin.
The nursing that I do in my house
Is not the nursing of a base clown.
It is Jesus with the men of Heaven
Near my heart every night.

Young Jesukin, my eternal good!
For heed of Him he is not slack—
The King who controls all things.
Not to beseech Him will cause repentance.
It is Jesu, noble, angelic, not a boorish cleric
Who is fostered by me in my little hermitage
Jesus, son of the Hebrew woman.

Though sons of princes, sons of kings,
Should come into my country,
Not from them do I expect profit.
More likely from Jesukin.
Sing ye a chorus, O maidens, to Him who has a right
To your tribute. Who sits in His place above,
Though as Jesukin he sits at my breast.

9TH CENTURY.
Translator Whitley Stokes.

He That Never Read A Line

'Tis sad to see the sons of learning
In everlasting Hellfire burning
While he that never read a line
Doth in eternal glory shine.

9TH CENTURY.
Translator Robin Flower.

On A Dead Scholar

LONGARAD WHITEFOOT: a master in theology, in history, in
the Brehon law and in poetry was he. To him came Columcille
to be his guest and Lon hid his books from him. So Columcille
left a curse on the books: "May that which thou grudgest
be useless after thee," said he. And so it was, for the books
abide still, but no man can read them. Now when Longarad
died the men of learning say that all the book-satchels of Ireland fell down that night. Or rather it was the book-satchels in
Columcille's oratory that fell, and Columcille and all they that
were with him there fell silent at the noise of the falling of the
books. Then said Columcille: "Longarad is dead in Ossory
to-day, the master of every art." "May it be long ere that come
true!" said Baothin. "Unfaith on the man that takes thy office
after thee for that!" says Columcille.
Et dixit Columcille:

Lon's away,
Cill Garad[1] is sad today;
Many-familied Eire weeps,
Learning sleeps and finds no stay.

---
[1] A place name, Kilgarrow.

Lon's no more,
Cill Garad is weeping sore;
Learning lies bereft and poor
All along the Irish shore.

9TH CENTURY.
Translator Robin Flower.

The Church Bell in the Night

Sweet little bell
That is struck in the windy night,
I liefer go to a tryst with thee
Than to a tryst with a foolish woman.

9TH CENTURY.
Translator Kuno Meyer.

Starry Sky

O King of the starry sky,
Lest Thou from me withdraw Thy light—
Whether my house be dark or bright,
My door shall close on none tonight.

9TH CENTURY.
Translator Sean O'Faolain.

The Desire for Hermitage

Ah! To be all alone in a little cell
With nobody near me;
Beloved that pilgrimage
Before the last pilgrimage to Death.

To be cleansing my flesh with good habits,
Trampling it down like a man;
To be weeping wearily,
Paying for my passions.

A cold bed of fear—
The lying down of a doomed man;
A short sleep, waking to danger;
Tears from early morning.

Dry bread portioned out
A good thing to hollow the face;
An end to gossip; no more fables;
The knees constantly bent.

That will be an end to evil
When I am alone
In a lovely little corner among tombs
Far from the houses of the great.

Ah! To be all alone in a little cell,
To be alone, all alone,
Alone as I came into the world—
And as I shall go from it.

8TH-9TH CENTURY.
Translator Sean O'Faolain.

The Wish of Manchín of Liath

I wish, O son of the Living God, ancient eternal King, for a secret hut in the wilderness that it may be my dwelling.

A very blue shallow well to be beside it, a clear pool for washing away sins through the grace of the Holy Ghost.

A beautiful wood close by around it on every side, for the nurture of many-voiced birds, to shelter and hide it.

Facing the south for warmth, a little stream across its enclosure, a choice ground with abundant bounties which would be good for every plant.

A few sage disciples—I will tell their number—humble and obedient, to pray to the King.

Four threes, three fours, ready for every need, two sixes in the church, both south and north.

Six couples in addition to me myself, praying through the long ages to the King who moves the sun.

A lovely church decked with linen, a dwelling for God of Heaven; then, bright candles over the holy white Scriptures.

One room to go to for the care of the body, without ribaldry, without boasting, without meditation of evil.

This is the housekeeping I would get. I would choose it without concealing. Fragrant fresh leeks, hens, salmon, trou' bees.

My fill of clothing and of food from the King of good fame,
and for me to be sitting for a while praying to God in every
place.

9TH CENTURY.
Translator Kenneth Jackson.

The Pilgrim at Rome

To go to Rome
Is much of trouble, little of profit:
The King whom thou seekest here,
Unless thou bring Him with thee, thou wilt not find.

9TH CENTURY.
Translator Kuno Meyer.

Winter Has Come

Winter has come with scarcity,
Lakes have flooded on all sides,
Frosts crumble the leaves,
The merry wave mutters.

9TH CENTURY.
Translator Kenneth Jackson.

The Ivy Crest

In Tuaim Inbhir here I find
No great house such as mortals build,
A hermitage that fits my mind
With sun and moon and starlight filled.

'Twas Gobbán[1] shaped it cunningly
—This is a tale that lacks not proof—
And my heart's darling in the sky,
Christ, was the thatcher of its roof.

Over my house rain never falls,
There comes no terror of the spear;
It is a garden without walls
And everlasting light shines here.

9TH CENTURY.
Translator Robin Flower.

---

[1] The great artificer of Celtic mythology.

Summer Is Gone

I have but one story—
The stags are moaning,
The sky is snowing,
Summer is gone.

Quickly the low sun
Goes drifting down
Behind the rollers,
Lifting and long.

The wild geese cry
Down the storm;
The ferns have fallen,
Russet and torn.

The wings of the birds
Are clotted with ice.
I have but one story—
Summer is gone.

> 9TH CENTURY.
> Translator Sean O'Faolain.

May

May's the merriest time of all,
   Life comes back to everything,
While a ray of light remains
   The never weary blackbirds sing.

That's the cuckoo's strident voice,
   "Welcome summer great and good!"
All the fierceness of the storm
   Lost in tangles of the wood.

Summer stems the languid stream,
   Galloping horses rush the pool,
Bracken bristles everywhere,
   White bog cotton is in bloom.

Scant of breath the burdened bees
   Carry home the flowery spoil,
To the mountains go the cows,
   The ant is glutted with his meal.

The woodland harp plays all day long,
   The sail falls and the world's at rest,
A mist of heat upon the hills
   And the water full of mist.

The corncrake drones, a mighty bard,
   The cold cascade that leaps the rock
Sings of the snugness of the pool,
   Their season come, the rushes talk.

The man grows strong, the virgin blooms
   In all her glory, firm and light,
Bright the far and fertile plain,
   Bright the wood from floor to height.

And here among the meadowlands
   An eager flock of birds descends,
There a stream runs white and fast
   Where the murmuring meadow bends.

And you long to race your horse
   Wildly through the parted crowd,
The sun has scarcely touched the land
   Yet the waterflags are gold.

Frightened, foolish, frail, a bird
   Sings of it with throbbing breast,
The lark that flings its praise abroad,
   May the brightest and the best.

      9TH-10TH CENTURY.
      Translator Frank O'Connor.

A Song of Winter

Cold, cold!
Cold to-night is broad Moylurg,
Higher the snow than the mountain-range,
The deer cannot get at their food.

Cold till Doom!
The storm has spread over all:
A river is each furrow upon the slope,
Each ford a full pool.

A great tidal sea is each loch,
A full loch is each pool:
Horses cannot get over the ford of Ross,
No more can two feet get there.

The fish of Ireland are a-roaming,
There is no strand which the wave does not pound,
Not a town there is in the land,
Not a bell is heard, no crane talks.

The wolves of Cuan-wood get
Neither rest nor sleep in their lair,
The little wren cannot find
Shelter in her nest on the slope of Lon.

Keen wind and cold ice
Has burst upon the little company of birds,
The blackbird cannot get a lee to her liking,
Shelter for its side in Cuan-wood.

Cozy our pot on its hook,
Crazy the hut on the slope of Lon:
The snow has crushed the wood here,
Toilsome to climb up Ben-bo.

Glenn Rye's ancient bird
From the bitter wind gets grief;
Great her misery and her pain,
The ice will get into her mouth.

From flock and from down to rise—
Take it to heart!—were folly for thee
Ice in heaps on every ford—
That is why I say "cold"!

     10TH CENTURY.
     Translator Kuno Meyer.

To Crinog[1]

Crinog, melodious is your song.
Though young no more you are still bashful.
We two grew up together in Niall's northern land,
When we used to sleep together in tranquil slumber.

That was my age when you slept with me,
O peerless lady of pleasant wisdom:
A pure-hearted youth, lovely without a flaw,
A gentle boy of seven sweet years.

We lived in the great world of Banva[2]
Without sullying soul or body,
My flashing eye full of love for you,
Like a poor innocent untempted by evil.

Your just counsel is ever ready,
Wherever we are we seek it:
To love your penetrating wisdom is better
Than glib discourse with a king.

Since then you have slept with four men after me,
Without folly or falling away:
I know, I hear it on all sides,
You are pure, without sin from man.

---

[1] "Crinog was evidently what is known in the literature of early Christianity as ἀγαπητή, virgo subintroducta (συνεισάκτος) or con-hospita, i.e., a nun who lived with a priest, monk, or hermit like a sister or 'spiritual wife' (uxor spiritualis). This practice, which was early suppressed or abandoned everywhere else, seems to have survived in the Irish Church till the tenth century." (Translator)

[2] A name for Ireland.

At last, after weary wanderings,
You have come to me again,
Darkness of age has settled on your face:
Sinless your life draws near its end.

You are still dear to me, faultless one,
You shall have welcome from me without stint;
You will not let us be drowned in torment:
We will earnestly practise devotion with you.

The lasting world is full of your fame,
Far and wide you have wandered on every track:
If every day we followed your ways,
We should come safe into the presence of dread God.

You leave an example and a bequest
To every one in this world,
You have taught us by your life:
Earnest prayer to God is no fallacy.

Then may God grant us peace and happiness!
May the countenance of the King
Shine brightly upon us
When we leave behind us our withered bodies.

19TH CENTURY.
Translator Kuno Meyer.

The Old Woman of Beare[1]

I the old woman of Beare
Once a shining shift would wear,
Now and since my beauty's fall
I have scarce a shift at all.

Plump no more, I sigh for these
Bones bare beyond belief;
Ebbtide is all my grief,
I am ebbing like the seas.

It is pay
And not men ye love today,
But when we were young, ah then
We gave all our hearts to men.

Men most dear,
Horseman, huntsman, charioteer;
We gave them love with all our will
But the measure did not fill.

When today they ask so fine,
And small good they get of it,
They are wornout in their prime
By the little that they get.

---

[1] The Old Woman of Beare still figures in Irish legend as a hag or witch of fabulous age. She had seven periods of youth and fifty foster children.

And long since the foaming steed
And the chariot with its speed
And the charioteer went by—
God be with them all, say.

Luck has left me, I go late
To the dark house where they wait;
When the Son of God thinks fit
Let Him call me home to it.

For my hands as you may see
Are but bony wasted things,
Hands that once would grasp the hand,
Clasp the haughty neck of kings.

O my hands as may be seen
Are so scraggy and so thin
That a boy might start in dread
Feeling them about his head.

Girls are gay
When the year draws on to May,
But for me, so poor am I,
Sun will scarcely light the day.

Though I care
Nothing now to deck my hair,
I had headgear bright enough
When the kings for love went bare.

'Tis not age that makes my pain
But the eye that sees so plain
How when all it loves decays,
Femon's ways are gold again.

Femon, Bregon, sacring stone,
Sacring stone and Ronan's throne,
Storms have sacked so long that now
Tomb and sacring stone are one.

Winter overwhelms the land,
The waves are noisy on the strand,
So I may not hope today
Faramuid will come my way.

Where are they? Ah, well I know
Old and toiling bones that row
Alma's flood or by its deep
Sleep in cold that slept not so.

Welladay!
Every child outlives its play,
Year on year has worn my flesh
Since my fresh sweet strength went grey.

And, O God,
Once again for ill or good
Spring will come and I shall see
Everything but me renewed.

Summer sun and autumn sun;
These I knew and they are gone,
And the winter time of men
Comes and they come not again.

And "Amen" I cry and "Woe!"
That the boughs are shaken bare
And that candlelight and feast
Leave me to the dark and prayer.

I that had my day with kings
And drank deep of mead and wine,
Drink whey-water with old hags
Sitting in their rags and pine.

"That my cups be cups of whey!
That Thy will be done," I pray,
But the prayer, O Living God,
Stirs up madness in my blood.

And I cry "Your locks are grey"
At the mantle that I stroke,
Then I grieve and murmur "Nay,
I am grey and not my cloak."

And of eyes that loved the sun
Age, my grief, has taken one,
And the other too will take
Soon for good proportion's sake.

Floodtide!
Flood or ebb upon the strand?
What floodtide brings to you,
Ebbtide carries from your hand.

Floodtide
And the swifter tides that fall,
All have reached me, ebb and flow,
Ay, and now I know them all.

Floodtide!
Not a man answers my call
Nor in darkness seeks my side,
A cold hand lies on them all.

Happy island of the main,
To you the tide will come again.
But to me it comes no more
Over the blank deserted shore.

Seeing it, I can scarcely say
"Here is such a place" today,
What was water far and wide
Changes with the ebbing tide.

10TH CENTURY.
Translator Frank O'Connor.

I Should Like to Have a Great Pool of Ale[1]

I should like to have a great pool of ale for the King of Kings; I should like the Heavenly Host to be drinking it for all eternity.

I should like to have the fruit of Faith, of pure devotion; I should like to have the couches of Holiness in my house.

I should like to have the men of Heaven in my own dwelling; I should like the vats of Long-Suffering to be at their disposal.

I should like to have the vessels of Charity to dispense; I should like to have the pitchers of Mercy for their company.

I should like there to be cheerfulness for their sake; I should like Jesus to be there too.

I should like to have the Three Marys of glorious renown; I should like to have the people of Heaven from every side.

I should like to be vassal to the Lord; if I should suffer distress he would grant me a good blessing.

10TH CENTURY.
Translator Kenneth Jackson.

---

[1] This poem is generally attributed to Brigid, the great saint of the fifth century.

St. Columcille the Scribe

My hand is weary with writing,
My sharp quill is not steady,
My slender-beaked pen juts forth
A black draught of shining dark-blue ink.

A stream of wisdom of blessed God
Springs from my fair-brown shapely hand:
On the page it squirts its draught
Of ink of the green-skinned holly.

My little dripping pen travels
Across the plain of shining books,
Without ceasing for the wealth of the great—
Whence my hand is weary with writing.

11TH CENTURY.
Translator Kuno Meyer.

A Storm at Sea

Tempest on the great seaborders!
Hear my tale, ye viking sworders:
Winter smites us, wild winds crying
Set the salty billows flying,
Wind and winter, fierce marauders.

Ler's[1] vast host of shouting water
Comes against us charged with slaughter;
None can tell the dread and wonder
Speaking in the ocean thunder
And the tempest, thunder's daughter.

With the wind of east at morning
All the waves' wild hearts are yearning
Westward over wastes of ocean
Till they stay their eager motion
Where the setting sun is burning.

When the northern wind comes flying,
All the press of dark waves crying
Southward surge and clamour, driven
To the shining southern heaven,
Wave to wave in song replying.

When the western wind is blowing
O'er the currents wildly flowing,
Eastward sets its mighty longing
And the waves go eastward, thronging
Far to find the sun-tree growing.

---

[1] Manannan macLir was god of the sea in Celtic mythology.

When the southern wind comes raining
Over shielded Saxons straining
Waves round Skiddy isle go pouring,
On Caladnet's beaches roaring,
In grey Shannon's mouth complaining.

Full the sea and fierce the surges,
Lovely are the ocean verges,
On the showery waters whirling
Sandy winds are swiftly swirling,
Rudders cleave the surf that urges.

Hard round Eire's cliffs and nesses,
Hard the strife, not soft the stresses,
Like swan-feathers softly sifting
Snow o'er Mile's folk[2] is drifting,
Manann's wife shakes angry tresses.

At the mouth of each dark river
Breaking waters surge and shiver,
Wind and winter met together
Trouble Alba[3] with wild weather,
Countless falls on Dremon quiver.

Son of God, great Lord of wonder,
Save me from the ravening thunder!
By the feast before Thy dying
Save me from the tempest crying
And from Hell tempestuous under!

11TH CENTURY.
Translator Robin Flower.

---

[2] I.e. the Irish people. Mil was the father of the sixth and last race
to invade Ireland.
[3] England.

The Praises of God

It is folly for any man in the world
To cease from praising Him,
When the bird does not cease
And it without a soul but wind.

11TH CENTURY.
Translator Kenneth Jackson.

The Blackbird

Ah, blackbird, thou art satisfied
Where thy nest is in the bush.
Hermit that clinkest no bell,
Sweet, soft, peaceful is thy note.

11TH-12TH CENTURY.
Translator Kuno Meyer.

St. Columcille's Island Hermitage

Delightful I think it to be in the bosom of an isle, on the peak of a rock, that I might often see there the calm of the sea.

That I might see its heavy waves over the glittering ocean, as they chant a melody to their Father on their eternal course.

That I might see its smooth strand of clear headlands, no gloomy thing; that I might hear the voice of the wondrous birds, a joyful course.

That I might hear the sound of the shallow waves against the rocks; that I might hear the cry by the graveyard, the noise of the sea.

That I might see its splendid flocks of birds over the full-watered ocean; that I might see its mighty whales, greatest of wonders.

That I might see its ebb and its flood-tide in their flow; that this may be my name, a secret I tell, "He who turned his back on Ireland."

That contrition of heart should come upon me as I watch it; that I might bewail my many sins, difficult to declare.

That I might bless the Lord who has power over all, Heaven with its pure host of angels, earth, ebb, flood-tide.

That I might pore on one of my books, good for my soul; a while kneeling for beloved Heaven, a while at psalms.

A while gathering dulse from the rock, a while fishing, a while giving good to the poor, a while in my cell.

A while meditating upon the Kingdom of Heaven, holy is the redemption; a while at labour not too heavy; it would be delightful!

12TH CENTURY.
Translator Kenneth Jackson.

PART II

Myth, Saga, and Romance

TRANSLATIONS FROM THE GAELIC

The Dream of Oenghus[1]

OENGHUS was asleep one night, when he saw a girl coming towards him as he lay on his bed. She was the loveliest that had ever been in Ireland. Oenghus went to take her hand, to bring her to him in his bed. As he looked, she sprang suddenly away from him; he could not tell where she had gone. He stayed there till morning, and he was sick at heart. The apparition which he had seen, and had not talked with, made him fall ill. No food passed his lips. She was there again the next night. He saw a lute in her hand, the sweetest that ever was; she played a tune to him, and he fell asleep at it. He remained there till morning, and that day he was unable to eat.

He passed a whole year while she visited him in this way, so that he fell into a wasting sickness. He spoke of it to no one.

---

[1] Oenghus Mac Oc (Angus Og), the master of love in Celtic mythology, was the son of the Dagda, chieftain of the Tuatha De Danann—one of the ancient peoples who invaded Ireland—and Boann, a river goddess who gave her name to the Boyne river.

So he fell into wasting sickness, and no one knew what was wrong with him. The physicians of Ireland were brought together; they did not know what was wrong with him in the end. They went to Fínghen, Conchobhar's[2] physician, and he came to him. He would tell from a man's face what his illness was, and would tell from the smoke which came from the house how many people were ill in it.

He spoke to him aside. "Ah, unhappy plight!" said Fínghen, "you have fallen in love in absence." "You have diagnosed my illness," said Oenghus. "You have fallen into a wretched state, and have not dared to tell it to anyone," said Fínghen. "You are right," said Oenghus; "a beautiful girl came to me, of the loveliest figure in Ireland, and of surpassing form. She had a lute in her hand, and played it to me every night." "No matter," said Fínghen, "it is fated for you to make a match with her. Send someone to Boann, your mother, that she should come to speak with you."

They went to her, and Boann came then. "I am attending this man," said Fínghen, "a serious illness has fallen upon him." They told his story to Boann. "Let his mother take care of him," said Fínghen; "a serious illness has fallen on him. Have the whole of Ireland scoured to see if you find a girl of this figure which your son has seen."

They spent a year at this. Nothing like her was found. Then Fínghen was called to them again. "No help has been found in this matter," said Boann. Said Fínghen, "Send to the Daghdhae, that he should come to speak with his son." They went to the Daghdhae, and he came back with them. "Why have I been summoned?" "To advise your son," said Boann; "it is as well for you to help him, for it is sad that he is perishing. He is wasting away. He has fallen in love in absence, and no help is to be found for him." "What is the use of talking to me?" said the Daghdhae, "I know no more than you do." "More indeed," said Fínghen, "you are the king of the fairy folk

---

[2] Conchubor (Conor), the son of Nessa, was king of Ulster and one of the central figures in the Ulster cycle of tales. See Introduction, p. xiii.

of Ireland. Send someone to Bodhbh, king of the fairies of
Munster; his knowledge is noised throughout Ireland."

They went to him. He welcomed them. "Welcome to you,
men of the Daghdhae," said Bodhbh. "That is what we have
come for." "Have you news?" said Bodhbh. "We have; Oenghus the son of the Daghdhae has been wasting away for two
years." "What is the matter with him?" said Bodhbh. "He has
seen a girl in his sleep. We do not know where in Ireland
is the girl whom he has seen and loved. The Daghdhae bids
you seek throughout Ireland for a girl of that figure and form."
"She shall be sought," said Bodhbh, "and let me have a year's
delay to find out the facts of the case."

They came back at the end of the year to Bodhbh's house at
the Fairy Hill beyond Feimhen. "I went round the whole of
Ireland until I found the girl at Loch Bél Dragon, at Crotta
Cliach,"[1] said Bodhbh. They went to the Daghdhae, and they
were made welcome. "Have you news?" said the Daghdhae.
"Good news; the girl of that figure which you described has
been found. Bodhbh bids you let Oenghus come away with us
to him, to know whether he recognises the girl when he sees
her."

Oenghus was taken in a chariot to the Fairy Hill beyond
Feimhen. The king had a great feast ready for them, and he
was made welcome. They were three days and three nights at
the feast. "Come away now," said Bodhbh, "to know whether
you recognise the girl when you see her. Even if you do recognise her, I have no power to give her to you, and you may only
see her."

They came then to the lake. They saw three times fifty
grown girls, and the girl herself among them. The girls did not
reach above her shoulder. There was a chain of silver between
each couple; and a necklet of silver round her own throat, and
a chain of refined gold. Then Bodhbh said, "Do you recognise
that girl?" "I do indeed," said Oenghus. "I can do no more for
you," said Bodhbh. "That is no matter, then," said Oenghus,

---

[1] The Galtee mountains.

"since it is she that I saw; I cannot take her this time. Who is this girl, Bodhbh?" said Oenghus. "I know, truly," said Bodhbh, "she is Caer Ibhormheith, daughter of Ethal Anbhuail from the fairy hill of Uamhan in the land of Connaught."

Then Oenghus and his people set off for their own country. Bodhbh went with him, and talked with the Daghdhae and Boann at Bruigh Maic ind Óaig.[1] They told them their news, and told how she seemed, in figure and form, just as they had seen; and they told her name and the name of her father and grandfather. "We feel it to be discourteous that we cannot content you," said the Daghdhae. "What you should do, Daghdhae," said Bodhbh, "is to go to Ailill and Medhbh,[2] for they have the girl in their province."

The Daghdhae went till he reached the lands of Connaught, with three score chariots in his company. The king and queen made them welcome. They spent a full week banqueting round the ale after that. "What has brought you?" said the king. "You have a girl in your country," said the Daghdhae, "and my son has fallen in love with her, and has become sick. I have come to you to find out whether you would give her to the lad." "Who?" said Ailill. "The daughter of Ethal Anbhuail." "We have no power over her," said Ailill and Medhbh, "if we had she should be given him." "This would be good—let the king of the fairy hill be summoned to you," said the Daghdhae.

Ailill's steward went to him. "You have been ordered by Ailill and Medhbh to go to speak with them." "I will not go," said he, "I will not give my daughter to the son of the Daghdhae." That is told to Ailill; "He cannot be made to come, but he knows why he is summoned." "No matter," said Ailill, "he shall come, and the heads of his warriors shall be brought with him." At that, Ailill's household troops and the men of the Daghdhae rose up against the fairy hill, and overran the whole hill. They brought out three score heads, and the king, so that he was in captivity at Cruachu.

---

[1] New Grange mound, on the Boyne.

[2] Ailill and Medhbh (Maeve) were king and queen respectively of Connaught and traditional enemies of Ulster.

Then Ailill said to Ethal Anbhuail, "Give your daughter to the son of the Daghdhae." "I cannot," said he, "her magic power is greater than mine." "What is this great magic power she has?" said Ailill. "Easily told; she is in the shape of a bird every other year, and in human shape the other years." "What year is she in the shape of a bird?" said Ailill. "It is not for me to betray her," said her father. "Off with your head, unless you tell us!" said Ailill. "I will not hold out any longer," said he; "I will tell you," said he, "since you are so persistent about her. Next All Hallows she will be at Loch Bél Dragon in the shape of a bird, and wonderful birds will be seen with her there, there will be three times fifty swans around her; and I have made preparations for them." "I do not care, then," said the Daghdhae; "since you know her nature, do you bring her."

Then a treaty was made between them, between Ailill and Ethal and the Daghdhae, and Ethal was let go. The Daghdhae bade them farewell and came to his house and told his news to his son. "Go next All Hallows to Loch Bél Dragon, and call her to you from the lake." The Mac Óag[1] went to Loch Bél Dragon. He saw three times fifty white birds with their silver chains, and curls of gold about their heads. Oenghus was in human shape on the brink of the lake. He called the girl to him. "Come to speak to me, Caer!" "Who calls me?" said Caer. "Oenghus calls you." "I will go, if you will undertake on your honour that I may come back to the lake again." "I pledge your protection," said he.

She went to him. He cast his arms about her. They fell asleep in the form of two swans, and went round the lake three times, so that his promise might not be broken. They went away in the form of two white birds till they came to Bruigh Maic ind Óaig, and sang a choral song so that they put the people to sleep for three days and three nights. The girl stayed with him after that.

8TH CENTURY.
Translator Kenneth Jackson.

---

[1] I.e. Oenghus.

The Boyhood Deeds of Cuchulain[1]

"THIS BOY," said Fergus, "was reared in his father's and his mother's house, by the seaside northwards in the plain of Muirthemne, where someone gave him an account of the macrad or 'boy-corps' of Emain Macha;[2] how that Conchobar divides his day into three parts: the first being devoted to watching the boy-corps at their sport, especially that of hurling; the second to the playing of chess and draughts; the third to pleasurable consuming of meat and drink until drowsiness sets in, which then is promoted by the exertions of minstrels and musicians to induce favorable placidity of mind and disposition. And, for all that we are banished from him," continued Fergus, "by my word I swear that neither in Ireland nor in Scotland is there a warrior his (i.e., Conchobar's) counterpart. The little lad, then, as aforesaid, having heard of all this, one day told his mother that he was bent on a visit to Emain Macha to test the boy-corps at their own sports. She objected that he was immature, and ought to wait until some grown warrior or other, or some confidential of Conchobar's should, in order to insure his safety, bind over the boy-corps to keep the peace toward him. He told his mother that that was too long an outlook, that he could not wait, and that all she had to do was to set him a course for Emain Macha, since he did not know in which direction it lay.

---

[1] The Achilles of the Ulster cycle was the son of Dechtire, sister of King Conchubor, by Lug, a prince of the Tuatha De Danann, or by Sualtach, an Ulster chieftain. His name Setanta was changed to Cuchulain (lit. the hound of Culann) when, at the age of seven, he destroyed the famous hound of Culann the smith. This story of Cuchulain's youth is taken from The Cattle Raid of Cooley, the great epic of the Ulster cycle and is told to Ailill and Maeve by several of the Ulster exiles serving in Maeve's army. See Introduction, p. xiii.

[2] The capital of Ulster near Armagh.

" 'It is a weary way from here,' said the mother, 'for between thee and it lies Sliab Fuait.'

" 'Give me the bearings,' said he; and she did so.

"Away he went then, taking with him his hurly of brass, his ball of silver, his throwing javelin, and his toy spear; with which equipment he fell to shortening the way for himself. He did it thus: with his hurly he would strike the ball and drive it a great distance; then he pelted the hurly after it, and drove it just as far again; then he threw his javelin, lastly the spear. Which done, he would make a playful rush after them all, pick up the hurly, the ball and the javelin, while, before the spear's tip could touch the earth, he had caught the missile by the other end.

"In due course Cu Chulainn reached Emain Macha, where he found the boy-corps, thrice fifty in number, hurling on the green and practising martial exercises with Conchobar's son Follamain at their head. The lad dived right in among them and took a hand in the game. He got the ball between his legs and held it there, not suffering it to travel higher up than his knees or lower down than his ankle-joints, and so making it impossible for them to get in a stroke or in any other way to touch it. In this manner he brought it along and sent it home over the goal. In utter amazement the whole corps looked on; but Follamain mac Conchobar cried: 'Good now, boys, all together meet this youngster as he deserves, and kill him; because it is taboo to have such a one join himself to you and interfere in your game, without first having had the civility to procure your guarantee that his life should be respected. Together then and at once attack him and avenge violation of your taboo; for we know that he is the son of some petty Ulster warrior, such as without safe-conduct is not accustomed to intrude into your play.'

"The whole of them assailed Cu Chulainn, and simultaneously sent their hurlies at his head; he, however, parried all the hundred and fifty and was unharmed. The same with the balls, which he fended off with fists, fore-arms, and palms alone.

Their thrice fifty toy spears he received in his little shield, and still was unhurt. In turn now, Cu Chulainn went among them, and laid low fifty of the best: five more of them," said Fergus, "came past the spot where myself and Conchobar sat at chess-play, with the young lad close in their wake.

" 'Hold, my little fellow,' said Conchobar, 'I see this is no gentle game thou playest with the boy-corps.'

" 'And good cause I have too,' cried Cu Chulainn: 'after coming out of a far land to them, I have not had a guest's reception.'

" 'How now, little one,' said the king, 'knowest thou not the boy-corps' conditions: that a newcomer must have them bound by their honor to respect his life?'

" 'I knew it not,' said the boy, 'otherwise I had conformed, and taken measures beforehand.'

" ' 'Tis well,' said the king: 'take it now upon yourselves to let the boy go safe.'

" 'We do,' the boy-corps answered.

"They resumed play; Cu Chulainn did as he would with them, and again laid out fifty of them on the ground. Their fathers deemed they could not but be dead. No such thing, however; it was merely that with his blows and pushes and repeated charges, he so terrified them that they took to the grass.

" 'What on earth is he at with them now?' asked Conchobar.

" 'I swear by my gods,' said Cu Chulainn, 'that until they in their turn come under my protection and guarantee, I will not lighten my hand from off them.'

"This they did at once. Now," said Fergus in conclusion, "I submit, that a youngster who did all this when he was just five years old, needs not to excite our wonder because, now being turned of seventeen years, he in this Cattle-Raid of Cooley cut a four-pronged pole and the rest, and that he should have killed a man, or two, or three men, or even, as indeed he has done, four."

Conchobar's son Cormac Conlonges spoke now, saying, "In the year after that, the same little boy did another deed."

"And what was that?" Ailill asked.

"Well," continued Cormac, "in Ulster there was a good smith and artificer, by name Culann. He prepared a banquet for Conchobar, and traveled to Emain Macha to bid him to it. He begged Conchobar to bring with him only a moderate number of warriors, because neither land nor domain had he, but merely the product of his hammer, of his anvil, and of his tongs. Conchobar promised that he would bring no more than a small company. Culann returned home to make his last preparations, Conchobar remaining in Emain Macha until the meeting broke up and the day came to a close. Then the king put on his light convenient travelling garb, and betook him to the green in order to bid the boy-corps farewell before he started. There, however, he saw a curious sight. One hundred and fifty youths at one end of the green, and at the other, a single one and he taking the goal against the crowd of them. Again, when they played the hole-game, and it was their turn to aim at the hole, it being his to defend it, he stopped all thrice fifty balls just at the edge of the hole, so that not one went in; when the defence was theirs and it was his turn to shoot, he would hole the entire set without missing one. When the game was to tear one another's clothes off, he would have the mantles off them all, while the full number could not even pull out his brooch. When it was to upset each other, he would knock over the hundred and fifty and they could not stretch him on the ground. All which when Conchobar had witnessed, he said: 'I congratulate the land into which the little boy has come; were his full-grown deeds to prove consonant with his boyish exploits, he would indeed be of some solid use.'

"To this doubtful expression Fergus objected, saying to Conchobar, 'That is not justly said; for according as the little boy grows, so also will his deeds increase with him.'

" 'Have the child called to us,' said the king, 'that he may come with us to share the banquet.'

" 'I cannot go thither just now,' said the boy.

" 'How so?' asked Conchobar.

" 'The boy-corps have not yet had enough of play.'

" 'It would be too long for us to wait until they had,' said the king.

" 'Wait not at all; I will follow after you.'

" 'But, young one, knowest thou the way?'

" 'I will follow the trail of the company, of the horses, and the chariots' tracks.'

"Thereupon Conchobar started; eventually he reached Culann's house, was received in becoming fashion, fresh rushes were laid, and they fell to the banquet. Presently the smith said to Conchobar, 'Good now, O king, has any one promised that this night he would follow thee to this dwelling?'

" 'No, not one,' answered Conchobar (quite forgetting the little boy); 'but wherefore do you ask?'

" ' It is only that I have an excellent ban-dog, from which when his chain is taken off no one may dare to be near him; for saving myself he knows not any man, and in him resides the strength of an hundred.'

"Conchobar said, 'Loose him then, and let him guard this place.'

"So Culann did; the dog made the circuit of his country, then took up his usual position whence to watch the house, and there he couched with his head on his paws. Surely an extraordinary, cruel, fierce and savage dog was he.

"As for the boy-corps, until it was time to separate, they continued in Emain Macha; then they dispersed, each one to his parent's house, or to his nurse's, or to his guardian's. But the little fellow, trusting to the trail, as aforesaid, struck out for Culann's house. With his club and his ball he shortened the way for himself as he went. So soon as ever he came to the green of Culann's fort, the ban-dog became aware of him and gave tongue in such a way as to be heard throughout all the countryside; not was it to carve the boy decently as for a feast that he was minded, but at one gulp to swallow him down. The child was without all reasonable means of defence; therefore as the dog charged at him open-jawed he threw his playing ball down his throat with great force, which mortally punished the creature's inwards. Cu Chulainn seized him by the hind legs and banged him against a rock to such purpose that he strewed all the ground in broken fragments.

"The whole company within had heard the ban-dog's challenge, at the sound of which Conchobar said, ' 'Tis no good luck has brought us on our present trip.'

" 'Your meaning?' asked the others.

" 'I mean that the little boy, my sister Dechtire's son, Setanta mac Sualtach, had promised to come after me; and he even now must be killed by the ban-dog.'

"To a man the heroes rose; and though the fort's doors were thrown open, out they stormed over the ramparts to seek him. Speedy as they were, yet did Fergus outstrip them; he picked up the boy, hoisted him on his shoulder, and carried him to Conchobar. Culann himself had come out, and there he saw his ban-dog lie in scraps and pieces; which was a heart's vexation to him. He went back indoors and said, 'Thy father and thy mother are welcome both, but most unwelcome thou.'

" 'Why, what hast thou against the little fellow?' asked Conchobar.

" 'It was no good luck that inspired me to make my feast for thee, O Conchobar: my dog now being gone, my substance is but substance wasted; my livelihood, a means of living set all astray. Little boy,' he continued, 'that was a good member of my family thou tookest from me: a safeguard of raiment, of flocks, and of herds.'

" 'Be not angered thereat,' said the child; 'for in this matter myself will pronounce a just award.'

" 'And what might that be?' inquired Conchobar.

"The little boy replied, 'If in all Ireland there be a whelp of that dog's breed, by me he shall be nurtured till he be fit for action as was his sire. In the meantime I, O Culann, myself will do thee a ban-dog's service, in guarding of thy cattle and substance and stronghold.'

" 'Well hast thou made the award,' said Conchobar; and Cathbad the druid, chiming in, declared that not in his own person could he have done it better, and that henceforth the boy must bear the name *Cu Chulainn*, 'Culann's Hound.' The youngster, however, objected; 'I like my own name better: Setanta mac Sualtach.'

" 'Say not so,' Cathbad remonstrated; 'for all men in the world shall have their mouths full of that name.'

"The boy answered that on those terms the name would be well pleasing to him, and in this way it came to pass that it stuck to him. Now the little fellow," continued Cormac Conlonges the narrator of all this, "who when just touching six years of age slew the dog which even a great company did not dare to approach, it were not reasonable to be astonished though the same at seventeen should come to the border of the province, and kill a man, or two, or three, or four, on the Cattle-Raid of Cooley."

Another exiled Ulsterman, Fiacha mac Firaba, taking up the recital, said that in the very year following that adventure of the dog, the little boy had performed a third exploit.

"And what was that?" Ailill asked.

"Why, it was Cathbad the druid," continued Fiacha, "who to the north-east of Emain Macha taught his pupils, there being with him eight from among the students of his art. When one of them questioned him as to what purpose that day was more especially favorable, Cathbad told him that any stripling who on that day should for the first time assume arms and armor, the name of such an one forever would surpass those of all Ireland's youths besides. His life, however, must be fleeting, short. The boy was some distance away on the south side of Emain Macha; nevertheless he heard Cathbad's speech. He put off his playing suit and laid aside his implements of sport; then he entered Conchobar's sleeping house and said, 'All good be thine, O king.'

"Conchobar answered, 'Little boy, what is thy request?'

" 'I desire to take arms.'

" 'And who prompted thee to that?'

" 'Cathbad the druid,' answered the boy.

" 'Thou shalt not be denied,' said the king, and forthwith gave him two spears with sword and shield. The boy suppled and brandished the weapons and in the process broke them all to shivers and splinters. In short, whereas in Emain Macha Conchobar had seventeen weapon-equipments ready for the boy-corps' service—since whenever one of them took arms, Conchobar it was who invested him with the outfit and brought him luck in the using of it—the boy made fragments of them all. Which done, he said, 'O my master, O Conchobar, these arms are not good; they suffice me not.' Thereupon the king gave him his own two spears, his own sword, and his own shield. In every possible way the boy tested them; he even bent them point to hilt and head to butt, yet never broke them: they endured him. 'These arms are good,' said he, 'and worthy of me. Fair fall the land and the region which for its king has him whose arms and armor are these.'

"Just then it was that Cathbad the druid came into the house and wondering asked, 'Is the little boy assuming arms?'

" 'Ay, indeed,' said the king.

" 'It is not his mother's son we would care to see assume them on this day,' said the druid.

" 'How now,' said the king, 'was it not thyself that prompted him?'

" 'Not I, of a surety.'

" 'Brat,' cried the king, 'what meanest thou by telling me that it was so, wherein thou hast lied to me?'

" 'O king, be not wroth,' the boy pleaded; 'for he it was that prompted me when he instructed his other pupils. For when they asked him what special virtue lay in this day, he told them that the name of whatsoever youth should therein for the first time take arms, would top the fame of all other Erin's men; nor thereby should he suffer resulting disadvantage, save that his life must be fleeting, short.'

" 'And it is true for me,' said Cathbad; 'noble and famous indeed thou shalt be, but transitory, soon gone.'

" 'Little care I,' said Cu Chulainn, 'nor though I were but one day or one night in being, so long as after me the history of myself and doings may endure.'

"Then said Cathbad again, 'Well then, get into a chariot, boy, and proceed to test in thine own person whether mine utterance be truth.'

"So Cu Chulainn mounted a chariot; in divers ways he tried

its strength, and reduced it to fragments. He mounted a second, with the same result. In brief, whereas in Emain Macha for the boy-corps' service Conchobar had seventeen chariots, in like wise the little fellow smashed them all; then he said, 'These chariots of thine, O Conchobar, are no good at all, nor worthy of me.'

" 'Where is Iubar mac Riangabra?'[1] cried Conchobar.

" 'Here I am,' he answered.

" 'Prepare my own chariot and harness my own horses for him there.'

"The driver did his will, Cu Chulainn mounted, tested the chariot, and it endured him. 'This chariot is good,' he said, 'and my worthy match.'

" 'Good now, little boy,' said Iubar, 'let the horses be turned out to grass.'

" 'Too early for that yet, Iubar; drive on and round Emain Macha.'

" 'Let the horses go out to graze.'

" 'Too early yet, Iubar; drive ahead, that the boy-corps may give me salutation on this the first day of my taking arms.'

"They came to the place where the boy-corps was, and the cry of them resounded, 'These are arms that thou hast taken.'

" 'The very thing indeed,' he said.

"They wished him success in spoil-winning and in first-slaying, but expressed regret that he was weaned away from them and their sports. Cu Chulainn assured them that it was not so, but that it was something in the nature of a charm that had caused him to take arms on this day of all others. Again Iubar pressed him to have the horses taken out, and again the boy refused. He questioned the driver, 'Whither leads this great road here running by us?' Iubar answered that it ran to Ath an Foraire (the Lookout Ford) in Sliab Fuait. In answer to further questions with which he plied the charioteer, Cu Chulainn learned that the ford had that name from the fact that daily

---

[1] Conchubor's charioteer. His brother Loeg became Cuchulain's charioteer.

there some prime warrior of the Ulstermen kept watch and ward to see that no foreign champion came to molest them, it being his duty to do single combat on behalf of his whole province. Should poets and musicians be coming away from Ulster dissatisfied with their treatment, it was his duty, acting for the whole province, to solace them with gold and other gifts. On the other hand, did poets and musicians enter his province, his duty was to see that they had safe-conduct up to Conchobar's bed-side. This sentinel's praise then would be the theme of the first pieces, in divers forms of verse, the poets would rehearse upon arriving in Emain Macha.

"Cu Chulainn inquired whether Iubar knew who it was that on this particular day mounted guard. 'I know it well,' the charioteer replied; 'it is Conall mac Amergin, surnamed Cernach (the Victorious), Ireland's pre-eminent warrior.'

" 'Onward to that ford, then, driver!" cried the boy.

"Sure enough at the water's edge they came upon Conall, who received them with, 'And is it arms that you have taken today, little boy?'

" 'It is indeed,' Iubar answered for him.

" 'May his arms bring him triumph and victory and drawing of first blood,' said Conall. 'The only thing is that in my judgment thou hast prematurely assumed them, seeing that as yet thou art not fit for exploits.'

"For all answer the boy said, 'And what dost thou here, Conall?'

" 'On behalf of the province I keep watch and ward.'

" 'Come,' said the youngster, 'for this day let me take the duty'

" 'Never say it,' replied Conall, 'for as yet thou art not up to coping with a real fighting man.'

" 'Then will I go down to the shallows of Loch Echtra, to see whether I may draw blood on either friend or foe.'

" 'And I,' said Conall, 'will go to protect thee and to safeguard, so that thou wilt not run into dangers on the border.'

" 'Nay,' said Cu Chulainn, 'come not.'

" 'I will so,' Conall insisted, 'for were I to permit thee all alone to frequent the border, the Ulstermen would avenge it on me.'

"Conall had his chariot made ready and his horses harnessed; he started on his errand of protection, and soon overtook Cu Chulainn, who had cut the matter short and had gone on before. They now being abreast, the boy deemed that, in event of opportunity to do some deed of mortal daring, Conall would never allow him to execute it. From the ground therefore he picked up a stone about the size of his fist, and took very careful aim at Conall's chariot-yoke. He broke it in two, the vehicle came down, and Conall was hurled prone, so falling that his mouth was brought over one shoulder.

" 'What's all this, boy?'

" 'It was I: in order to see whether my marksmanship was good and whether there was in me the material of a good warrior.'

" 'Poison take both thy shot and thyself as well; and though thy head should fall as a prize to some foe over yonder, yet never a foot further will I budge to save thee!'

" 'The very thing I crave of thee,' said the boy; 'and I do this in this particular manner because to you Ulstermen it is taboo to persist after violence is done to you.' With that Conall went back to his post at the ford.

"As for the little boy, southwards he went his way to the shallows of Loch Echtra, and until the day's end abode there. Then spoke Iubar: 'If to thee we might venture to say so much, little one, I should be more than rejoiced that we made instant return to Emain Macha. For already for some time the carving has been going on there; and whereas there thou hast thine appointed place kept till thou come—between Conchobar's knees—I on the contrary can do nothing but join the messengers and jesters of his house, to fit in where I may; for which reason I judge it now fitting that I were back in time to scramble with them.'

"Cu Chulainn ordered him to harness the chariot; which being done, they drove off, and Cu Chulainn inquired the name of a mountain that he saw. He learned that it was Sliab Morne,

and further asked the meaning of a white cairn which appeared
on a summit. It was Finnchairn; the boy thought it inviting,
and ordered the driver to take him thither. Iubar expressed
great reluctance and Cu Chulainn said, 'Thou art a lazy loon,
considering that this is my first adventure-quest, and this is
thy first trip with me.'

" 'And if it is,' said Iubar, 'and if I ever reach Emain Macha,
for ever and for ever may it be my last!'

" 'Good now, driver,' said the boy when they were on the top
of the hillock; 'in all directions point out to me the topography
of Ulster, a country in which I know not my way about.' The
charioteer from that position pointed out the hills and the plain
lands and the strongholds of the province.

" ' 'Tis well, O driver; and what now is yon well-defined glen-
seamed plain before us to the southward?'

" 'That is the plain of Bray (Mag Breg).'

" 'Proceed then and instruct me concerning the strongholds
and forts of that plain.' Then Iubar pointed out to him Tara and
Tailltiu, Cletty and Knowth and the brug of Angus mac Oc on
the Boyne, and the stronghold of Nechtan Sceine's sons.

" 'Are they those sons of Nechtan of whom it is said, that the
number of Ulstermen now alive exceeds not the number of
them fallen by their hands?'

" 'The same,' said Iubar.

" 'Away with us then to the stronghold of Nechtan's sons.'

" 'Woe waits on such a speech; and whosoever he be that
goes there, I will not be the one.'

"Cu Chulainn said, 'Alive or dead, thither shalt thou go,
however.'

" 'Alive I go then, and dead I shall be left there.'

"They made their way to the stronghold, and the little boy
dismounted upon the green, a green with this particular feature:
in its center stood a pillar stone, encircled with an iron collar,
test of heroic accomplishment; for it bore graven writing to the
effect that any man (if only he were one that carried arms) who
should enter on this green, must hold it taboo to him to depart
from it without challenging to single combat some of the

dwellers in the stronghold. The little boy read the Ogam,[1] threw his arms around the stone to start it, and eventually pitched it, collar and all, into the water close at hand.

" 'In my poor opinion,' ventured Iubar, 'it is no better so than it was before; and I well know that this time at all events thou wilt find the object of thy search: a prompt and violent death.'

" 'Good, good, O driver, spread me now the chariot-coverings that I may sleep a little while.'

" 'Alas that one should speak so; for a land of foemen and not of friends is this.'

"Iubar obeyed, and on the green at once the little fellow fell asleep. Just then it was that Foill mac Nechtain issued forth, and, at the sight of the chariot, called out, 'Driver, do not unharness those horses!' Iubar made answer that he still held the reins in his hand—a sign that he was not about to unharness them.

" 'What horses are these?'

" 'Conchobar's two piebalds.'

" 'Even such at sight I took them to be,' said Foill; 'and who has brought them into these borders?'

" 'A young bit of a little boy; one who for luck has taken arms to-day, and for the purpose of showing off his form and fashion has come into the borders.'

" 'Never let it thrive with him,' said Foill; 'were it sure that he is capable of action, it is dead in place of alive that he would go back to Emain Macha.'

" 'Indeed he is not capable, nor could it be rightly imputed to him; this is but the seventh year since his birth.' Here the little one lifted his face from the ground; not only that but his whole body to his feet, blushed deep at the affront which he had overheard, and said, 'Ay, I am fit for action!'

"But Foill rejoined, 'I rather would incline to hold that thou art not.'

---

[1] An alphabet of twenty characters used by the ancient British and Irish. NED.

" 'Thou shalt know what to hold in this matter, only let us repair to the ford; but first, go fetch thy weapons; in cowardly guise thou art come hither, for nor drivers nor messengers nor folk unarmed slay I.' Foill rushed headlong for his weapons, and Iubar advised the boy that he must be careful with him. Cu Chulainn asked the reason, and was told that the man was Foill mac Nechtain Sceine, invulnerable to either point or edge of any kind.

" 'Not to me should such a thing be spoken,' he replied, 'for I will take in hand my special feat: the tempered and refined iron ball, which shall land in his forehead's midst and backwards through his skull shall carry out his brain, so leaving his head traversed with a fair conduit for the air.' With that, out came Foill mac Nechtain again; the little lad grasped his ball, hurled it with the exact effect foretold, and he took Foill's head.

"Out of the stronghold now the second son emerged on the green, whose name was Tuachall mac Nechtain, and he said, 'Belike thou art inclined to boast of that much.' Cu Chulainn replied that the fall of a single warrior was for him no matter of boast, and Tuachall told him that in that case he should not boast at all, because straightway he would perish by his hand. 'Then make haste for thy weapons,' said the boy, 'for in cowardly guise thou comest hither.'

"Away went Tuachall; Iubar repeated his admonitions. 'Who is that?' asked the boy. He was told not only that he was a son of Nechtan but also that he must be slain by the first stroke or shot or other attempt of whatsoever sort, or not at all; and this because of the extraordinary activity and skill which in front of weapons' points he displayed to avoid them. Again Cu Chulainn objected that such language ought not to be addressed to him. Said he, 'I will take in my hand Conchobar's great spear, the Venomous; it shall pierce the shield over his breast and, after holing the heart within him, shall break three ribs in his side that is the farthest from me.' This also the boy performed, and took the victim's head before his body touched the ground.

"Now came out the youngest of the sons, Fainnle mac

Nechtain, and said, 'But simpletons they were with whom thou hast had to do.' Cu Chulainn asked him what he meant, and Fainnle invited him to come away down and out upon the water where his foot would not touch bottom, himself on the instant darting to the ford. Still Iubar warned the boy to be on his guard. 'How is that then?' said Cu Chulainn.

" 'Because that is Fainnle mac Nechtain; and the reason why he bears that name is that as it were a *fáinnle* (swallow) or a weasel, even so for swiftness he travels on the water's surface, nor can the whole world's swimmers attempt to cope with him.'

" 'Not to me ought such a thing to be said,' objected the boy again; 'for thou knowest the river which we have in Emain Macha, the Callan: well, when the boy-corps break off from their sports and plunge into it to swim, on either shoulder I take a lad of them, on either palm another, nor in the transit across that water ever wet as much as my ankles.'

"Then he and Fainnle entered the ford and there wrestled. The youngster clasped his arms around him and got him just flush with the water; then he dealt him a stroke with Conchobar's sword and took his head, letting the body go with the current. To finish up, Cu Chulainn entered the stronghold and harried it; then he and Iubar fired it and left it burning brightly, then turned about to retrace their steps through Sliab Fuait, not forgetting to carry with them the heads of Nechtan Sceine's sons.

"Soon they saw in front of them a herd of deer, and the boy sought to know what were those numerous and restless cattle. Iubar explained that they were not cattle, but a herd of wild deer that kept in the dark glens of Sliab Fuait. He being urged to goad the horses in their direction, did so; but the king's fat horses could not attain to join company with the hard-conditioned deer. Cu Chulainn dismounted therefore and by sheer running and mere speed captured in the moor two stags of the greatest bulk, which he made fast to the chariot with thongs. Still they held a course for Emain Macha, and by-and-by, when nearing it, perceived a certain flock of whitest swans. The boy

asked were they pet birds or wild, and learned that they were
wild swans which used to congregate from rocks and islands of
the sea, and for feeding's sake, infest the country. Cu Chulainn
questioned further, and wished to know which was the rarer
thing: to bring some of them back to Emain Macha alive, or to
bring them dead. Iubar did not hesitate to say that bringing
them back living would be the more creditable by far; 'for,' said
he, 'you may find plenty to bring them in dead; perhaps not
one to bring them in living.'

"Into his sling Cu Chulainn laid a little stone, and with it at
a cast brought down eight swans of the number. Again he
loaded, this time with a larger stone, and now brought down
sixteen. 'Driver, bring along the birds,' he said.

"But Iubar hesitated. 'I hardly can do that.'

" 'And why not?' said the boy.

" 'Because if I quit my present position, the horses' speed
and the action being what they are, the chariot wheels will cut
me into pieces; or else the stags' antlers will pierce and otherwise wound me.'

" 'No true warrior art thou, Iubar; but come, the horses I
will gaze upon with such a look that they shall not break their
regulation pace; as for the gaze that I will bend upon the stags,
they will stoop their heads for awe.'

"At this Iubar ventured down and retrieved the swans, which
with more of the thongs and ropes he secured to the chariot.
In this manner they covered the rest of the way to Emain
Macha.

"Leborcham, daughter of Aed and messenger to the king,
perceived them now and cried, 'A solitary chariot-fighter draws
near to thee now, O Conchobar, and terribly he comes! The
chariot is graced with the bleeding heads of his enemies; beautiful white birds he has which in the chariot bear him company,
and wild unbroken stags bound and tethered to the same. Indeed if measures be not taken to receive him prudently, the best
of the Ulstermen must fall by his hand.'

" 'I know that little chariot-fighter,' Conchobar said: 'the little boy, my sister's son, who this very day went to the border. Surely he will have reddened his hand; and should his fury not be timely met, all Emain Macha's young men will perish by him.'

"At last they hit upon a method to abate his manly rage (the result of having shed blood), and it was this: Emain Macha's women all (six score and ten in number) bared their bosoms, and without subterfuge of any kind trooped out to meet him (their manoeuver being based on Cu Chulainn's well-known modesty, which, like all his other qualities, was excessive). The little fellow leaned his head against the rail of the chariot and shut them from his sight. Then was the desired moment; all unawares he was seized, and soused in a vat of cold water ready for the purpose. In this first vessel the heat generated by his immersion was such that the staves and hoops flew asunder instantly. In a second vat the water escaped (by boiling over); in yet a third the water still was hotter than one could bear. By this time, however, the little boy's fury had died down in him; from crown to sole he blushed a beautiful pink red all over, and they clad him in his festive clothes. Thus his natural form and feature were restored to him.

"A beautiful boy indeed was that: seven toes to each foot he had, and to either hand as many fingers; his eyes were bright with seven pupils apiece, each one of which glittered with seven gem-like sparkles. On either cheek he had four moles: a blue, a crimson, a green, and a yellow one. Between one ear and the other he had fifty clear-yellow long tresses that were as the yellow wax of bees, or like a brooch of white gold as it glints in the sun unobscured. He wore a green mantle silver-clasped upon his breast, a gold-thread shirt. The small boy took his place between Conchobar's knees, and the king began to stroke his hair. Now the stripling who by the time seven years were completed since his birth, had done such deeds: had destroyed the champions by whom two-thirds of the Ulstermen had fallen unavenged,—I hold," said Fiacha mac Firaba, the narrator, "that there is scant room for wonder though at seventeen he comes to the border, and kills a man, ay, two or three, or four, all in the Cattle-Raid of Cooley."

9TH CENTURY.
Translator Standish Hayes O'Grady.

The Tragic Death of Connla[1]

WHAT WAS the cause for which Cu Chulainn slew his son?

Not hard to tell. Cu Chulainn went to be taught craft of arms by Scathach, daughter of Ardgeimm, in Letha,[2] until he attained mastership of feats with her. And Aife, a neighboring princess, went to him, and he left her pregnant. And he said to her that she would bear a son. "Keep this golden thumb-ring," said he, "until it fits the boy. When it fits him, let him come to seek me in Ireland. Let no man put him off his road, let him not make himself known to any man, nor let him refuse combat to any."

That day seven years the boy went forth to seek his father. The men of Ulster were at a gathering by Tracht Eisi (Strand of the Track), when they saw the boy coming towards them across the sea, a skiff of bronze under him, and gilt oars in his hand. In the skiff he had a heap of stones. He would put a stone in his staff-sling, and launch a stunning shot at the sea-birds, so that he brought them down, and they alive. Then would he let them up into the air again. He would perform his palate-feat, between both hands, so that it was too quick for the eye to perceive. He would tune his voice for them, and bring them down for the second time. Then he revived them once more.

"Well, now," said Conchobar, "woe to the land into which yonder lad comes! If grown-up men of the island from which he comes were to come, they would grind us to dust, when a

---

[1] See Introduction, p. xvii.
[2] Brittany or the continent in general.

small boy makes that practice. Let some one go to meet him! Let him not allow the boy to come on land at all!"

"Who shall go to meet him?"

"Who should it be," said Conchobar, "but Condere son of Eochaid?"

"Why should Condere go?" said the others.

"Not hard to tell," said Conchobar. "If it is reason and eloquence he practises, then Condere is the proper person."

"I shall go to meet him," said Condere.

So Condere went just as the boy took the beach. "Thou hast come far enough, my good boy," said Condere, "for us to know whither thou goest and whence is thy race."

"I do not make myself known to any one man," said the lad, "nor do I avoid any man."

"Thou shalt not land," said Condere, "until thou hast made thyself known."

"I shall go whither I have set out," said the lad.

The boy turned away. Then said Condere: "Turn to me, my boy; Conchobar will protect thee. Turn to Conchobar, the valiant son of Nessa; to Sencha, the son of Coscra; to Cethern, the red-bladed son of Fintan, the fire that wounds battalions; to Amergin the poet; to Cumscraid of the great hosts. Welcome he whom Conall the Victorious protects."

"Thou hast met us well," said the lad. "Therefore shalt thou have thy answer. Turn back again!" said the lad. "For though thou hadst the strength of a hundred, thou art not able to check me."

"Well," said Condere, "let someone else go to speak to thee!" So Condere went to the men of Ulster and told them.

"It shall not be," said Conall the Victorious, "that the honor of Ulster be carried off while I am alive." Then he went towards the boy. "Thy play is pretty, my good boy," said Conall.

"It will not be less pretty against thee," said the lad. The lad put a stone in his sling. He sent it into the air, so that its noise and thunder as it went up reached Conall, and threw him on his back. Before he could rise, the lad put the strap of his shield upon his arms.

"Someone else against him!" said Conall. In that way the boy made mockery of the host of Ulster.

Cu Chulainn, however, was present at the time, going towards the boy, and the arm of Emer, Forgall's daughter, over his neck. "Do not go down!" said she. "It is a son of thine that is down there. Do not murder thy only son! It is not fair fight nor wise to rise up against thy son. Turn to me! Hear my voice! My advice is good. Let Cu Chulainn hear it! I know what name he will tell, if the boy down there is Connla, the only son of Aife," said Emer.

Then said Cu Chulainn: "Forbear, woman! Even though it were he who is there," said he, "I would kill him for the honor of Ulster."

Then he went down himself. "Delightful, my boy, is the play which thou makest," said he.

"Your play, though, is not so," said the little boy, "that two of you did not come, so that I may make myself known to them."

"It would have been necessary to bring a small boy along with me," said Cu Chulainn. "However, thou wilt die unless thou tellest thy name."

"Let it be so!" said the lad. The boy made for him. They exchanged blows. The lad, by a properly measured stroke with the sword, cropped off Cu Chulainn's hair. "The mockery has come to a head!" said Cu Chulainn: "Now let us wrestle!"

"I cannot reach thy belt," said the boy. He got upon two stones, and thrust Cu Chulainn thrice between two pillar-stones, while the boy did not move either of his feet from the stones until his feet went into the stones up to his ankles. The track of his feet is there still. Hence is the Strand of the Track (Tracht Eisi) in Ulster.

Then they went into the sea to drown each other, and twice the boy ducked him. Thereupon Cu Chulainn went at the boy from the water, and played him false with the *gae bulga;*[1] for to

[1] A mysterious weapon, probably some kind of spear (*gae*), given to Cuchulain by Scathach.

no man had Scathach ever taught the use of that weapon save to
Cu Chulainn alone. He sent it at the boy through the water, so
that his bowels fell about his feet.

"Now, this is what Scathach never taught me!" cried the boy.
"Woe that thou has wounded me!"

"It is true," said Cu Chulainn. He took the boy between his
arms, and carried him till he let him down before the men of
Ulster. "Here is my son for you, men of Ulster," said he.

"Alas!" said the men; and "It is true," said the boy. "If I
were among you to the end of five years, I should vanquish the
men of the world before you on every side, and you would hold
kingship as far as Rome. Since it is as it is, point out to me the
famous men that are on the spot, that I may take leave of
them!"

Thereupon he put his arms round the neck of one after
another, bade farewell to his father, and forthwith died. Then
his cry of lament was raised, his grave made, his stone set up,
and to the end of three days no calf was let to their cows by the
men of Ulster, to commemorate him.

9TH CENTURY.
Translator Kuno Meyer.

Fand Yields Cuchulain to Emer[1]

Emer, he is your man, now,
And well may you wear him.
When I can no longer hold him,
I must yield him.

Many a man has wanted me,
But I have kept my vows.
I have been an honest woman,
Under the roofs and boughs.

Pity the woman loves a man,
When no love invites her.
Better for her to fly from love
If unloved, love bites her,

       9TH CENTURY.
       Translator Sean O'Faolain.

---

[1] In this poem taken from *The Sick-Bed of Cuchulain*, a story preserved in *The Book of the Dun Cow*, Fand, a woman of the other world, yields to Emer, her earthly rival for the love of Cuchulain.

Cuchulain's Lament for Ferdiad[1]

Play was each, pleasure each,
Till Ferdiad faced the beach;
One had been our student life,
One in strife of school our place,
One our gentle teacher's grace
    Loved o'er all and each.

Play was each, pleasure each,
Till Ferdiad faced the beach;
One had been our wonted ways,
One the praise for feat of fields,
Scathach gave two victor shields
    Equal prize to each.

Play was each, pleasure each,
Till Ferdiad faced the beach;
Dear that pillar of pure gold
Who fell cold beside the ford.
Hosts of heroes felt his sword
    First in battle's breach.

---

[1] In the war between Ulster and Connaught, which is the theme
of *The Cattle Raid of Cooley*, Cuchulain vanquishes Ferdiad, his
boyhood friend and sworn brother, who with other Ulster warriors
had gone over to the enemy after the betrayal of the sons of Usnech
by Conchubor king of Ulster.

Play was each, pleasure each,
Till Ferdiad faced the beach;
Lion fiery, fierce and bright,
Wave whose might no thing withstands,
Sweeping, with the shrinking sands,
 Horror o'er the beach.

Play was each, pleasure each,
Till Ferdiad faced the beach;
Loved Ferdiad, dear to me:
I shall dree his death for aye—
Yesterday a mountain he,
 A shade today.

9TH CENTURY.
Translator George Sigerson.

The Death of Cuchulain[1]

WHEN Cu Chulainn's foes came for the last time against him, his land was filled with smoke and flame, the weapons fell from their racks, and the day of his death drew nigh. The evil tidings were brought to him, and the maiden Leborcham bade him arise, though he was worn out with fighting in defence of the plain of Muirthemne, and Niam, wife of Conall the Victorious, also spoke to him; so he sprang to his arms, and flung his mantle around him; but the brooch fell and pierced his foot, forewarning him. Then he took his shield and ordered his charioteer Loeg to harness his horse, the Gray of Macha.

"I swear by the gods by whom my people swear," said Loeg, "though the men of Conchobar's province were around the Gray of Macha, they could not bring him to the chariot. I never refused thee till today. If thou wilt, come thou, and speak with the Gray himself."

Cu Chulainn went to him. And thrice did the horse turn his left side to his master. On the night before, the Morrigu[2] had broken the chariot, for she liked not Cu Chulainn's going to the battle, for she knew that he would not come again to Emain Macha. Then Cu Chulainn reproached his horse, saying that he was not wont to deal thus with his master.

Thereat the Gray of Macha came and let his big round tears of blood fall on Cu Chulainn's feet. And then Cu Chulainn leaped into the chariot, and drove it suddenly southwards along the Road of Midluachar.

And Leborcham met him and besought him not to leave them; and the thrice fifty queens who were in Emain Macha and who loved him cried to him with a great cry. And when he turned his chariot to the right, they gave a scream of wailing and

---

[1] See Introduction, p. xviii.
[2] A female demon associated with battle and slaughter.

lamentation, and smote their hands, for they knew that he would not come to them again.

The house of his nurse that had fostered him was before him on the road. He used to go to it whenever he went driving past her southwards and from the south. And she kept for him always a vessel with drink therein. Now he drank a drink and fared forth, bidding his nurse farewell. Then he saw three Crones, blind of the left eye, before him on the road. They had cooked on spits of rowantree a dog with poisons and spells. And one of the things that Cu Chulainn was bound not to do, was going to a cooking-hearth and consuming the food.[1] And another of the things that he must not do, was eating his namesake's flesh.[2] He sped on and was about to pass them, for he knew that they were not there for his good.

Then said a Crone to him: "Visit us, O Cu Chulainn."

"I will not visit you in sooth," said Cu Chulainn.

"The food is only a hound," said she. "Were this a great cooking-hearth thou wouldst have visited us. But because what is here is little, thou comest not. Unseemly are the great who endure not the little and poor."

Then he drew nigh to her, and the Crone gave him the shoulder-blade of the hound out of her left hand. And then Cu Chulainn ate it out of his left hand, and put it under his left thigh. The hand that took it and the thigh under which he put it were seized from trunk to end, so that the normal strength abode not in them.

Then he drove along the Road of Midluachar around Sliab Fuait; and his enemy Erc son of Cairbre saw him in his chariot, with his sword shining redly in his hand, and the light of valor hovering over him, and his three-hued hair like strings of golden thread over the edge of the anvil of some cunning craftsman.

"That man is coming towards us, O men of Erin!" said Erc; "await him." So they made a fence of their linked shields, and

---

[1] Because of his geasa or taboos.

[2] Since his name was Cu (hound), he was forbidden to eat dog's flesh.

at each corner Erc made them place two of their bravest feign-
ing to fight each other, and a satirist with each of these pairs,
and he told the satirists to ask Cu Chulainn for his spear, for
the sons of Calatin had prophesied of his spear that a king
would be slain by it, unless it were given when demanded. And
he made the men of Erin utter a great cry. And Cu Chulainn
rushed against them in his chariot, performing his three
thunder-feats; and he plied his spear and sword; so that the
halves of their heads and skulls and hands and feet, and their
red bones were scattered broadcast throughout the plain of
Muirthemne, in number like to the sands of the sea and stars
of heaven and dewdrops of May, flakes of snow, hailstones,
leaves in the forest, buttercups on Mag Breg, and grass under
the hoofs of herds on a day in summer. And gray was the field
with their brains after that onslaught and plying of weapons
which Cu Chulainn dealt unto them.

Then he saw one of the pairs of warriors contending together,
and the satirist called on him to intervene, and Cu Chulainn
leaped at them, and with two blows of his fist dashed out their
brains.

"That spear to me!" said the satirist.

"I swear what my people swear," said Cu Chulainn, "thou
dost not need it more than I do. The men of Erin are upon me
here and I am attacking them."

"I will revile thee if thou givest it not," said the satirist.

"I have never yet been reviled because of my niggardliness or
my churlishness."

With that Cu Chulainn flung the spear at him with its
handle foremost, and it passed through his head and killed
nine on the other side of him.

And Cu Chulainn drove through the host, but Lugaid son of
Cu Roi got the spear.

"What will fall by this spear, O sons of Calatin?" asked
Lugaid.

"A king will fall by that spear," said the sons of Calatin.

Then Lugaid flung the spear at Cu Chulainn's chariot, and it reached the charioteer, Loeg mac Riangabra, and all his bowels came forth on the cushion of the chariot.

Then said Loeg, "Bitterly have I been wounded," etc.

Thereafter Cu Chulainn drew out the spear, and Loeg bade him farewell. Then said Cu Chulainn: "Today I shall be warrior and I shall be charioteer also."

Then he saw the second pair contending, and one of them said it was a shame for him not to intervene. And Cu Chulainn sprang upon them and dashed them into pieces against a rock.

"That spear to me, O Cu Chulainn!" said the satirist.

"I swear what my people swear, thou dost not need the spear more than I do. On my hand and my valor and my weapons it rests today to sweep the four provinces of Erin today from the plain of Muirthemne."

"I will revile thee," said the satirist.

"I am not bound to grant more than one request this day, and, moreover, I have already paid for my honor."

"I will revile Ulster for thy default," said the satirist.

"Never yet has Ulster been reviled for my refusal nor for my churlishness. Though little of my life remains to me, Ulster shall not be reviled this day."

Then Cu Chulainn cast his spear at him by the handle and it went through his head and killed nine behind him, and Cu Chulainn drove through the host even as he had done before.

Then Erc son of Cairbre took the spear. "What shall fall by this spear, O sons of Calatin?" said Erc son of Cairbre.

"Not hard to say: a king falls by that spear," said the sons of Calatin.

"I heard you say that a king would fall by the spear which Lugaid long since cast."

"And that is true," said the sons of Calatin. "Thereby fell the king of the charioteers of Erin, namely Cu Chulainn's charioteer, Loeg mac Riangabra."

Now Erc cast the spear at Cu Chulainn, and it lighted on his horse, the Gray of Macha. Cu Chulainn snatched out the spear. And each of them bade the other farewell. Thereat the Gray of

Macha left him with half the yoke under his neck and went into the Gray's Linn in Sliab Fuait.

Thereupon Cu Chulainn again drove through the host and saw the third pair contending, and he intervened as he had done before, and the satirist demanded his spear and Cu Chulain at first refused it.

"I will revile thee," said the satirist.

"I have paid for my honor today. I am not bound to grant more than one request this day."

"I will revile Ulster for thy fault."

"I have paid for Ulster's honor," said Cu Chulainn.

"I will revile thy race," said the satirist.

"Tidings that I have been defamed shall never reach the land I have not reached. For little there is of my life remaining."

So Cu Chulainn flung the spear to him, handle foremost, and it went through his head and through thrice nine other men.

" 'Tis grace with wrath, O Cu Chulainn," said the satirist.

Then Cu Chulainn for the last time drove through the host, and Lugaid took the spear, and said:

"What will fall by this spear, O sons of Calatin?"

"I heard you say that a king would fall by the spear that Erc cast this morning."

"That is true," said they, "the king of the steeds of Erin fell by it, namely the Gray of Macha."

Then Lugaid flung the spear and struck Cu Chulainn, and his bowels came forth on the cushion of the chariot, and his only horse, the Black Sainglenn, fled away, with half the yoke hanging to him, and left the chariot and his master, the king of the heroes of Erin, dying alone on the plain.

Then said Cu Chulainn, "I would fain go as far as that loch to drink a drink thereout."

"We give thee leave," said they, "provided that thou come to us again."

"I will bid you come for me," said Cu Chulainn, "if I cannot come myself."

Then he gathered his bowels into his breast, and went forth to the loch.

And there he drank his drink, and washed himself, and came forth to die, calling on his foes to come to meet him.

Now a great mearing went westwards from the loch and his eye lit upon it, and he went to a pillar-stone which is in the plain, and he put his breast-girdle round it that he might not die seated nor lying down, but that he might die standing up. Then came the men all around him, but they durst not go to him, for they thought he was alive.

"It is a shame for you," said Erc son of Cairbre, "not to take that man's head in revenge for my father's head which was taken by him."

Then came the Gray of Macha to Cu Chulainn to protect him so long as his soul was in him and the "hero's light" out of his forehead remained. And the Gray of Macha wrought three red routs all around him. And fifty fell by his teeth and thirty by each of his hoofs. This is what he slew of the host. And hence is the saying, "Not keener were the victorious courses of the Gray of Macha after Cu Chulainn's slaughter."

And then came the battle goddess Morrigu and her sisters in the form of scald-crows and sat on his shoulder. "That pillar is not wont to be under birds," said Erc son of Cairbre.

Then Lugaid arranged Cu Chulainn's hair over his shoulder, and cut off his head. And then fell the sword from Cu Chulainn's hand, and smote off Lugaid's right hand, which fell on the ground. And Cu Chulainn's right hand was cut off in revenge for this. Lugaid and the hosts then marched away, carrying with them Cu Chulainn's head and his right hand, and they came to Tara, and there is the "Sick-bed" of his head and his right hand, and the full of the cover of his shield of mould.

From Tara they marched southwards to the river Liffey. But meanwhile the hosts of Ulster were hurrying to attack their foes, and Conall the Victorious, driving in front of them, met the Gray of Macha streaming with blood. Then Conall knew that Cu Chulainn had been slain. And he and the Gray of Macha sought Cu Chulainn's body. They saw Cu Chulainn at the pillar-stone. Then went the Gray of Macha and laid his head on Cu Chulainn's breast. And Conall said, "A heavy care to the Gray of Macha is that corpse."

And Conall followed the hosts meditating vengeance, for he was bound to avenge Cu Chulainn. For there was a comrades' covenant between Cu Chulainn and Conall the Victorious, namely, that whichever of them was first killed should be avenged by the other. "And if I be the first killed," Cu Chulainn had said, "how soon wilt thou avenge me?"

"The day on which thou shalt be slain," said Conall, "I will avenge thee before that evening. And if I be slain," said Conall, "how soon wilt thou avenge me?"

"Thy blood will not be cold on earth," said Cu Chulainn, "before I shall avenge thee." So Conall pursued Lugaid to the Liffey.

Then was Lugaid bathing. "Keep a lookout over the plain," said he to his charioteer, "that no one come to us without being seen."

The charioteer looked. "One horseman is here coming to us," said he, "and great are the speed and swiftness with which he comes. Thou wouldst deem that all the ravens of Erin were above him. Thou wouldst deem that flakes of snow were specking the plain before him."

"Unbeloved is the horseman that comes there," said Lugaid. "It is Conall the Victorious, mounted on the Dewy-Red. The birds thou sawest above him are the sods from that horse's hoofs. The snow-flakes thou sawest specking the plain before him are the foam from that horse's lips and from the curbs of his bridle. Look again," said Lugaid, "what road is he coming?"

"He is coming to the ford," said the charioteer, "the path that the hosts have taken."

"Let that horse pass us," said Lugaid. "We desire not to fight against him." But when Conall reached the middle of the ford he spied Lugaid and his charioteer and went to them.

"Welcome is a debtor's face!" said Conall. "He to whom he oweth debts demands them of him. I am thy creditor for the slaying of my comrade Cu Chulainn, and here I am suing thee for this."

They then agreed to fight on the plain of Argetros, and there Conall wounded Lugaid with his javelin. Thence they went to a place called Ferta Lugdach.

"I wish," said Lugaid, "to have the truth of men from thee."

"What is that?" asked Conall the Victorious.

"That thou shouldst use only one hand against me, for one hand only have I."

"Thou shalt have it," said Conall the Victorious.

So Conall's hand was bound to his side with ropes. There for the space between two of the watches of the day they fought, and neither of them prevailed over the other. When Conall found that he prevailed not, he saw his steed the Dewy-Red by Lugaid. And the steed came to Lugaid and tore a piece out of his side.

"Woe is me!" said Lugaid, "that is not the truth of men, O Conall."

"I gave it only on my own behalf," said Conall. "I gave it not on behalf of savage beasts and senseless things."

"I know now," said Lugaid, "that thou wilt not go till thou takest my head with thee, since we took Cu Chulainn's head from him. So take," said he, "my head in addition to thine own, and add my realm to thy realm, and my valor to thy valor. For I prefer that thou shouldst be the best hero in Erin."

Thereat Conall the Victorious cut off Lugaid's head. And Conall and his Ulstermen then returned to Emain Macha. That week they entered it not in triumph. But the soul of Cu Chulainn appeared there to the thrice fifty queens who had loved him, and they saw him floating in his phantom chariot over Emain Macha, and they heard him chant a mystic song of the coming of Christ and the Day of Doom.

8TH CENTURY.
Translator Whitley Stokes.

The Story of Deirdre

THE MEN of Ulster were drinking in the house of Feidhlimidh son of Dall, Conchobhar's story-teller. Now Feidhlimidh's wife was waiting on the company, standing before them, and she was pregnant. Drinking-horns and servings of food went round, and the men raised a howl of drunkenness. When they were about to go to bed, the woman came to her couch. As she crossed the middle of the house the baby shrieked in her womb, so that it was heard throughout the courtyard. Everyone inside jumped up at each other at that screech, so that they were face to face in the house. Then Senchae son of Ailill restrained them. "Do not move," said he, "let the woman be brought to us so that the cause of this noise may be discovered." The woman was brought to them then . . . Then she ran to Cathbhadh, because he was a seer; . . . and Cathbhadh said:

> "Under the cradle of your womb
> cried a woman of curling yellow golden hair,
> with slow grey-pupilled eyes.
> Like the foxglove are her purple cheeks,
> to the colour of snow we compare
> the spotless treasure of her teeth.
> Bright are her lips, of vermilion red.
> A woman for whom there will be many slaughters
> among the chariot-warriors of Ulster." . . .

Then Cathbhadh put his hand on the woman's belly, so that the baby stormed under his hand. "Truly," said he, "it is a girl there, and *Deirdriu* shall be her name, and evil will come of her." The girl was born after that. . . .

"Let the girl be killed," said the warriors. "Not so," said Conchobhar, "the girl shall be taken by me to-morrow," said Conchobhar, "and shall be brought up under my own control,

and shall be the woman who will be in my company." And
the Ulstermen did not dare correct him in this.

It was done, then. She was brought up by Conchobhar until
she was the most wonderfully beautiful girl in Ireland. In a
court apart she was reared, so that none of the Ulstermen might
see her until the time when she should sleep with Conchobhar;
and there was no one who might be allowed into that court but
her foster-father and her foster-mother, and also Lebhorcham,
for she could not be excluded because she was a satirist.

Now once upon a time the girl's foster-father was skinning a
trespassing calf in the snow outside, in the winter, to cook it for
her. She saw a raven drinking the blood on the snow. Then she
said to Lebhorcham, "I should dearly love any man with those
three colours, with hair like the raven and cheek like the blood
and body like the snow." "Dignity and good luck be yours,"
said Lebhorcham, "it is not far from you. He is in the house
beside you, Noísi the son of Uisliu." "I shall not be well, truly,"
said she, "until I see him." . . .

Now when he, this same Noísi, was alone outside, she stole
away out to him as if to pass him by, and he did not recognise
her. "Pretty is the heifer which passes by us," said he. "The
heifers are bound to be well-grown," said she, "where there are
no bulls." "You have the bull of the province, the king of
Ulster," said he. "I would choose between you two," said she,
"and I would take a young little bull like you." "Not so," said
he, "because of Cathbhadh's prophecy." "Is it to reject me that
you say that?" said she. "It is indeed," said he. At that she
leaped at him and seized his ears on his head. "Two ears of
shame and derision are these," she said, "unless you carry me
off with you." "Away from me, woman," said he. "That will
happen to you," she said. At this his bass call went up from
him. When the Ulstermen beyond heard the call, every one
of them fell upon the other. The sons of Uisliu came out to
restrain their brother. "What is the matter with you?" they
said, "do not let the Ulstermen kill each other because of your
fault." Then he told them what had been done to him. "Evil
will come of it," said the warriors. "Though it should, you

shall not be in disgrace as long as we are alive. We will go with
her into another land. There is not a king in Ireland who will
not make us welcome." This was their conclusion. They went
off that night, with a hundred and fifty warriors of theirs and
a hundred and fifty women and a hundred and fifty hounds and
a hundred and fifty servants, and Deirdriu along with the others
with them.

They were in sanctuary for a long while throughout Ireland,
so that their destruction was often attempted by the kings of
Ireland through the plots and wiles of Conchobhar, round from
Assaroe southwest to Howth again to the northeast. However
the Ulstermen hounded them across to the land of Scotland,
and they settled down in the wilds there. When the hunting of
the mountain failed them they turned to taking the cattle of the
men of Scotland for themselves. These went to destroy them
in a single day, whereupon they went to the king of Scotland,
and he admitted them into his household, and they took service
with him; and they set up their huts on the green. Because of
the girl the huts were made, so that no one with them should
see her, for fear they would be killed for her sake.

Once upon a time then, the steward went early in the morning so that he went round their house. He saw the couple
asleep. He went thereupon and woke the king. "I have not
found a woman worthy of you until to-day," said he; "there is
a woman worthy of the King of the Western World with
Noísi son of Uisliu. Let Noísi be killed immediately, and let the
woman sleep with you," said the steward. "No," said the king,
"but you do go to woo her for me secretly every day." That
was done. But what the steward used to say to her by day,
she would tell her husband straightway the same night. Since
nothing was got from her, the sons of Uisliu were ordered to go
into risks and fights and difficulties, so that they might be killed.
Nevertheless they were so brave in every slaughter that it was
impossible to do anything to them in these attacks.

After taking counsel about it against her, the men of Scotland
were mustered to kill them. She told Noísi. "Go away," said
she, "for if you have not gone away by to-night you will be

killed to-morrow." They went away that night, so that they were on an island of the sea. This was told to the Ulstermen. "It is sad, Conchobhar," said the Ulstermen, "that the sons of Uisliu should fall in a hostile land through the fault of a bad woman. It would be better to escort them and feed them, and not to kill them, and for them to come to their land, rather than to fall before their enemies." "Let them come, then," said Conchobhar, "and let sureties go for them." That was brought to them. "It is welcome to us," they said; "we shall go, and let Ferghus and Dubhthach and Cormac son of Conchobhar come as sureties for us." These went and escorted them from the sea.

Now, through the counsel of Conchobhar people rivalled each other to invite Ferghus to ale-feasts, for the sons of Uisliu declared that they would not eat food in Ireland except the food of Conchobhar first.[1] Then Fiachu son of Ferghus went with them, and Ferghus and Dubhthach stayed behind, and the sons of Uisliu came until they were on the green at Emhain. Then too Éoghan son of Durthacht, the king of Fernmhagh, came to make peace with Conchobhar, for he had been at war with him for a long time. It was he who was entrusted with killing the sons of Uisliu, with the soldiers of Conchobhar around him so that they might not come at him.

The sons of Uisliu were standing in the middle of the green, and the women were sitting on the rampart of Emhain. Then Éoghan went against them with his troop over the green, but the son of Ferghus came so that he was beside Noísi. Éoghan welcomed them with a thrusting blow of a great spear into Noísi, so that his back broke within him. At that the son of Ferghus threw himself and put his arms round Noísi and bore him under, so that he cast himself down on him. And so it is

---

[1] Conchubor's strategy was to separate the Sons of Uisliu from Fergus, their surety, who was under taboo not to refuse an invitation to an ale-feast. Conchubor also knew that the Sons of Uisliu, on the other hand, were obligated to refuse such an invitation since they had sworn, for their own protection, to partake only of his food according to the rule of hospitality.

that Noísi was struck from above, right through the son of
Ferghus. They were killed then all over the green, so that none
escaped but those who went by point of spear and edge of
sword; and she was brought across to Conchobhar so that she
was beside him, and her hands were bound behind her back.

Then this was told to Ferghus and Dubhthach and Cormac.
They came and did great deeds straightway; that is to say,
Dubhthach killed Maine son of Conchobhar, and Fiachna son
of Feidhelm, daughter of Conchobhar, was slain by a single
thrust, and Ferghus killed Traighthrén son of Traighlethan and
his brother; and this was an outrage to Conchobhar. And a
battle was fought between them after that on the same day, so
that three hundred Ulstermen fell between them; and Dubhthach killed the girls of Ulster before morning and Ferghus
burned Emhain. Then they went to Ailill and Medhbh, because they knew that couple would be able to support them;
but it was no love-nest for the Ulstermen. Three thousand was
the number of the exiles. Till the end of sixteen years, weeping
and trembling never ceased in Ulster at their hands, but there
was weeping and trembling at their hands every single night.

She was a year with Conchobhar, and during that time she
did not smile, and did not take her fill of food or sleep, and did
not raise her head from her knee . . . "What do you see that you
most hate?" said Conchobhar. "Yourself, surely," said she,
"and Éoghan son of Durthacht." "Then you shall be a year
with Éoghan," said Conchobhar. He brought her then beside
Éoghan. They went the next day to the assembly of Macha.
She was behind Éoghan in a chariot. She had vowed that she
would not see her two husbands together on earth. "Well,
Deirdriu," said Conchobhar, "it is the eye of a ewe between
two rams that you make between me and Éoghan." There was
a great boulder of stone before her. She dashed her head on
the stone so that she made fragments of her head, so that she
died.

8TH OR 9TH CENTURY.
Translator Kenneth Jackson.

The Colloquy of the Old Men[1]

WHEN THE Battle of Comar, the Battle of Gabra, and the Battle of Ollarba had been fought, and after the fian[2] were for the most part extinguished, the residue of them had dispersed in small bands and in companies throughout all Ireland, until at the time which concerns us there remained of them two good warriors only: Oisin son of Finn, and Cailte son of Crunnchu son of Ronan (whose lusty vigor and power of spear-throwing were now dwindled down), and so many fighting men as with themselves made twice nine. These twice nine came out of the flowery-soiled and well-wooded borders of Sliab Fuait and into the Lugbarta Bana, at the present day called Lugmad, where at the falling of the evening clouds that night they were melancholy, dispirited.

Cailte said to Oisin then, "Good now, Oisin, before the day's end what path shall we take in quest of entertainment for the night?"

Oisin answered, "I know not, seeing that of the ancients of the fian, and of Finn's former people but three survive: I and thyself, Cailte, with Cama, the female-chief and female-custodian who, from the time he was a boy until the day he died, kept Finn mac Cumaill safe."

Cailte said, "We are entitled to this night's lodging and provision from her; for it is not possible to rehearse nor to show the quantity which Finn, captain of the fian, bestowed on her of precious things and of treasures, including the third best thing of price that Finn ever acquired, namely, the Anga-

----

[1] See Introduction, p. xix.

[2] A band of semi-nomadic guerrilla fighters, particularly that commanded by Finn. The modern English word *Fenian*, meaning follower of Finn, derives not from Finn's name but from *fian* (plu *fianna*). See "The Fianna," p. 95.

lach or drinking horn which Moriath daughter of the king of
Greece gave to Finn, and Finn to Cama."

With Cama, therefore, they got hospitality for the night;
their names she inquired of them and at their sound wept
vehement showers of tears; then she and they, each of the
other, sought to have tidings. Next they entered into the bed-
house disposed for them, and Cama the female chief prescribed their repast: that the freshest of all kinds of meats and
the oldest of all sorts of drink be given them, for she knew in
what fashion they used to be fed. She knew also how much it
was that many a time before the present had constituted a
sufficiency for Oisin and Cailte. Languidly and feebly she
arose and held forth on the fian and on Finn mac Cumaill; of
Oisin's son Oscar too she spoke, of Mac Lugach, of the Battle
of Gabra with other matters; and by reason of this in the end
a great silence settled on them all.

Then Cailte said, "Such matters we hold to be not more
painful than the way in which the twice nine that we are of
the remnant of that great and goodly fellowship must perforce
part, and separate from each other."

Oisin answered, "Since they have departed, in me, by my
word, there is no more fight and pith."

Valiant as were these warrior-men, here nevertheless with
Cama they wept, in gloom, in sadness, and in dejection. Their
adequate allowance of meat and drink was given them; they
tarried there for three days and three nights, then bade Cama
farewell, and Oisin said:

> Cama to-day is sorrowful: she is come to the point
> where she must swim; Cama without either son or grand-
> son: it has befallen her to be old and blighted.

Forth from the enclosure they came now, and out upon the
green; there they took a resolve, which was this: to separate,
and this parting of theirs was a sundering of soul and body.
Even so they did: for Oisin went to the fairy-mound of Uch
Cletigh, where was his mother, Blai daughter of Derc Dian-

scothach; while Cailte took his way to Inber Bic Loingsigh which at present is called Mainister Droichid Atha (the monastery of Drogheda) from Beg Loigsech son of Arist that was drowned in it, that is, the king of the Romans' son, who came to invade Ireland; but a tidal wave drowned him there in his *inber* (river-mouth). He went on to Linn Feic (Fiacc's Pool), on the bright-streaming Boyne; southwards over the Old Mag Breg, and to the rath (stronghold) of Drum Derg, where Patrick mac Calpuirn was.

Just then Patrick was chanting the Lord's order of the canon (*i.e.*, Mass), and lauded the Creator, and pronounced a benediction on the rath where Finn mac Cumaill had been, the rath of Drum Derg. The clerics saw Cailte and his band draw near them; and fear fell upon them before the tall men with their huge wolf-dogs that accompanied them, for they were not people of one epoch or of one time with the clergy.

Then Heaven's distinguished one, that pillar of dignity and angel on earth, Calpurn's son Patrick, apostle of the Gael, rose and took the sprinkler to sprinkle holy water on the great men; floating over whom until that day there had been and were now a thousand legions of demons Into the hills and brush wood, into the outer borders of the region and of the country, the demons departed forthwith in all directions; after which the enormous men sat down.

"Good now," said Patrick to Cailte, "what name hast thou?"

"I am Cailte son of Crunnchu son of Ronan."

For a long while the clergy marvelled greatly as they gazed upon them; for the largest man of them reached but to the waist, or else to the shoulder of any given one of the others, and they sitting.

Patrick said again, "Cailte, I wish to beg a favor of thee."

He answered, "If I have but that much strength or power, it shall be had; at all events, tell me what it is."

"To have in our vicinity here a well of pure water, from which we might baptize the tribes of Breg, of Meath, and of Usnech."

"Noble and righteous one," said Cailte, "that have I for thee," and they, crossing the rath's wall, came out; in his hand Cailte took Patrick's staff and in a little while right in front of them they saw a loch-well, sparkling and very clear. The size and thickness of the cress and of the brooklime that grew on it was a wonderment to them; then Cailte began to tell its fame and qualities, in doing of which he said:

O Well of Traig Da Ban (Strand of the Two Women), beautiful thy cresses, luxurious-branching. Since thy produce is neglected on thee thy brooklime is not suffered to grow. Forth from thy banks thy trout are to be seen, thy wild swine in the neighboring wilderness; the deer of thy fair hunting cragland, thy dappled and red-chested fawns! Thy mast all hanging on the branches of thy trees; thy fish in estuaries of thy rivers; lovely the color of thy purling streams, O thou that thyself art azure-hued, and again green with reflection of surrounding copsewood! . . .

" 'Tis well," Patrick said; "hath our dinner and our provisions reached us yet?"

"It has so," answered the bishop Sechnall.

"Distribute it," said Patrick, "and one half give to yon nine tall warriors of the survivors of the fian." Then his bishops and his priests and his psalmodists arose and blessed the meat; and of both meat and liquor they consumed their full sufficiency, yet so as to serve their soul's welfare.

Patrick said then, "Was he not a good lord with whom ye were, that is, Finn mac Cumaill?"

Upon which Cailte uttered this little tribute of praise:

Were but the brown leaf which the wood sheds from it gold—were but the white billows silver—Finn would have given it all away.

"Who or what was it that maintained you so in your life?" Patrick inquired; and Cailte answered, "Truth that was in our hearts, and strength in our arms, and fulfillment in our tongues."

"Good, Cailte," Patrick went on; "in the houses which

before our time thou didst frequent were there drinking-horns, or cups, or goblets of crystal and of pale gold?"

And Cailte answered, "The number of the horns that were in my lord's house was as follows:

> Twelve drinking-horns and three hundred made of gold Finn had; whenever they came to the pouring out, the quantity of liquor they held was immense.

"Were it not for us an impairing of the devout life, an occasion of neglecting prayer, and of deserting converse with God, we, as we talked with thee, would feel the time pass quickly, O warrior."

Then Cailte began to rehearse the drinking-horns, with the chiefs and lords whose they had been:

> Horns that were in Finn's house, their names I bear in mind.

.   .   .   .

"Success and benediction attend thee, Cailte," Patrick said; "this is to me a lightening of spirit and of mind; and now tell us another tale."

"I will indeed; but say what story thou wouldst be pleased to have."

"In the fian had ye horses or cavalry?"

Cailte answered, "We had so; thrice fifty foals from one mare and a single sire."

"Whence were they procured?"

"I will tell thee the truth of the matter:

"A young man that served with Finn, Arthur son of Beine Brit, his company being thrice nine men. Finn set on foot the hunting of Benn Etair (which indeed turned out to be a bountiful and fruitful hunt). They slipped their hounds accordingly, while Finn took his seat on Carn an Feinneda (Cairn of the Fian) between Etar's top and the sea; there his spirit was gay within him when he listened to the maddened stags' bellowing as by the hounds of the fian they were rapidly killed.

"Where Arthur son of Beine Brit was stationed was between

the main body of the hunt and the sea in order that the deer should not take to the sea and elude them by swimming. But Arthur, being thus on the outside and close against the shore, marked three of Finn's hounds, Bran, Sceolaing, and Adnuall, and he resolved on a plan, which was: himself and his three nines to depart away across the sea, he carrying off with him into his own land those same three hounds. This plot was put into action then; for well I know that they, having with them those three hounds, crossed the sea's surface and at Inber Mara Gaimiach in Britainland took harbor and haven. They landed there, proceeded to the mountain of Lodan son of Lir, and hunted it.

"After this occurrence the fian made an end of their hunting and of their woodland slaughter, and camped on the eminence of Etgaeth's son Etar (Benn Etair), and as the custom was then, Finn's hounds were counted. Now his hounds were many in number, as the poet said:

> An enumerating of branches on the tree was that of Finn's full-grown hounds with his sleek melodious pack of youngsters; three hundred of the first there were, and puppy-hounds two hundred.

"Many men they must have been who owned those," said Patrick.

"True for you indeed," Cailte answered, "for the tale that used to be in Finn's house was this:

> They that dwelt in the house of Finn were three times fifty of joyous leaders of the fian; three hundred confidential servitors as well, and two hundred fosterlings that were worthy of their chiefs.

"But when the hounds were counted, a great shortcoming was discovered in them: Bran, Sceolaing, Adnuall were missing, and it was told to Finn. 'Have all three battalions of the fian searched out,' he said; yet though the search was made the hounds were not found.

"To Finn then was brought a long basin of pale gold; he washed his kingly face, put his thumb under his tooth of knowledge,[1] truth was revealed to him, and he said, 'The king of the Britons' son has deprived you of your hounds; pick ye therefore nine men to go in quest of them!' They were chosen, their names being these: Diarmuid O'Duibne, of the Erna of Munster in the south; Goll mac Morna—"

"Was Goll a chief's son, or a simple warrior's?" Patrick inquired.

"A chief's," answered Cailte:

> He was son of Teigue son of Morna of the Mag, that was son of Feradach son of Fiacha son of Art of the Mag son of Muiredach son of Eochaid.

"There was Cael Croda the hundred-slayer, grandson of Nemnann, a champion that Finn had, and endowed with a deadly property, that his arm never delivered a cast that missed its mark, and that never was his hand bloodied on a man but that the same would before a nine days' term were out be dead; there was Finn's son Oisin—he that, if only a man had a head to eat with and legs to go upon and carry off his largess, never refused any."

---

[1] According to a passage in a twelfth century text (*The Boyhood Deeds of Finn*) Finn, while still a young man, went to study the art of poetry under a master named Finneces, who for seven years had been engaged in fishing the river Boyne for the fabulous salmon of knowledge. When he finally caught the salmon he gave it to his pupil to cook with instructions not to eat any of it. "The youth brought him the salmon after cooking. 'Hast thou eaten any of the salmon, my lad?' said the poet. 'No,' said the youth, 'but I burned my thumb and put it into my mouth afterwards.' 'What is thy name, my lad?' said he. 'Demne,' said the youth. 'Finn is thy name, my lad,' said he; 'and to thee was the salmon given to be eaten, and indeed thou art Finn.' Thereupon the youth ate the salmon. It is that which gave the knowledge to Finn, so that whenever he put his thumb into his mouth and sang by means of chewing marrow whatever he had been ignorant of would be revealed to him."

"Cailte," said Patrick, "that is a great character."

"And though it be so is it a true one," Cailte answered, and said:

> In the matter of gold, of silver, or concerning meat, Oisin never denied any man; nor, though another's generosity were such as might fit a chief, did Oisin ever seek ought of him.

"There was Oisin's son Oscar, the chief's son that in all Ireland was best for spear-throwing and for vigorous activity; also Ferdoman son of Bodb Derg son of the Dagda; Finn's son Raigne Wide-eye; his son Caince the Crimson-red; Glas son of Enchard Bera mac Lugach; and myself. Now, saintly Patrick, we the aforesaid within ourselves were confident that from Taprobane in the east to the garden of the Hesperides in the world's westernmost part were no four hundred warriors but, on the battle-field and hand-to-hand, we were a match for them. We had not a head without a helmet, nor a shoulder without a whitened shield, nor a right fist that grasped not two great and lengthy spears. On this expedition we went our way then until we reached Lodan mac Lir's mountain in Britain, where we had been no long time before we heard talk of men that hunted in the field.

"As regards Beine Brit's son Arthur, he just then, with his people, sat on his hunting ground. Them we charged in lively fashion, and killed all Arthur's people; but round him Oscar knit both his arms, gave him quarter, and we brought off our three hounds. Here Goll mac Morna chancing to look about him saw an iron-grey horse, flecked with spots, and wearing a bridle fitted with wrought ornaments of gold. At another glance that he threw to his left he discerned a bay horse, one not easy to lay hold of, having a wrought bridle of twice-refined silver fitted with a golden bit. This second horse Goll also seized and put into the hand of Oisin, who passed him on to Diarmuid. After successful execution and due celebration of our slaughter we came away, bringing with us the heads of those thrice nine, our hounds, and the horses, too, with

Arthur himself a prisoner, and so back to where Finn was on Benn Etair. We reached his tent, and Cailte said, 'We have brought Arthur.' This latter entered into bonds with Finn, and thereafter, up to the day on which he died, was Finn's follower. The two horses we gave to Finn, horse and mare, of whose seed were all the horses of the fian, who hitherto had not used any such. The mare bred eight times, at every birth eight foals, which were made over to the various detachments and notables of the fian, and these afterwards had chariots made." . . .

"Success and benediction be thine, Cailte. All this is to us a recreation of spirit and of mind, were it only not a destruction of devotion and a dereliction of prayer."

There they were until the morrow's morning came, when Patrick robed himself and emerged upon the green; together with his three score priests, three score psalmodists, and holy bishops three score as well, that with him spread faith and piety throughout Ireland. Patrick's two guardian angels came to him now—Aibellan and Solusbretach, of whom he inquired whether in God's sight it were convenient for him to be listening to stories of the fian. With equal emphasis, and concordantly, the angels answered him, "Holy cleric, no more than a third part of their stories do those ancient warriors tell, by reason of forgetfulness and lack of memory; but by thee be it written on tables of poets, and in learned men's words; for to the companies and nobles of the later time to give ear to these stories will be a pastime." Which said, the angels departed.

From Patrick messengers were accordingly dispatched to fetch Cailte, and he, along with the nine that were in his company, were brought to the saint; whose names were Failbe son of Flann, Eogan the Red-weaponed the King of Ulster's son, Flann son of Fergus king of Kinelconnell, Conall the Slaughterer son of Angus king of Connacht, Scannlan son of Ailill king of Ossory, Baedan son of Garb king of Corkaguiney, Luamnech Linn son of the king of Dalaradia's sons out of the north, with Fulartach son of Fingin king of the peoples of Breg and of Meath.

Patrick said, "Know ye why ye are brought to confer with me?"

"In truth we do not," they answered.

"To the end you should conform to the gospel of Heaven's and of Earth's king, the most glorious God." Then and there the water of Christ's baptism was by Patrick sprinkled on them preparatory to the baptism and conversion of all Ireland.

Then with his right hand Cailte reached across him to the rim of his shield, and gave to Patrick a ridgy mass of gold in which there were three times fifty ounces; this as a fee for the baptism of the nine with him. He said, "That was Finn's, the chief's, last wage to me and, Patrick, take it for my soul's and for my chief's soul's weal." The extent to which this mass reached on Patrick was from his middle finger's tip to his shoulder's highest point, while in width and in thickness it measured a man's cubit. Now this gold was bestowed upon the Tailchenn's[1] canonical hand-bells, on psalters, and on missals.

Patrick said again, "It is well, Cailte. What was the best hunting that the fian ever had, whether in Ireland or in Scotland?"

"The hunting of Arran."

Patrick asked, "Where is that land?"

"Between Scotland and Pictland. On the first day of the Trogan-month (which is now called Lugnasad i.e., Lammas-tide) we, to the number of the three battalions of the fian used to repair thither and there have our fill of hunting until such time as from the tree-tops the cuckoo would call in Ireland. More melodious than all music whatsoever it was to give ear to the voices of the birds as they rose from the billows and from the island's coast-line; thrice fifty separate flocks there were that encircled her, and they clad in gay brilliance of all colors, as blue and green and azure and yellow." Here Cailte uttered a lay:

---

[1] Literally "adze-head," an epithet applied to St. Patrick.

Arran of the many stags—the sea impinges on her very shoulders! an island in which whole companies are fed—and with ridges among which blue spears are reddened! Skittish deer are on her pinnacles, soft blackberries on her waving heather; cool water there is in her rivers, and mast upon her russet oaks! Greyhounds there were in her, and beagles; berries and sloes of the dark blackthorn; dwellings with their backs set close against her woods, and the deer fed scattered by her oaken thickets! A crimson crop grew on her rocks, in all her glades a faultless grass; over her crags, affording friendly refuge, leaping went on and fawns were skipping! Smooth were her level spots—her wild swine, they were fat; cheerful her fields (this is a tale that may be credited), her nuts hung on her forest-hazels' boughs, and there was sailing of long galleys past her! Right pleasant their condition all when the fair weather sets in: under her rivers' brinks trout lie; the sea-gulls wheeling round her grand cliff answer one the other—at every fitting time delectable is Arran!

"Victory and blessing wait on thee, Cailte!" said Patrick; "for the future thy stories and thyself are dear to us."

Straightway now before him Patrick saw a stronghold, a fair dwelling, and, "Cailte," he said, "what is yon town?"

"That is the proudest place that ever I was in, in Ireland or in Scotland."

"Who lived there?"

"The three sons of Lugaid Menn son of Angus, that is, the king of Ireland's three sons: Ruide and Fiacha and Eochaid were their names."

"What procured them their great wealth?"

"It was once upon a time that they came to have speech of their father to Fert na Druad northwest of Tara. 'Whence come ye, young men?' he inquired. They made answer, 'From Echlais Banguba to the southward, out of our nurse's and our guardian's house.' 'My lads, what set you on your way?' 'To crave a heritage of you, a domain.' For a space the king was silent, and then said, 'No father it was that on me conferred either country or domain, but my own luck and bright achievement. Lands therefore I will not bestow on you, but win lands for yourselves.' Whereupon they, with the ready rising of one man, rose and took their way to the green of the Brug upon the Boyne[1] where, none other in their company, they sat down. Ruide said, 'What is your plan tonight?' His brothers answered, 'Our project is to fast on the Tuatha De Danann, aiming thus to win from them good fortune in the shape of a country, of a domain, of lands, and to have vast riches.' Nor had they been long there when they marked a cheery-looking young man of a peaceful demeanor that came towards them. He saluted the king of Ireland's sons, and they replied in like manner. 'Young man, whence art thou? Whence camest thou?' 'Out of yonder brug checkered with the many lights hard by you here.' 'What name wearest thou?' 'I am the Dagda's son Bodb Derg; and to the Tuatha De Danann it was revealed that you would come to fast here to-night for lands and for great fortune. But come with me.' Simultaneously they rose and entered into the brug; supper was served to them, but they ate it not. Bodb inquired of them why it was they took no meat. 'Because the king of Ireland, our father, denied us territory and lands. Now there are in Ireland but two tribes that are equal: the sons of Mil and the Tuatha De Danann; to the alternative one of which we have come now.'

"Then the Tuatha De Danann went into council, he that in such council was most noble in rank, and authoritative, being Mider Yellow-mane son of the Dagda, who said, 'Accommodate those yonder now with three wives, since it is from wives that either fortune or misfortune is derived.' Whereat were given to them Mider's three daughters, Doirenn and Aife and Ailbe. Said Mider, 'Tell us, Bodb, what gifts shall be given them?' Bodb said, 'I will tell you. Three times fifty sons of kings are in this fairy-mound; every king's son shall give them thrice

---

[1] A famous fairy dwelling, now a group of prehistoric mounds on the river Boyne in Leinster

fifty ounces of red gold, while from me they shall have in addition thrice fifty suits of raiment various with all hues.' Aed son of Aeda Nabusach from Cnoc Ardmulla out in the sea, which to-day is called Rachrainn, a youth of the Tuatha De Danann, said, 'From me too a gift for them, viz. a horn and a vat; regarding which it needs but to fill the vat with pure water, and of this it will make mead both drinkable and having virtue to intoxicate; into the horn put bitter brine out of the deep, and on the instant it shall turn into wine.' 'A gift for them from me,' said Lir of the fairy-mound of Finnachad; 'three times fifty swords, and thrice fifty well-riveted spears of length.' 'A gift from me to them,' said the Dagda's son Angus Oc; 'a fort and stronghold, and a most excellent spacious town with lofty stockades, with light-admitting bowers, with houses of clear outlook and very roomy; all this in whatsoever place it shall please them between Rath Cobtaig and Tara.' 'A gift for them from me," said Aine daughter of Modarn; 'a she-cook that I have, to whom it is taboo to refuse meat to any; but according as she serves out, so too is her store replenished.' 'A gift from me to them,' said Bodb Derg; 'a good minstrel that I have (Fertuinne mac Trogain is his name), and though saws were being plied where there were women in sharpest pains of childbirth, and brave men that were wounded early in the day, nevertheless would they be put to sleep by the wistful melody that he makes. Yet to the dwelling in which for the time being he actually is he is not minstrel more effectively than to that whole country's inhabitants in general, for all they as well may hear him.' For three days and three night they abode in the fairy-mound.

"Angus told them to carry away out of Fid Omna three apple-trees; one in full bloom, another shedding its blossoms, and another covered with ripe fruit. Then they repaired to the stronghold given them by Angus, where they abode for three times fifty years, and until those kings disappeared; for in virtue of marriage alliance they returned again to the Tuatha De Danann and from that time forth have remained there. And that, Patrick, is the stronghold concerning which you inquired of me," said Cailte. And he sang this lay:

Three things in great plenty, and O great plenty of three things, that out of Ruide's high fort issued! a crowd of young men, a great troop of horses, the numerous greyhounds of Lugaid's three sons. Three sorts of music and O music of three kinds, that comely kings enjoyed! music of harps, melody of sweet timpans, humming of Trogan's son Fertuinne. A triple stronghold and a stronghold of three fold! sound of tramping ascending from the green of that stronghold, uproar of racing, boom of lowing kine. Three noises, and O noises three! sound of its swine, span-thick in fat and excellent, buzz of the crowd upon the palace lawn, hilarity of revellers with mead-begotten clamor. Fruit-crops in three stages, and O crops in stages three, that used to be there hanging on its boughs! a tree shedding, a tree in bloom, and yet another laden ripe. Three sons it was that Lugaid left (though their great deeds are passed away): Ruide, spacious Lugaid's son, Eochaid, and manly Fiacha. I will testify to Eochaid that never took a step in flight: never was he without his customary music, nor ever for any time without quaffing of ale. I will testify to Fiacha, though the fame of his depredations be obscured: never he uttered an expression that was excessive, and in his time was none that excelled more in valor. I will testify to Ruide, to whom those aforesaid three things (young men, horses, hounds) in great plenty flowed in: that never a thing he denied to any man, nor of a man sought anything at all. Thirty chieftains, thirty leaders, thirty champions that might befit a king: while the strength of his hundredfold host was hundreds thirtyfold thrice told.

12TH CENTURY.
Translator Standish Hayes O'Grady.

The Fianna

THIS IS the enumeration of Finn's people. Their strength was seven-score-and-ten officers, each man of these having thrice nine warriors, every one bound (as was the way with Cuchulain in the time when he was there) to certain conditions of service, namely that in satisfaction of a guarantee violated they must not accept material compensation in the matter of valuables or of meat, must not deny any guarantee, nor any single individual of them fly before nine warriors.

Not a man was taken into the Fianna nor admitted whether to the great Gathering of Usnach, to the Convention of Taillte, or to Tara's Feast, until both his paternal and his maternal correlatives, his *tuatha*[1] and kindreds, had given securities for him to the effect that though at the present instant he were slain, yet should not claim be urged in lieu of him, and this in order that to none other but to themselves alone should the Fianna look to avenge themselves. On the other hand, in case it were they that inflicted great mischiefs upon others, reprisals were not to be made upon their relatives.

Again not a man was taken until he was a prime poet versed in the twelve books of poetic composition. No man was taken till in the ground a large hole had been made (such as to reach the fold of his belt) and he put into it with his shield and a forearm's length of a hazel stick. Then must nine warriors, having nine spears, with a ten furrows width betwixt them and him, assail him and in concert let fly at him. If past that guard of his he were hurt then, he was not received into Fianship.

Not a man of them was taken till his hair had been interwoven into braids on him and he started at a run through Ireland's woods; while they, seeking to wound him, followed in his wake, there having been between him and them but one forest bough by way of interval at first. Should he be overtaken,

---

[1] People.

he was wounded and not received into the Fianna after. If his weapons had quivered in his hand, he was not taken. Should a branch in the wood have disturbed anything of his hair out of its braiding, neither was he taken. If he had cracked a dry stick under his foot as he ran he was not accepted. Unless that at full speed he had both jumped a stick level with his brow and stooped to pass under one even with his knee, he was not taken. Also, unless without slackening his pace he could with his nail extract a thorn from his foot, he was not taken into Fianship. But if he performed all this he was of Finn's people.

15TH OR 16TH CENTURY.
Translator Standish Hayes O'Grady.

The Headless Phantoms

This is a fair in Magh Eala of the king: the fair of Liffey with its brilliancy: happy for each one that goes thither, he is not like Guaire the Blind.

Guaire the Blind was not in truth my name when I used to be in the king's house, in the house of excellent Fearghus on the strand over Bearramhain.

The horses of the Fiana would come to the race, and the horses of the Munstermen of the great races: they once held three famous contests on the green of the sons of Muiridh.

A black horse belonging to Dil, son of Da Chreag, in each race that they held at the rock above Loch Goir, he won the three chief prizes of the fair.

Fiachra then besought the horse from the druid, his grand-father, gave him a hundred cattle of each kind, that he might give it in return.

"There is the fast black horse for thee," said Fiachra to the Fiana's chief: "here I give thee my sword of fame, and a horse for thy charioteer.

"Take my helmet equal to a hundred, take my shield from the lands of the Greeks, take my fierce spears and my silvern weapons.

"If it please thee better than to have nothing, chief of the Fiana, handsome king, thou shalt not go off without a gift, chief of the blade-blue Fiana."

Thereupon Fionn himself arose: he was thankful to Eoghan's son: they salute each other: not without stir was their rising together.

Fionn went before us on the way: we come with him three score hundred; to Cathair to Dún-over-Lake, 'tis there we went from the fair.

Three days and three nights in high honour we spent in Cathair's house, without lack of ale or food for Cumhall's son[1] from the great king.

Fifty rings Fionn gave him, fifty horses and fifty cows: Fionn gave the worth of his ale to Cathaoir son of Oilill.

Fionn went to try the black steed to the strand over Bearramhain; I and Caoilte follow in sportiveness, and we race right cunningly.

Even we were not slow, full swift were our bounds: one of us on his left, one on his right—there is no deer we could not have outrun.

When the king (Fionn) noticed this, he spurred his horse to Tráigh Lí, from Tráigh Lí over Tráigh Doimh Ghlais, over Fraochmhagh and over Fionn-ghlais.

Over Magh Fleisge, over Magh Cairn, over the Sean-umair of Druim Garbh, over the brink of the silvery Flesk, over the "Bedside" of the Cochrainn. Over Druim Eadair, over Druim Caoin, over Druim Dha Fhiach, over Formaoil.

When we had come to the hill, we were first by eight times: though it was we that got there first, the king's horse was nowise slow.

"This is night, the day is ended," said Fionn in good sooth "folly it was that brought us here, let us go seek a hunting booth."

---

[1] I.e. Finn.

As the king glanced aside at the crag to his left, he saw a great
house with a fire in the valley before him.

Then said Caoilte a stout saying that was no matter for boasting: "Till this night I have never seen a house in this valley
though I know it well."

"Let us start off," quoth Caoilte, "and visit it; there are many
things that I am in ignorance of:" a welcome, best of all
things, was given to the son of Cumhall of Almhain.

After this we went in on a night's visit that was rued: we were
met with screeching, wailing, and shouting, and a clamorous
rabbly household.

Within stood a grey-haired churl in the midst: he quickly seizes
Finn's horse: he takes down the door on this side from its
iron hinges.

We sit down on the hard couch that has to rest us all at once:
the log of elder that is on the hearth has all but quenched the
fire.

The unmusical churl spoke a speech that did not greatly please
us: "Rise up, ye folk that are within: sing a song for the
king-feinnidh."[1]

Nine bodies rise out of the corner from the side next to us: nine
heads from the other side on the iron couch.

They set up nine horrid screeches: though matched in loudness,
they were not matched in harmony: the churl answered in
turn, and the headless body answered.

Though each rough strain of theirs was bad, the headless body's
strain was worse: there was no strain but was tolerable compared to the shriek of the one-eyed man.

The song they sang for us would have wakened dead men out of
the clay: it well-nigh split the bones of our heads: it was not
a melodious chorus.

After that the churl gets up and takes his firewood hatchet,
comes and kills our horses, flays and cuts them up at one task.

---

[1] Literally member of the fian. Finn was called rig-feinid, king-
Fenian.

Fifty spits that were pointed, the which were spits of rowan—
 on each in turn he puts two joints and sticks them round the
 fireplace.

No spit of them had to be taught, as he took them up from the
 fire; and he brought before Fionn his horse's flesh on spits of
 rowan.

"Thou churl, take off thy food: horse-flesh I have never eaten,
 and never yet will I eat, for the matter of going foodless for
 one mealtime."

"If for this my house has been visited, to refuse food," quoth
 the churl, "it will fall out pleasantly for you, Caoilte, Fionn
 and Oisin."

With that we started up to get our swords of temper: each man
 seized another's sword—it was an omen of fist-play.

The fire that was set is quenched, so that neither flame nor
 embers were visible: a dark and murky corner is narrowed
 round us three in one place.

When we were man to man, who should prove our stay but
 Fionn: slain outright were we, but for Fionn of the Fian.

Man against man we were in the house, the whole long night till
 morning, until the sun came in at rising time on the morrow.

When the sun rose, down fell each man eastward or westward:
 into each man's head a black mist came, till they lay lifeless
 in that hour.

Not long we were in our swoon: we rise up hale and sound: the
 house had vanished from us, and vanished from us are the
 inmates.

The party that had fought with us were the Nine Phantoms
 from Yewvalley, to avenge on us their sister whose name was
 Cuilleann broad of foot.

In this manner rose Fionn—his horse's reins in his hand: the
 horse was whole, head and foot: every injury had left him.

I am Caoilte the beloved, left behind the faultless heroes:
 greatly I miss it out and out that I no longer see the Fair.

17TH CENTURY.
Translator Eoin MacNeill.

The Bathing of Oisin's Head

Woman, bathe this head of mine: long since it parted with the Fian of Finn: this year and five, a long space, it has had no woman to bathe it.

This night sixteen years agone, happy was I with my fine head of hair: hard to know in it that head since it lost its wave-yellow torch-flame.

Ah, me! that is the poor head that hounds used to raise their hound-cry round: if it was the day on Leitir Lon, it would have women to bathe it.

Its outing to Leitir Lon—an outing on which great spoils used to be taken—when we killed brown stags above the brink of Loch Liathdroma.

An argument we had over there, I and light-footed Caoilte, when we divided the pleasant chase through quarrel and contention.

Darling Caoilte said—a man that was no shirker of combat, that excelled in bestowing cow and horse—that he was the greater champion.

I said he spoke untruly, the true prince,—it is no falsehood: though it fell out that I said so, dear Caoilte was indeed my friend.

Caoilte went to Ceann Con, I go to Leitir Lon: Caoilte with his fortunate folk, and I my lief alone.

Caoilte of the battles did not kill that day with his swift shooting—the man that often won fame—but one doe and one stag.

I vow to you, woman—it is no time for me to tell lies—that there came out with me over the plain thrice fifty fierce stags.

By thy hand, young woman, the cooking of Formaoil profited: thrice fifty stately stags in this place, with fifty pigs thrown in.

My shooting on Leitir Laoigh was not the tender shooting of a stripling: thrice fifty deer on the field, with the threescore wild pigs.

The hound I held in my active land—Gaillfheith, Fionn mac

Cumhaill's hound—there never touched the warm earth a hound that could win the day from Gaillfheith.

The small spear I had in my hand—seven rivets holding it—often had my hand been on its shaft, along the slope it was not unsteady.

A good spear was Fionn's spear: there was great venom in its steel-blue point: anyone whose blood it ever let never tasted food in his life again.

If it were that day, woman, to come to me above any man, thou wouldst wash my two hands, thou wouldst not avoid me.

It is a pity thou didst not do this for me, thou quiet, fair-haired girl, to lay my head on the cold pile of stone, and to wash for burial my poor bald pate.

Fine was the beauty of the fair hair that all men saw on my head: it has left me for good and all, till I am a disease-smitten grey-face.

Fine was the lustre of my hair, it was a fine setting for a body: never came through head's bone hair so good but the hair of Fionn.

Aye, and these teeth up here, away up in the old head, they were once on a time that they would crunch yellow-topt nuts.

They could gnaw a stag's haunch, hard and hungry and hound-like: they would not leave joint or jot of it but they would make mince-meat of.

Aye, and these eyes up here, away up in the old head, though they are roots of blood to-night, they were once thin pearly gems.

On a night of dark blind weather, they would not cause a stray step: to-night, though I should look out, I cannot see the fair.

Aye, and these legs below, nothing could have wearied them: to-night they are bowed and bent, pitiful, shrunken-sided.

Though they are without power or vigour—I cannot even turn them—they were swift on a time to follow the phantom of Fionnmhagh.

The phantom of Fionnmhagh or Magh Maoin, we got a turn of his ill-nature: on Sunday he was on the plain of Meath, when Cormac took . . . .

The Fiana ran towards him, sure they were that they would

overtake the phantom: they did not overtake him, though
fierce their effort, except Oisin in Argadros.

The poor Oisin thou seest here, he encountered great harm and
hardship, following the phantom southwards to cold Bearnan
of edge-feats.

There he leapt a bold leap, highly, terribly, outlandishly, and
he reached its arm with swiftness, up in the air he struck it.

I dealt a brave and hardy blow over its hideous clammy arm: I
smote, without scarcity, on the eastward, the gold from its
paw into the shield.

The little shield that was on my arm, over which I hewed the
monster's paw, even had it desired the gold, it would have
had it in its middle.

Ten rings in it of gold for Fionn, and ten for Croibhfinn, ten
of them for Goll's daughter, and ten for the daughter of
Iorgholl.

The reckoning of its gold from that out, besides gold that was
hidden, even a seer does not know, for the greatness of its
treasures.

I know ten hiding-places of Fionn's of treasures that I remember: pity they should be under the warm earth, each hiding-
place having ten treasures.

His handsome drinking-horns are these, beside the pillar-stone
of Carn Aodha: on the hillock hitherward from it he hid ten
garments.

Beneath it are hunting spears wherewith red-headed stags were
wounded: dear was the hero's hand that grasped them, meetly
the stone of Almhain hath covered it.

Goblets that held the ale are there, beside the waterfall of
Modhorn: let whoso seek them might and main, they shall
not be found till the end of all.

These and the other treasures of Fionn, above all men might I
reveal: I know no treasure of them all without its mounting
of white bronze.

All we get in the lasting world, they would be numerous to re-
count: all that we laid in peopled earth will not be found till
doom, woman.

I am left behind all these—it is right to thank the Lord for it—
without vigour, without power while I live, at the back of
Cionaodh's fortress.

Patrick's baptism is better for me than the deceitful bathing of
women, protecting churches and peoples and habitations: if
God permits it, do it, woman.

17TH CENTURY.
Translator Eoin MacNeill.

Goll's[1] Parting with his Wife

"Woman, take away my tunic: rise up and go from me: prepare
to depart, clear one of rosy cheeks, the morn before my slaying."

"O Goll, what way shall I take? alas for those whose friends are
few! rare is the woman that has grace, when she is left without head, without lord."

"Seek the camp of Fionn of the Fiana in its place on this westward side; wed there, gentle one of red lips, some good man
worthy of thee."

"What man there might I wed, my great Goll that wast kind to
me? where might I find west or east thy equal for a bed-
fellow?"

"Wilt thou have Oisin son of Fionn, or Aonghus son of Aodh
Rinn, or muscular bloodstained Caireall, or the hundred-
wounding Corr Chos-luath?"

"Conall of Cruachain is my father: I am fellow-fosterling[2] to
Conn of the Hundred Battles: brother to me in the northern
land is Ceidghein son of shaft-stout Conall.

---

[1] Although Goll Mac Morna opposed Finn at the battle of Cnucha
and killed his father Cumall they were eventually reconciled when
each commanded a clan in the same *fian*. But violence once more
arose between them and Goll, after being cornered by his enemy on a
narrow crag, was destroyed.

[2] The Celtic infant was not reared by his own parents but turned
over to other parents to be brought up.

"It is the harder for me to leave thee, that thou art my gentle sweet first husband: seven years of bravery agone, thou broughtest me, husband, to thy couch.

"From that night until to-night, thou hast not shown me a harsh mind: from this night out I will not be light-minded, I will belong to no man on the surface of earth.

"Thirty days living without food scarcely was ever man before thee: a hundred heroes, Goll, by thy hand have fallen on the narrow crag."

"Wide is the sea around us, and I on the narrow of the crag: hunger for food is betraying me, and thirst is overmatching me.

"Though hunger for food is betraying me, though fierce is the warfare of the five battalions, still more it takes the beauty from my cheek, to have to drink bitter-strong brine.

"My own twenty-nine brothers if one man of the Fian had killed, it would make my peace with him (were he) to relieve me for one night from thirst."

"Goll son of Morna from Magh Maoin, eat those bodies at thy side: it will relieve thy thirst after [eating of] the men to drink the milk of my breasts."

"Daughter of Conall, I will not hide it—ah! it is pitiful how this thing has befallen—woman's bidding north or south I will not do and have never done."

"Ah! Goll, it is a woeful plight, five battalions or six against thee, and thou on the corner of a hard crag, a bare lofty chilly crag."

"That, O red mouth that wast musical, was my one fear on wave or land—Fionn and his Fian pressing on me and I without food in a narrow corner.

"I have stained my shafts right well in the bodies of the House of Tréanmhór: I have inflicted on them suffering and hardship, I have killed shaft-strong Cumhall.

"I brought the Munstermen to grief on the Tuesday in Magh Léana: I delivered battle bravely on the morn in Magh Eanaigh.

"Eochaidh Red-spot son of Mál, of Ulster's proud-faced over-

king, I plunged into that hero my spear: I brought them to
sorrow, woman."

17TH CENTURY.
Translator Eoin MacNeill.

Oisin in the Land of Youth

BY Michael Comyn[1]

PROLOGUE

Patrick.   O noble Oisin, son of the king,
                Whose deeds men sing this day in song!
                Thy grief abate and to us relate
                By what strange fate thou hast lived so long!

Oisin.   O Patrick, here's the tale for thee,
                Tho' sad to me its memories old—
                'Twas after Gabra—I mind me well,
                The field where fell my Oscar bold!

I. GOLDEN-HAIRED NIAMH

One day the generous Finn my sire
    With olden fire led forth the chase—
    But our band was small when gather'd all,
    For past recall were the hosts of our race.

---

[1] Michael Comyn was a Gaelic poet who died in 1760. *Oisin in the
Land of Youth* is based on the Fenian tradition of Oisin's visit to
Tir-na-n-Og, the land of eternal youth in the otherworld, and his return to earth on a marvelous white steed from which he had been
warned not to dismount.

'Twas a summer's morn and a mist hung o'er
    The winding shore of sweet Loch Lein,
    Where fragrant trees perfume the breeze
    And birds e'er please with a joyous strain.

We soon awoke the woodland deer
    That forced by fear fled far away—
    Keenly our hounds with strenuous bounds
    O'er moors and mounds pursued their prey.

When lo! into sight came a figure bright,
    In a blaze of light from the west it rushed—
    A lady fair of radiance rare
    Whom a white steed bore to our band, now
        hush'd!

Amazed we halt, though hot the chase,
    To gaze on the face of the fair young queen—
    A marvel to Finn and his fian band,
    Who ne'er in the land such beauty had seen!

A golden crown on her brow she bore,
    A mantle she wore of silken sheen
    All studded with stars of bright red gold—
    Ample each fold fell on herbage green.

Her golden hair all fair to view
    In golden curls on her shoulders fell—
    Bright and pure were her eyes of blue
    As drops of the dew in a blue harebell.

Ruddier far her cheek than the rose,
　　Her bosom more white than the swan's so free,
　　Sweeter the breath of her balmy mouth
　　Than spice of the south from over the sea.

Her milk-white steed was of worth untold
　　Nor bridle of gold did the charger lack—
　　A saddle all covered with purple and gold
　　Lay bright to behold on the steed's proud back.

Four shoes of gold his hoofs did guard,
　　Of gold unmarred by mixture base,
　　A silver wreath on his crest was shown—
　　Such steed was unknown on the earth's fair face.

To Finn's great presence drew the maid
　　Thus bright array'd and softly spake—
　　"O King of the fian host," she cried
　　"Far have I hied for sweet love's sake!"

"Who art thou, pray, O princess rare,
　　Of form most fair, of face divine?
　　Gently thy errand to us make known—
　　What land's thine own, what name is thine?"

"Niam the Golden-haired I'm named,
　　—O Finn far-famed for wisdom and truth!—
　　My praise harps ring, and bards e'er sing,
　　And my sire's the King of the Land of Youth!"

"Then tell us, most lovely lady now,
  Why comest thou o'er seas so far?
  Has heartless husband left thee to weep
  With grief most deep, thy mind to mar!"

"No husband has left me, O lordly Finn,
  —My heart within ne'er man did gain,
  Till hero of Erin, thy famous son,
  Its young love won, for aye to reign!"

"On which of my gallant sons, O maid,
  Is thy heart's love laid, so frankly free?
  Now hide not from us, O princess dear,
  The causes clear of thy visit to me!"

"His name, O Finn, then I'll declare—
  'Tis thy famed son, so fair, so brave,
  Oisin the warrior, Erin's bard,
  My fair reward for crossing the wave!"

"Then why hast thou hastened to give thy love,
  O maiden above all maids most fair—
  To Oisin my own beyond all known
  Of princes high both rich and rare?"

"Good cause I ween for my course shall be seen,
  O king of the Fian, when I tell thee truth:
  Oisin's high deeds and noble name
  Have won him fame in the Land of Youth.

"Full many a prince of high degree
  Hath offered me both heart and hand;
  But whoso appealed, I ne'er did yield
  But my heart kept sealed for my hero grand!"

Oisin.   O Patrick stern, how my soul did yearn
  And with ardor burn for the peerless maid—
  No shame to tell—each word was a spell,
  That bound me well past mortal aid.

I took her gentle hand in mine
  And with every sign of love I said,
  "Welcome a hundred thousand times,
  From fairy climes, O royal maid!

"Of women the rarest, fairest seen,
  Thou art O queen, without compeer!
  My soul, my life, my chosen wife,
  Star of my way of ray most clear!"

II. THE DELIGHTS OF THE LAND OF YOUTH

"Request refused by no true knight
  Who knoweth aright the knightly vogue,
  I make of thee now—'tis hence to speed
  With me on my steed to *Tír na n-Óg!*

"Delightful land beyond all dreams!
  Beyond what seems to thee most fair—
  Rich fruits abound the bright year round
  And flowers are found of hues most rare.

"Unfailing there the honey and wine
And draughts divine of mead there be,
No ache nor ailing night or day—
Death or decay thou ne'er shalt see!

"The mirthful feast and joyous play
And music's sway all blest, benign—
Silver untold and store of gold
Undreamt by the old shall all be thine!

"A hundred swords of steel refined,
A hundred cloaks of kind full rare,
A hundred steeds of proudest breed,
A hundred hounds—thy meed when there!

"A hundred coats of mail shall be thine,
A hundred kine of sleekest skin,
A hundred sheep with fleece of gold,
And gems none hold these shores within.

"A hundred maidens young and fair
Of blithesome air shall tend on thee,
Of form most meet, as fairies fleet
And of song more sweet than the wild thrush free!

"A hundred knights in fights most bold
Of skill untold in all chivalry,
Full-armed, bedight in mail of gold
Shall in Tír na n-Óg thy comrades be.

"A corslet charmed for thee shall be made
  And a matchless blade of magic power,
  Worth a hundred blades in a hero's hands,
  Most blest of brands in battle's hour!

"The royal crown of the King of Youth
  Shall shine in sooth on thy brow most fair,
  All brilliant with gems of luster bright
  Whose worth aright none might declare.

"All things I've named thou shalt enjoy
  And none shall cloy—to endless life—
  Beauty and strength and power thou'lt see
  And I'll e'er be thy own true wife!"

"Refusal of mine thou ne'er shalt hear,
  O maid without peer, of the locks of gold!
  My chosen wife for life I know
  And gladly I'll go to *Tír na n-Óg!*"

III. THE DEPARTURE TO TIR-NA-N-OG

Forthwith the steed I then bestrode;
  Before me rode my royal queen,
  Who said, "O Oisin with caution ride
  Till side of dividing sea we've seen!"

Then up rose that steed with a mighty bound,
　　Gave forth three sounding startling neighs,
　　His mane he shook, then with fiery look
　　His riders he took to the sea's known ways.

Now when from Finn and the fian host
　　The steed to the coast was coursing so,
　　There burst from the chief a cry of grief,
　　A wail of grief not brief nor low.

"Oh Oisin," cried Finn with faltering voice—
　　"My son most choice must I then lose,
　　With never a hope to see thee again?
　　—My heart in twain 'twill break and bruise!"

His noble features now clouded o'er
　　And tears did pour in showers free
　　Till breast and beard in tears were drowned—
　　"My grief! he e'er found this maid from the Sea!"

Oh Patrick, I grieve to tell thee the tale,
　　My words now fail to find their way—
　　How the father did part from the son of his heart,
　　My tears e'er start when I think of the day.

I drew up the steed for a moment's rest
　　And tenderly pressed on my sire a kiss,
　　Then bade farewell to the fian band,
　　Tho' the tears did stand in my eyes, I wis

Full many a day great Finn and I
   And our host all nigh in gay array
   Held glorious feast where harps ne'er ceased
   And highest and least had their choice alway.

Full oft our race held a royal chase
   While at boldest pace ran our sweet-voiced
      hounds—
   Anon in battle our javelins rattle
   And men like cattle fall in heaps and mounds!

Patrick. O vain old Oisin, dwell no more
   On thy deeds of yore in the fian ranks,
   How didst thou go to *Tír na n-Óg?*
   Come let me know and I'll owe much thanks.

Oisin. We turned away as I truly said
   And our horse's head we gave to the west,
   When lo! the deep sea opened before
   While behind us bore the billows that pressed.

Anon we saw in our path strange sights,
   Cities on heights and castles fair,
   Palaces brilliant with lights and flowers—
   The brightest of bowers were gleaming there.

And then we saw a yellow young fawn
   Leap over a lawn of softest green,
   Chased by a graceful, snow-white hound
   That with airy bound pressed on most keen.

We next beheld—I tell thee true,
   A maid in view on a bright bay steed,
   An apple of gold in her hand did she hold,
   O'er the waves most bold she hied with speed.

And soon we saw another sight,
   A youthful knight who a white steed rode,
   The rider in purple and crimson array'd
   Whilst a glittering blade in his hand he showed.

"Yon youthful pair both knight and maid—
   Pray tell," I said, "who they may be—
   The lady mild as a summer's morn
   And knight high-born that fares so free."

"In all thy sight may light on here,
   O Oisin dear, I say with truth,
   There's nought of beauty, nought of strength,
   Till we reach at length the Land of Youth!"

IV. FOMOR OF THE BLOWS

And now as we rode we came in sight
   Of a palace bright, high-placed, and strong,
   Shapely its hall and lofty its wall
   Far beyond all e'er famed in song.

"What royal fort is yon, O queen,
   That stands serene on yon hill-side,
   Whose towers and columns so stately spring—
   What prince or king doth there abide?"

"In yonder fort a sad queen dwells
　　Whom force compels her life to mourn—
　　Whom Fomor fierce of the Mighty Blows
　　Doth there enclose from friends' arms torn.

"But captive though to that pirate proud,
　　She yet hath vowed by taboos grave,
　　Never for life to be his wife
　　Till won in strife 'gainst champion brave!"

"Blessing and bliss be thine," I cried
　　"O maid bright eyed, for thy welcome word,
　　Tho' grieved that woman such fate should meet,
　　Music more sweet I ne'er have heard!

"For now we'll go to that high-placed fort
　　And help full soon that maid distressed;
　　A champion's steel shall Fomor feel
　　And 'neath my heel shall his neck be pressed!"

To Fomor's stronghold then we rode—
　　Unblest abode for a captive sweet!
　　At once the queen with joyous mien,
　　Came forth on the green with welcome meet.

In robe of rich-hued silk arrayed
　　Was this queenly maid with the brow of snow,
　　Her neck all fair could with swan's compare
　　Her cheeks did wear the rose's glow.

Of golden hue was her hair, 'tis true,
    Of heavenly blue her bright eyes clear,
    Her lips were red as berries on bough,
    Shapely each brow with rare compeer!

To seat ourselves we then were told—
    In a chair of gold each one sat down,
    Most royal fare was set forth there
    In royal ware of great renown.

Now when of food we had had our fill
    And of wine as will might fancy e'en,
    Thus spoke the queen, her face now pale,
    "Now list my tale, with ears all keen!"

From first to last she told her tale
    Her cheek all pale and wet with tears—
    How kith and kin ne'er more she'd see
    Whilst Fomor free provoked her fears.

"Then weep no more, O fair young queen,
    Henceforth, I ween, thou needst not mourn,
    Fomor shall pay with his life this day
    In mortal fray for the wrongs thou'st borne!"

"Alas! no champion can be found
    On earth's great round, I fear me much,
    Could hand to hand such foe withstand
    Or free me from this tyrant's clutch."

"I tell thee truly, lady fair,
  I'll boldly dare him to the field,
  Resolved to save thee or in strife
  Never while life doth last to yield!"

Ere cease my words, in savage trim
  The giant grim against us hies—
  In skins of beasts uncouthly clad,
  Whilst a club he had of monstrous size.

No salutation from him came,
  But his eyes aflame glared all around;
  Forthwith he challenged me to fight
  And I with delight took up my ground.

For full three nights and eke three days
  Our deadly fray's end seemed in doubt,
  Till at length his head with my sword I sped
  O'er the plain now red with the blood pour'd out!

Now when the two young maids beheld
  Fierce Fomor felled by my good sword,
  They gave three shouts of joy and glee
  Of joy for freedom now restored.

We then returned to the giant's fort,
  Where faint in swoon at last I fell,
  Faint from wounds and loss of blood
  That still in flood gushed like a well.

But now the maid from Fomor freed
　　Ran up with speed, to help me fain—
My wounds she washed, and bathed with balm,
　　And health and calm I found again.

The giant grim we buried him
　　Deep down in earth in widest grave—
We raised a stone his grave to note
　　And his name we wrote in Ogam-craev.

A merry feast we then did hold
　　And stories told of olden days—
And when night fell we rested well
　　On couches such as poets praise.

When morning fair the sun did greet,
　　From slumbers sweet we fresh awoke—
"Dear friend, to my land now depart—"
　　'Twas thus my lovely princess spoke.

We soon equipped us for our way,
　　For longer stay was needed not,
Sad, sorrowful the leave we took,
　　And sad the maiden's look, I wot.

The further fate of that sweet maid,
　　O Patrick staid, I could not tell,
No word of her I've heard one say
　　E'er since the day we said farewell.

V. IN THE LAND OF YOUTH

We turned once more upon our course,
  And fleetly sped our horse along—
  No wind that sweeps the mountain drift
  Was half so swift or half so strong.

But now the sky began to lower,
  The wind in power increased full fast—
  Red lightning lights the mad sea-waves,
  And madly raves the thunder past!

A while we cowered 'neath the storm,
  —All nature's form in darkness dread—
  When lo! the winds' fierce course was run,
  And bright the sun appear'd o'erhead!

And now there spread before our sight
  A land most bright, most rich, and fair,
  With hill and plain and shady bower
  And a royal tower of splendor rare.

And in this roval mansion fair
  All colors were that eye hath seen—
  The blue most bright, the purest white
  With purple and yellow and softest green.

To left and right of this palace bright
  Rose many a hall and sun-lit tower,
  All built of brilliant gems and stones
  By hands, one owns, of wondrous power.

"What lovely land is that we see?
　　Pray answer me with maiden's truth—
　　Is't penned in page that man may read,
　　Or is it indeed the Land of Youth?"

"It is indeed the Land of Youth—
　　And maiden's truth I've ever told—
　　No joy or bliss I've promised thee
　　But thou shalt see this land doth hold!"

And now there rode from the king's abode
　　To meet us on the lawn of green
　　Thrice fifty champions of might,
　　In armor bright, of noble mien.

And then there came in hues arrayed
　　A hundred maids in maiden vogue—
　　In silken garments bright and brave
　　Who welcome gave to Tír na n-Óg.

And next marched forth a chosen band
　　Of the troops of that land, a lovely sight—
　　A king at their head of kingly tread
　　Of mighty name and fame in fight.

A yellow shirt of silken weft,
　　A cloak most deftly broidered o'er
　　On the king in folds hung freely down
　　Whilst a glittering crown on his head he wore.

And close behind him there was seen
  His youthful queen—a consort meet—
  With fifty maidens in her train
  Who sang a strain divinely sweet.

Then spoke the king in kindly voice,
  "O friends, rejoice, for here you see
  Oisin the famous son of Finn,
  Who spouse of our Niam shall be!"

He takes me warmly by the hand,
  Then as we stand he speaks anew—
  "Welcome," he cries, "I give thee now,
  A hundred thousand welcomes true!

"This kingdom which o'er seas and lands
  Thou'st sought, now stands reveal'd to thee;
  Long shalt thou live our race among
  And ever young as thou shalt see.

"No pleasure e'er that entered mind
  But here thou'lt find without alloy,
  This is the land thy bards e'er sing,
  And I am the King of this Land of Joy.

"Here is our gentle, fair young queen.
  Mother of Niam the Golden-haired,
  Who crossed for thee the stormy sea
  And thine to be all dangers dared!"

I thanked the king with grateful heart,
   To the queen apart I bowed me low—
   We tarried no longer without the walls
   But entered the halls of Rí na n-Óg.[1]

There came the nobles of all that land,
   The great and grand to sing our praise—
   And feast was held with all delights
   For ten long nights and ten long days.

I then was wedded to Gold-haired Niam—
   And there to leave the tale were well—
   Thus did I go to Tír na n-Óg,
   Though grief and woe 'tis now to tell.

Patrick.   Come, finish the charming tale thou'st told,
   O Oisin of gold, of the weapons of war—
   Why from such land didst thou e'er return?
   I fain would learn what the causes are.

And say whilst there thou didst abide
   If thee thy bride any children bore,
   Or wast thou for long in the Land of Youth?
   —I long in truth to list such lore!

Oisin.   I had by Niam of the Golden Hair
   Three children fair as ever smiled,
   Whose sweetness gave us daily joys—
   Two gallant boys and a maiden mild.

---

[1] "King of [the Land of] the Young."

Patrick. O sweet-voiced Oisin, do not grieve,—
    Where didst thou leave those children sweet?
    Tell me the names of thy offspring fair,
    And tell me where they mirthful meet.

Oisin. Those children three rich heirs would be
    To kingdoms free and fair and great,
    To royal scepter, crown of gold
    And wealth untold, no tongue could state.

My gentle Niam on her boys bestowed
    The names I owed most honor to—
    Finn the bright of the hosts of might,
    And Oscar who'd fight for the right and true.

And I my daughter fair did call
    By a name which all fair names o'ershades—
    In beauty's virtue and sweetness' power
    By rightful dower—the Flower-of-Maids!

VI. THE RETURN FROM TIR-NA-N-OG

Long lived I there as now appears,
    Tho' short the years seemed e'er to me,
    Till a strong desire of my heart took hold
    Finn and my friends of old to see.

One day of the king I asked for leave
    And of loving Niam who grieved the while,
    To visit dear Erin once again
    My native plain, my native isle.

"I will not hinder thee," she cried,
 "From crossing the tide for duty dear,
 Tho' it bodes me ill and my heart doth fill
 With doubts that chill and deadly fear!"

"Why shouldst thou fear, O queen my own,
 When the way shall be shown by the magic
     steed—
 The steed that bore us o'er the sea—
 And home to thee I'll safely speed?"

"Remember then what now I say—
 If thou shouldst lay a foot to ground,
 There's no return for thee e'ermore
 To this fair shore when home thou'st found!

"I tell thee truly, vain's thy might
 Shouldst thou alight from thy white steed,
 For never again shouldst thou in truth
 See Land of Youth or hither speed.

"A third time now I thee implore
 And beg thee sore thy seat to hold,
 Or else at once thy strength shall go,
 And thou shalt grow both blind and old!

" 'Tis woe to me, Oisin, to see
 How thou canst be so anxious-soul'd
 About green Erin, changed for aye—
 For past's the day of the fian bold.

"In Erin green there's now nought seen
　　But priests full lean and troops of saints—
　　Then Oisin, here's my kiss to thee,
　　Our last, may be—my heart now faints!"

I gazed into her soft sad eyes
　　Whilst the tears did rise and well in my own—
　　O saint severe, thou'dst weep a tear
　　To hear that dear wife's hopeless moan!

By solemn vow I then was bound,
　　To Erin's ground ne'er to descend
　　And if to keep this vow I failed
　　No power availed or could befriend.

I pledged to keep my solemn vow
　　And do all now enjoined had been,
　　I mounted then my magic steed
　　And said farewell to king and queen.

I kissed once more my Gold-haired Niam,
　　—My heart doth grieve as I tell the tale—
　　I kissed my sons and daughter young,
　　Whose hearts were wrung and cheeks were pale.

I turned my steed at last to the strand
　　And passed from the Land of Lasting Youth—
　　Boldly my horse pursued his course
　　And the billows' force was nought in sooth.

O Patrick of the orders pure,
   No lie, full sure, I've told but truth,
   Thus have I tried my tale to weave
   And thus did I leave the Land of Youth.

If of good bread I could get my fill
   As Finn at will gave to each guest,
   Each day I'd pray to the King of Grace
   That Heaven might be thy place of rest.

Patrick.   Those shalt of bread have quite thy fill
   And drink at will, O ancient bard!
   Dear to me thy pleasant tale!
   It ne'er can fail to win regard.

Oisin.   I need not tell each thing befell
   Me and my spell-borne steed each day,
   But at length green Erin's isle we reach,
   And up the beach we bend our way.

When once I found my steed trod ground,
   I looked around on every side,
   Anxious for tidings small or great
   Of Finn and his state, once Erin's pride.

Not long in doubt had I thus stayed
   When a cavalcade came up the way—
   Strange crowd, I thought, of women and men,
   And past my ken their strange array.

Right gently they saluted me
 But marvell'd much to see my size,
 They marvell'd at my wondrous steed,
 For on such breed they'd ne'er set eyes.

I asked—with fear my heart within—
 If the noble Finn were yet alive,
 Or if his hosts that kept the coasts
 Of Erin safe, did yet survive.

"Of Finn," they said, "we oft have heard—
 His name and fame are now world-wide,
 But full three hundred years have passed
 Since Finn and the last of the fian died.

"Many a book and many a tale
 Have bards of the Gael that treat of Finn—
 Of this strength and valor and wisdom bright,
 Of his race of might and mighty kin.

"We've also heard of Finn's great son—
 A youth of wondrous mien and mould,
 That a lady came hither from over the sea
 And with her went he to *Tír na n-Óg!*"

Now when those words fell on mine ear—
 That Finn and his heroes were no more—
 My heart was chilled—my soul was filled
 With woe unwilled ne'er felt before.

I stopped no longer upon my course
    But swift my horse urged onward flew,
    Till Almu's hill o'er Leinster's plain
    Rose once again before my view.

What shock I felt none could report,
    To see the court of Finn of the steeds
    A ruin lone, all overgrown
    With nettles and thorns and rankest weeds!

I found alas, 'twas a vain pursuit,
    A bootless, fruitless, visit mine!
    Great Finn was dead and the hosts he led—
    For this I'd sped thro' ocean's brine!

But let me tell my story all—
    Tho' Almu's roofless hall I'd seen
    I still would see spots dear to me
    Where the fian free and Finn had been.

In passing through the Thrushes' Glen
    A crowd of men in straits I see;
    Full thrice five score and haply more
    At toil full sore awaited me.

Then forth there spoke a man of that herd,
    With suppliant word to me address'd—
    "Come to our help, O champion brave,
    Come quick to save us thus distress'd!"

I rode up briskly to the crowd
    And found them bow'd beneath a weight—
    A flag of marble great and long
    Bore down the throng who moaned their fate.

Now all who tried to lift that stone
    Did pant and groan most piteously—
    Till some its crushing weight drove mad
    And some fell dead, most sad to see!

Then cried a steward of that crowd,
    And said aloud, "O haste and hie,
    O gallant chief to our relief,
    Or else 'tis brief ere all shall die!

"A shameful thing it is to say
    —For such array of men these days—
    They're powerless of blood and bone
    Full easily that stone to raise!

"If Oscar, Oisin's valiant son
    Laid hold upon that marble stone,
    With right hand bare he'd hurl't in air,
    Flinging it fair, with ne'er a groan!"

Asked thus for help, I did not lag
    But 'neath the flag I placed one hand—
    Full perches seven that stone I hurl
    And scare each churl in all the band!

But scarce alas! that stone had passed
  With that fair cast when ah! the strain—
  The strain it broke the white steed's girth,—
  I fell to earth, doomed now to pain!

No sooner had I touched the ground
  Than with a bound my steed took fright—
  Away, away, to the west he rushed!
  Whilst all stood hush'd at such strange sight!

At once I lost the sight of my eyes,
  My youth's bloom died, lean age began,
  And I was left of strength bereft,
  A helpless, hopeless, blind old man!

O Patrick, now the tale thou hast,
  As each thing passed, indeed, in truth,
  My going away, my lengthened stay,
  .And return for aye from the Land of Youth!

18TH CENTURY.
Translator Tomás O'Flannghaile.

The Voyage of Bran[1]

'TWAS FIFTY quatrains the woman from unknown lands sang on the floor of the house to Bran son of Febal, when the royal house was full of kings, who knew not whence the woman had come, since the ramparts were closed.

This is the beginning of the story. One day, in the neighborhood of his stronghold, Bran went about alone, when he heard music behind him. As often as he looked back, 'twas still behind him the music was. At last he fell asleep at the music, such was its sweetness. When he awoke from his sleep, he saw close by him a branch of silver with white blossoms, nor was it easy to distinguish its bloom from the branch. Then Bran took the branch in his hand to his royal house. When the hosts were in the royal house, they saw a woman in strange raiment therein. 'Twas then she sang the fifty[2] quatrains to Bran, while the host heard her, and all beheld the woman.

And she said:

> A branch of the apple-tree from Emain
> I bring, like those one knows;
> Twigs of white silver are on it,
> Crystal brows with blossoms.

> There is a distant isle,
> Around which sea-horses[3] glisten:
> A fair course against the white-swelling surge,—
> Four feet uphold it.[4]

---

[1] See Introduction, p. xxi.
[2] Only twenty-eight quatrains are given in the manuscripts.
[3] A kenning for "crested sea-waves."
[4] I.e. the island is supported by four pillars.

A delight of the eyes, a glorious range,
Is the plain on which the hosts hold games:
Coracle contends against chariot
In southern Mag Findargat[1]

Feet of white bronze under it
Glittering through beautiful ages.
Lovely land throughout the world's age,
On which the many blossoms drop.

An ancient tree there is with blossoms,
On which birds call to the Hours.[2]
'Tis in harmony it is their wont
To call together every Hour.

Splendors of every color glisten
Throughout the gentle-voiced plains.
Joy is known, ranked around music,
In southern Mag Argatnel[3]

Unknown is wailing or treachery
In the familiar cultivated land,
There is nothing rough or harsh,
But sweet music striking on the ear.

Without grief, without sorrow, without death,
Without any sickness, without debility,
That is the sign of Emain—
Uncommon is an equal marvel.

---

[1] Literally the "White-Silver Plain."
[2] I.e. the canonical hours.
[3] Literally "Silver-Cloud Plain."

A beauty of a wondrous land,
Whose aspects are lovely,
Whose view is a fair country,
Incomparable is its haze.

Then if Aircthech[1] is seen,
On which dragon-stones and crystals drop,
The sea washes the wave against the land,
Hair of crystal drops from its mane.

Wealth, treasures of every hue,
Are in Ciuin,[2] a beauty of freshness,
Listening to sweet music,
Drinking the best of wine.

Golden chariots in Mag Rein,[3]
Rising with the tide to the sun,
Chariots of silver in Mag Mon,[4]
And of bronze without blemish.

Yellow golden steeds are on the sward there,
Other steeds with crimson hue,
Others with wool upon their backs
Of the hue of heaven all-blue.

---

[1] Literally "Bountiful Land."
[2] Literally "Gentle Land."
[3] Literally "Plain of the Sea."
[4] Literally "Plain of Sports."

At sunrise there will come
A fair man illumining level lands;
He rides upon the fair sea-washed plain,
He stirs the ocean till it is blood.

A host will come across the clear sea,
To the land they show their rowing;
Then they row to the conspicuous stone,
From which arise a hundred strains.

It sings a strain unto the host
Through long ages, it is not sad,
Its music swells with choruses of hundreds—
They look for neither decay nor death.

Many-shaped Emne[1] by the sea,
Whether it be near, whether it be far,
In which are many thousands of motley women,
Which the clear sea encircles.

If he has heard the voice of the music,
The chorus of the little birds from Imchiuin,[2]
A small band of women will come from a height
To the plain of sport in which he is.

---

[1] Emne is the nominative of Emain.
[2] Literally "Very Gentle Land."

There will come happiness with health
To the land against which laughter peals,
Into Imchiuin at every season
Will come everlasting joy.

It is a day of lasting weather
That showers silver on the lands,
A pure-white cliff on the range of the sea,
Which from the sun receives its heat.

The host race along Mag Mon,
A beautiful game, not feeble,
In the variegated land over a mass of beauty.
They look for neither decay nor death.

Listening to music at night,
And going into Ildathach,[1]
A variegated land, splendor on a diadem of beauty,
Whence the white cloud glistens.

There are thrice fifty distant isles
In the ocean to the west of us;
Larger than Erin twice
Is each of them, or thrice.

A great birth[2] will come after ages,
That will not be in a lofty place,
The son of a woman whose mate will not be known,
He will seize the rule of the many thousands.

---

[1] Literally "Many-colored Land."
[2] I.e. Christ's.

A rule without beginning, without end,
He has created the world so that it is perfect,
Whose are earth and sea,
Woe to him that shall be under His unwill!

'Tis He that made the heavens,
Happy he that has a white heart,
He will purify hosts under pure water,
'Tis He that will heal your sicknesses.

Not to all of you is my speech,
Though its great marvel has been made known:
Let Bran hear from the crowd of the world
What of wisdom has been told to him.

Do not fall on a bed of sloth,
Let not thy intoxication overcome thee;
Begin a voyage across the clear sea,
If perchance thou mayst reach the land of women.

Thereupon the woman went from them, while they knew not whither she went. And she took her branch with her. The branch sprang from Bran's hand into the hand of the woman, nor was there strength in Bran's hand to hold the branch.

Then on the morrow Bran went upon the sea. The number of his men was three companies of nine. One of his foster-brothers and mates[1] was set over each of the three companies of nine. When he had been at sea two days and two nights, he saw a man in a chariot coming towards him over the sea. That man also sang thirty[2] other quatrains to him, and made himself known to him, and said that he was Manannan son of Lir,[3]

---

[1] Literally "men of the same age."

[2] Again only twenty-eight quatrains are given in the manuscripts.

[3] Manannan macLir was god of the sea in Celtic mythology.

and said that it was upon him to go to Ireland after long ages,
and that a son would be born to him, Mongan son of Fiachna—
that was the name which would be upon him.

So Manannan sang these thirty quatrains to Bran:

> Bran deems it a marvellous beauty
> In his coracle across the clear sea:
> While to me in my chariot from afar
> It is a flowery plain on which he rides about.

> What is a clear sea
> For the prowed skiff in which Bran is,
> That is a happy plain with profusion of flowers
> To me from the chariot of two wheels.

> Bran sees
> The number of waves beating across the clear sea:
> I myself see in Mag Mon[1]
> Red-headed flowers without fault.

> Sea-horses glisten in summer
> As far as Bran has stretched his glance:
> Rivers pour forth a stream of honey
> In the land of Manannan son of Lir.

> The sheen of the main, on which thou art,
> The white hue of the sea, on which thou rowest about,
> Yellow and azure are spread out,
> It is land, and is not rough.

> Speckled salmon leap from the womb
> Of the white sea, on which thou lookest:
> They are calves, they are colored lambs
> With friendliness, without mutual slaughter.

---

[1] Literally "Plain of Sports."

Though but one chariot-rider is seen
In Mag Mell[1] of many flowers,
There are many steeds on its surface,
Though them thou seest not.

The size of the plain, the number of the host,
Colors glisten with pure glory,
A fair stream of silver, cloths of gold,
Afford a welcome with all abundance.

A beautiful game, most delightful,
They play sitting at the luxurious wine,
Men and gentle women under a bush,
Without sin, without crime.

Along the top of a wood has swum
Thy coracle across ridges,
There is a wood of beautiful fruit
Under the prow of thy little skiff.

A wood with blossom and fruit,
On which is the vine's veritable fragrance,
A wood without decay, without defect,
On which are leaves of golden hue.

We are from the beginning of creation
Without old age, without consummation of earth,[2]
Hence we expect not that there should be frailty;
The sin has not come to us.

---

[1] Literally "Pleasant, or Happy Plain."
[2] I.e. of the grave.

An evil day when the Serpent went
To the father to his city![1]
She has perverted the times in this world,
So that there came decay which was not original.

By greed and lust he[2] has slain us,
Through which he has ruined his noble race:
The withered body has gone to the fold of torment,
And everlasting abode of torture.

It is a law of pride in this world
To believe in the creatures,[3] to forget God,
Overthrow by diseases, and old age,
Destruction of the soul through deception.

A noble salvation will come
From the King who has created us,
A white law will come over seas;
Besides being God, He will be man.

This shape, he on whom thou lookest,
Will come to thy parts;[4]
'Tis mine to journey to her house,[5]
To the woman in Line-Mag.

---

[1] I.e. to Adam in Paradise.
[2] I.e. Adam.
[3] I.e. to worship idols.
[4] I.e. to Ireland.
[5] I.e. to the wife of Fiachna, an Ulster king, whose royal seat was in Line-Mag (Moylinny), county Antrim.

For it is Manannan son of Lir,
From the chariot in the shape of a man;
Of his progeny will be a very short while
A fair man in a body of white clay.[1]

Manannan the descendant of Lir will be
A vigorous bed-fellow to Caintigern:[2]
He shall be called to his son in the beautiful world,
Fiachna will acknowledge him as his son.

He will delight the company of every fairy-knoll,
He will be the darling of every goodly land,
He will make known secrets—a course of wisdom—
In the world, without being feared.

He will be in the shape of every beast,
Both on the azure sea and on land,
He will be a dragon before hosts at the onset,
He will be a wolf of every great forest.

He will be a stag with horns of silver
In the land where chariots are driven,
He will be a speckled salmon in a full pool,
He will be a seal, he will be a fair-white swan.

---

[1] I.e. Mongan, fathered by Manannan upon Fiachna's wife.
[2] I.e. Fiachna's wife.

He will be throughout long ages
A hundred years in fair kingship,
He will cut down battalions,—a lasting grave—
He will redden fields, a wheel around the track.

It will be about kings with a champion
That he will be known as a valiant hero,
Into the strongholds of a land on a height
I shall send an appointed end from Islay.[1]

High shall I place him with princes,
He will be overcome by a son of error;[2]
Manannan the son of Lir
Will be his father, his tutor.

He will be—his time will be short—
Fifty years in this world:
A dragon-stone from the sea will kill him
In the fight at Senlabor.

He will ask a drink from Loch Lo,
While he looks at the stream of blood;
The white host[3] will take him under a wheel of clouds[4]
To the gathering where there is no sorrow.

Steadily then let Bran row,
Not far to the Land of Women,
Emne with many hues of hospitality
Thou wilt reach before the setting of the sun.

---

[1] The translation of this quatrain is uncertain because the Irish text is hopelessly corrupt in several places.

[2] Mongan was killed by Arthur, son of Bicor of Britain.

[3] I.e. the angels.

[4] I.e. in a chariot.

Thereupon Bran went from him. And he saw an island.
He rowed round about it, and a large host was gaping and
laughing. They were all looking at Bran and his people, but
would not stay to converse with them. They continued to give
forth gusts of laughter at them. Bran sent one of his people
on the island. He ranged himself with the others, and was
gaping at them like the other men of the island. Bran kept
rowing round about the island. Whenever his man came past
Bran, his comrades would address him. But he would not converse with them, but would only look at them and gape at
them. The name of this island is the Island of Joy. Thereupon they left him there.

It was not long thereafter when they reached the Land of
Women. They saw the leader of the women at the port. Said
the chief of the women: "Come hither on land, O Bran son
of Febal! Welcome is thy advent!" Bran did not venture to go
on shore. The woman threw a ball of thread to Bran straight
over his face. Bran put his hand on the ball, which adhered to
his palm. The thread of the ball was in the woman's hand, and
she pulled the coracle towards the port. Thereupon they went
into a large house, in which was a bed for every couple, even
thrice nine beds. The food that was put on every dish vanished
not from them. It seemed a year to them that they were
there,—it chanced to be many years. No savor was wanting to
them.

Home-sickness seized one of them, even Nechtan son of
Collbran. Bran's kindred kept praying him that he should go
to Erin with them. The woman said to them their going would
make them rue. However, they went, and the woman said that
none of them should touch the land, and that they should visit
and take with them the man whom they had left in the Island
of Joy.

Then they went until they arrived at a gathering at Srub
Brain on the coast of Erin. The men asked of them who it was
came over the sea. Said Bran: "I am Bran the son of Febal."

One of the men said: "We do not know such a one, though the 'Voyage of Bran' is in our ancient stories."

The man[1] leaped from them out of the coracle. As soon as he touched the earth of Ireland, forthwith he was a heap of ashes, as though he had been in the earth for many hundred years. 'Twas then that Bran sang this quatrain:

> For Collbran's son great was the folly
> To lift his hand against age,
> Without anyone casting a wave of pure water[2]
> Over Nechtan, Collbran's son.

Thereupon, to the people of the gathering Bran told all his wanderings from the beginning until that time. And he wrote these quatrains in ogam, and then bade them farewell. And from that hour his wanderings are not known.

7TH OR 8TH CENTURY.
Translator Kuno Meyer.

Mad Sweeney[3]

FOR SEVEN whole years Sweeney wandered over Ireland from one point to another until one night he arrived at Glen Bolcain; for it is there stood his fortress and his dwelling-place, and more delightful was it to him to tarry and abide there than in any other place in Ireland; for thither would he go from every part of Ireland, nor would he leave it except through fear and terror. Sweeney dwelt there that night, and on the morrow morning Lynchehaun came seeking him. Some say that Lynchehaun was Sweeney's mother's son, others that he was a foster-brother, but, whichever he was, his concern for Sweeney was great, for he (Sweeney) went off three times in madness

---

[1] I.e. Nechtan, son of Collbran.
[2] I.e. holy water.
[3] See Introduction, p. xxi.

and thrice he brought him back. This time Lynchehaun was
seeking him in the glen, and he found the track of his feet
by the brink of the stream of which he was wont to eat the
watercress. He found also the branches that used to break
under his feet as he changed from the top of one tree to
another. That day, however, he did not find the madman, so
he went into a deserted house in the glen, and there he fell into
deep sleep after the great labour of the pursuit of Sweeney
whom he was seeking. Then Sweeney came upon his track so
that he reached the house, and there he heard Lynchehaun's
snore; whereupon he uttered this lay:

The man by the wall snores,
slumber like that I dare not;
for seven years from the Tuesday at Magh Rath[1]
I have not slept a wink.

O God of Heaven! would that I had not gone
to the fierce battle!
thereafter Sweeney Geilt[2] was my name,
alone in the top of the ivy.

Watercress of the well of Druim Cirb
is my meal at terce;
on my face may be recognized its hue,
'tis true I am Sweeney Geilt.

For certain am I Sweeney Geilt,
one who sleeps under shelter of a rag,
about Sliabh Liag if . . .
these men pursue me.

---

[1] I.e. the battle of Mag Rath (A.D. 637) at which Sweeney lost
his wits.
[2] Mad.

When I was Sweeney the sage,
I used to dwell in a lonely shieling,[1]
on sedgy land, on a morass, on a mountain-side;
I have bartered my home for a far-off land.

I give thanks to the King above
with whom great harshness is not usual;
'tis the extent of my injustice
that has changed my guise.

Cold, cold for me is it
since my body lives not in the ivy-bushes,
much rain comes upon it
and much thunder.

Though I live from hill to hill
in the mountain above the yew glen;
in the place where Congal Claon[2] was left
alas that I was not left there on my back!

Frequent is my groan,
far from my churchyard is my gaping house;
I am no champion but a needy madman,
God has thrust me in rags, without sense.

'Tis great folly
for me to come out of Glen Bolcain,
there are many apple-trees in Glen Bolcain
for . . . of my head.

---

[1] A rude hut.
[2] One of the chief participants in the battle of Mag Rath.

Green watercress
and a draft of pure water,
I fare on them, I smile not,
not so the man by the wall.[1]

In summer amid the herons of Cooley,
among packs of wolves when winter comes,
at other times under the crown of a wood;
not so the man by the wall.

Happy Glen Bolcain, fronting the wind,
around which madmen of the glen call,
woe is me! I sleep not there;
more wretched am I than the man by the wall.

After that lay he came the next night to Lynchehaun's mill
which was being watched over by one old woman, Lonnog,
daughter of Dubh Dithribh, mother of Lynchehaun's wife.
Sweeney went into the house to her and she gave him small
morsels, and for a long time in that manner he kept visiting the
mill. One day Lynchehaun set out after him, when he saw him
by the mill-stream, and he went to speak to the old woman, that
is, his wife's mother, Lonnog. "Has Sweeney come to the mill,
woman?" said Lynchehaun. "He was last here last night," said
the woman. Lynchehaun then put on the woman's garment and
remained in the mill after her; that night Sweeney came to the
mill and he recognised Lynchehaun. When he saw his eyes,
he sprang away from him at once out through the skylight
of the house, saying: "Pitiful is your pursuit of me, Lynchehaun, chasing me from my place and from each spot dearest
to me in Ireland; and as Ronan[2] does not allow me to trust you,

---

[1] "The man by the wall" is a serf, whose place was farthest from
the fire.
[2] Saint Ronan, whose curse upon Sweeney was responsible for
Sweeney's madness.

it is tiresome and importunate of you to be following me";
and he made this lay:

> O Lynchehaun, thou art irksome,
> I have not leisure to speak with thee,
> Ronan does not let me trust thee;
> 'tis he who has put me in a sorry plight
>
> I made the luckless cast
> from the midst of the battle at Ronan
> it pierced the precious bell
> which was on the cleric's breast.
>
> As I hurled the splendid cast
> from the midst of the battle at Ronan,
> said the fair cleric: "Thou hast leave
> to go with the birds."
>
> Thereafter I sprang up
> into the air above;
> in life I have never leaped
> a single leap that was lighter.
>
> Were it in the glorious morning,
> on the Tuesday following the Monday,
> none would be prouder than I am
> by the side of a warrior of my folk.
>
> A marvel to me is that which I see,
> O Thou that hast shaped this day;
> the woman's garment on the floor,
> two piercing eyes of Lynchehaun.

"Sad is the disgrace you would fain put upon me, Lynchehaun," said he; "and do not continue annoying me further,
but go to your house and I will go on to where Eorann is."

Now, Eorann at the time was dwelling with Guaire, son of
Congal, son of Scannlan, for it was Eorann who was Sweeney's
wife, for there were two kinsmen in the country, and they
had equal title to the sovereignty which Sweeney had abandoned, viz.: Guaire, son of Congal, son of Scannlan, and
Eochaidh, son of Condlo, son of Scannlan. Sweeney proceeded to the place in which Eorann was. Guaire had gone to
the chase that day, and the route he took was to the pass of
Sliabh Fuaid and by Sgirig Cinn Glinne and Ettan Tairbh.
His camp was beside Glen Bolcain—which is called Glenn
Chiach to-day—in the plain of Cinel Ainmirech. Then the
madman sat down upon the lintel of the hut in which Eorann
was, whereupon he said: "Do you remember, lady, the great
love we gave to each other what time we were together? Easy
and pleasant it is for you now, but not so for me"; whereupon
Sweeney said, and Eorann answered him as follows:

Sweeney: At ease art thou, bright Eorann,
              at the bedside with thy lover;
              not so with me here,
              long have I been restless.

              Once thou didst utter, O great Eorann,
              a saying pleasing and light,
              that thou wouldst not survive
              parted one day from Sweeney.

> To-day, it is readily manifest,
> thou thinkest little of thy old friend;
> warm for thee on the down of a pleasant bed,
> cold for me abroad till morn.

Eorann:
> Welcome to thee, thou guileless mad one!
> thou art most welcome of the men of the earth;
> though at ease am I, my body is wasted
> since the day I heard of thy ruin.

Sweeney:
> More welcome to thee is the king's son
> who takes thee to feast without sorrow;
> he is thy chosen wooer;
> you seek not your old friend.

Eorann:
> Though the king's son were to lead me
> to blithe banqueting-halls,
> I had liefer sleep in a tree's narrow hollow
> beside thee, my husband, could I do so.

> If my choice were given me
> of the men of Erin and Alba,[1]
> I had liefer bide sinless with thee
> on water and on watercress.

Sweeney:
> No path for a beloved lady
> is that of Sweeney here on the track of care;
> cold are my beds at Ard Abhla,
> my cold dwellings are not few.

---

[1] England.

More meet for thee to bestow love and affection
on the man with whom thou art alone
than on an uncouth and famished madman,
horrible, fearful, stark-naked.

Eorann: O toiling madman, 'tis my grief
that thou art uncomely and dejected;
I sorrow that thy skin has lost its colour,
briars and thorns rending thee.

Sweeney: I blame thee not for it,
thou gentle, radiant woman;
Christ, Son of Mary—great bondage—
He has caused my feebleness.

Eorann: I would fain that we were together,
and that feathers might grow on our bodies;
in light and darkness I would wander
with thee each day and night.

Sweeney: One night I was in pleasant Boirche,
I have reached lovely Tuath Inbhir,
I have wandered throughout Magh Fail,
I have happened on Cell Ui Suanaigh.

No sooner had he finished than the army swarmed into the
camp from every quarter, whereupon he set off in his headlong
flight, as he had often done. He halted not in his career until
before the fall of night he arrived at Ros Bearaigh—the first
church at which he tarried after the battle of Magh Rath—and
he went into the yew-tree which was in the church.

Muireadach mac Earca was erenach[1] of the church at the
time, and his wife happened to be going past the yew when

_____
[1] A church official in charge of secular affairs and responsible for
provisioning the establishment. He apparently farmed the church
land.

she saw the madman in it; she recognized that it was Sweeney was there and said to him: "Come out of the yew, king of Dal Araidhe; there is but one woman before you here." She said so in order to seize the madman, and to deceive and beguile him. "I will not go indeed," said Sweeney, "lest Lynchehaun and his wife come to me, for there was a time when it would have been easier for you to recognize me than it is to-day"; whereupon he uttered these staves:

O woman, who dost recognize me
with the points of thy blue eyes,
there was a time when my aspect was better
in the assembly of Dal Araidhe.

I have changed in shape and hue
since the hour I came out of the battle;
I was the slender Sweeney
of whom the men of Erin had heard.

Bide thou with thy husband and in thy house,
I shall not tarry in Ros Bearaigh;
until holy Judgment we shall not foregather,
I and thou, O woman.

He emerged then from the tree lightly and nimbly, and went on his way until he reached the old tree at Ros Earcain. (For he had three dwellings in his own country in which he was wont to reside, viz.: Teach mic Ninnedha, Cluain Creamha, and Ros Earcain). Thereafter for a fortnight and a month he tarried in the yew-tree without being perceived; but at length his place and dwelling were discovered, and the nobles of Dal Araidhe took counsel as to who should go to seize him. Everyone said that it was Lynchehaun who should

be sent. Lynchehaun undertook the task, and he went along
until he came to the yew in which Sweeney was, whereupon
he beheld the madman on the branch above him. "Sad is it,
Sweeney," said he, "that your last plight should be thus, without food, without drink, without raiment, like any bird of
the air, after having been in garments of silk and satin on splendid steeds from foreign lands with matchless bridles; with you
were women gentle and comely, likewise many youths and
hounds and goodly folk of every art; many hosts, many and
diverse nobles and chiefs, and young lords, and landholders
and hospitallers were at your command. Many cups and goblets and carved buffalo horns for pleasant-flavoured and enjoy-
able liquors were yours also. Sad is it for you to be in that wise
like unto any miserable bird going from wilderness to wilderness." "Cease now, Lynchehaun," said Sweeney; "that is what
was destined for us; but have you tidings for me of my country?"
"I have in sooth," said Lynchehaun, "for your father is dead."
"That has seized me," said he. "Your mother is also dead,"
said the young man. "Now all pity for me is at an end," said
he. "Dead is your brother," said Lynchehaun. "Gaping is my
side on that account," said Sweeney. "Dead is your daughter,"
said Lynchehaun. "The heart's needle is an only daughter,"
said Sweeney. "Dead is your son who used to call you 'daddy',"
said Lynchehaun. "True," said he, "that is the drop which
brings a man to the ground"; whereupon they, even Lynchehaun and Sweeney, uttered this lay between them:

Lynchehaun: O Sweeney from lofty Sliabh na nEach,
              thou of the rough blade wert given to wound-
                 ing;
              for Christ's sake, who hath put thee in bond-
                 age,
              grant converse with thy foster-brother.

Hearken to me if thou hearest me,
O splendid king, O great prince,
so that I may relate gently
to thee tidings of thy good land.

There is life for none in thy land after thee;
it is to tell of it that I have come;
dead is thy renowned brother there,
dead thy father and thy mother.

Sweeney: If my gentle mother be dead,
harder is it for me to go to my land;
'tis long since she has loved my body;
she has ceased to pity me.

Foolish the counsel of each wild youth
whose elders live not;
like unto a branch bowed under nuts;
whoso is brotherless has a gaping side.

Lynchehaun: There is another calamity there
which is bewailed by the men of Erin,
though uncouth be thy side and thy foot,
dead is thy fair wife of grief for thee.

Sweeney: For a household to be without a wife
is rowing a rudderless boat,
'tis a garb of feathers to the skin,
'tis kindling a single fire.

Lynchehaun: I have heard a fearful and loud tale
around which was a clear, fierce wail,
'tis a fist round smoke, however,
thou art without sister, O Sweeney.

Sweeney: A proverb this, bitter the . . . —
it has no delight for me—
the mild sun rests on every ditch,
a sister loves though she be not loved.

Lynchehaun: Calves are not let to cows
amongst us in cold Araidhe
since thy gentle daughter, who has loved thee,
    died,
likewise thy sister's son.

Sweeney: My sister's son and my hound,
they would not forsake me for wealth,
'tis adding loss to sorrow,
the heart's needle is an only daughter.

Lynchehaun: There is another famous story—
loth am I to tell it—
meetly are the men of the Arada
bewailing thy only son.

Sweeney: That is the renowned drop
which brings a man to the ground,
that his little son who used to say 'daddy'
should be without life.

It has called me to thee from the tree,
scarce have I caused enmity,
I cannot bear up against the blow
since I heard the tidings of my only son.

Lynchehaun: Since thou hast come, O splendid warrior,
within Lynchehaun's hands,
all thy folk are alive,
O scion of Eochu Salbuidhe.

Be still, let thy sense come,
in the east is thy house, not in the west,
far from thy land thou hast come hither,
this is the truth, O Sweeney.

More delightful deemest thou to be amongst
  deer
in woods and forests
than sleeping in thy stronghold in the east
on a bed of down.

Better deemest thou to be on a holly-branch
beside the swift mill's pond
than to be in choice company
with young fellows about thee.

If thou wert to sleep in the bosom of hills
to the soft strings of lutes,
more sweet wouldst thou deem under the oakwood
the belling of the brown stag of the herd.

Thou art fleeter than the wind across the valley,
thou art the famous madman of Erin,
brilliant in thy beauty, come hither,
O Sweeney, thou wast a noble champion.

When Sweeney heard tidings of his only son, he fell from
the yew, whereupon Lynchehaun closed his arms around him
and put manacles on him. He then told him that all his people
lived; and he took him to the place in which the nobles of Dal
Araidhe were. They brought with them locks and fetters to put
on Sweeney, and he was entrusted to Lynchehaun to take him
with him for a fortnight and a month. He took Sweeney away,
and the nobles of the province were coming and going during
that time; and at the end of it his sense and memory came to
him, likewise his own shape and guise. They took his bonds
off him, and his kingship was manifest. Harvest-time came
then, and one day Lynchehaun went with his people to reap.
Sweeney was put in Lynchehaun's bed-room after his bonds
were taken off him, and his sense had come back to him. The
bed-room was shut on him and nobody was left with him but
the mill-hag, and she was enjoined not to attempt to speak to
him. Nevertheless she spoke to him, asking him to tell some of
his adventures while he was in a state of madness. "A curse on
your mouth, hag!" said Sweeney; "ill is what you say; God will
not suffer me to go mad again." "I know well," said the hag,
"that it was the outrage done to Ronan that drove you to madness." "O woman," said he, "it is hateful that you should be
betraying and luring me." "It is not betrayal at all but truth";
and Sweeney said:

Sweeney: O hag of yonder mill,
              why shouldst thou set me astray?
              is it not deceitful of thee that, through women,
              I should be betrayed and lured?

The Hag:	'Tis not I who betrayed thee,
	O Sweeney, though fair thy fame,
	but the miracles of Ronan from Heaven
	which drove thee to madness among madmen.

Sweeney:	Were it myself, and would it were I,
	that were king of Dal Araidhe
	it were a reason for a blow across a chin;
	thou shalt not have a feast, O hag.

"O hag," said he, "great are the hardships I have encountered if you but knew; many a dreadful leap have I leaped from hill to hill, from fortress to fortress, from land to land, from valley to valley." "For God's sake," said the hag, "leap for us now one of the leaps you used to leap when you were mad." Thereupon he bounded over the bed-rail so that he reached the end of the bench. "My conscience!" said the hag, "I could leap that myself," and in the same manner she did so. He took another leap out through the skylight of the hostel. "I could leap that too," said the hag, and straightway she leaped. This, however, is a summary of it: Sweeney travelled through five cantreds of Dal Araidhe that day until he arrived at Glenn na nEachtach in Fiodh Gaibhle, and she followed him all that time. When Sweeney rested there on the summit of a tall ivy-branch, the hag rested on another tree beside him. It was then the end of harvest-time precisely. Thereupon Sweeney heard a hunting-call of a multitude in the verge of the wood. "This," said he, "is the cry of a great host, and they are the Ui Faelain coming to kill me to avenge Oilill Cedach, king of the Ui Faelain, whom I slew in the battle of Magh Rath." He heard the bellowing of the stag, and he made a lay wherein he eulogized aloud the trees of Ireland, and, recalling some of his own hardships and sorrows, he said:

O little stag, thou little bleating one,
O melodious little clamourer,
sweet to us is the music
thou makest in the glen.

Longing for my little home
has come on my senses—
the flocks in the plain,
the deer on the mountain.

Thou oak, bushy, leafy,
thou art high beyond trees;
O hazlet, little branching one,
O fragrance of hazel-nuts.

O alder, thou art not hostile,
delightful is thy hue,
thou art not rending and prickling
in the gap wherein thou art.

O little blackthorn, little thorny one;
O little black sloe-tree;
O watercress, little green-topped one,
from the brink of the ousel spring.

O minen[1] of the pathway,
thou art sweet beyond herbs,
O little green one, very green one,
O herb on which grows the strawberry.

---

[1] The name of some plant.

O apple-tree, little apple tree,
much art thou shaken;
O quicken, little berried one,
delightful is thy bloom.

O briar, little arched one,
thou grantest no fair terms,
thou ceasest not to tear me,
till thou hast thy fill of blood.

O yew-tree, little yew-tree,
in churchyards thou art conspicuous;
O ivy, little ivy,
thou art familiar in the dusky wood.

O holly, little sheltering one,
thou door against the wind;
O ash-tree, thou baleful one,
hand-weapon of a warrior.

O birch, smooth and blessed,
thou melodious, proud one,
delightful each entwining branch
in the top of thy crown.

The aspen a-trembling;
by turns I hear
its leaves a-racing—
meseems 'tis the foray!

My aversion in woods—
I conceal it not from anyone—
is the leafy stirk of an oak
swaying evermore.

Ill-hap by which I outraged
the honour of Ronan Finn,
his miracles have troubled me,
his little bells from the church.

Ill-omened I found
the armour of upright Congai,
his sheltering, bright tunic
with selvages of gold.

It was a saying of each one
of the valiant, active host:
"Let not escape from you through the narrow
    copse
the man of the goodly tunic.

"Wound, kill, slaughter,
let all of you take advantage of him;
put him, though it is great guilt,
on spit and on spike."

The horsemen pursuing me
across round Magh Cobha,
no cast from them reaches
me through my back.

Going through the ivy-trees—
I conceal it not, O warrior—
like good cast of a spear
I went with the wind.

O little fawn, O little long-legged one,
I was able to catch thee
riding upon thee
from one peak to another.

From Carn Cornan of the contests
to the summit of Sliabh Niadh,
from the summit of Sliabh Uillinne
I reach Crota Cliach.

From Crota Cliach of assemblies
to Carn Liffi of Leinster,
I arrive before eventide
in bitter Benn Gulbain.

My night before the battle of Congal,
I deemed it fortunate,
before I restlessly
wandered over the mountain-peaks.

Glen Bolcain, my constant abode,
'twas a boon to me,
many a night have I attempted
a stern race against the peak.

If I were to wander alone
the mountains of the brown world,
better would I deem the site of a single hut
in the Glen of mighty Bolcan.

Good its water pure-green,
good its clean, fierce wind,
good its cress-green watercress,
best its tall brooklime.

Good its enduring ivy-trees,
good its bright, cheerful sallow,
good its yewy yews,
best its melodious birch.

If thou shouldst come, O Lynchehaun,
to me in every guise,
each night to talk to me,
perchance I would not tarry for thee.

I would not have tarried to speak to thee
were it not for the tale which has wounded
    me—
father, mother, daughter, son,
brother, strong wife dead.

If thou shouldst come to speak to me,
no better would I deem it;
I would wander before morn
the mountains of Boirche of peaks.

By the mill of the little floury one
thy folk has been ground,
O wretched one, O weary one,
O swift Lynchehaun.

O hag of this mill,
why dost thou take advantage of me?
I hear thee revile me
even when thou art out on the mountain.

O hag, O round-headed one,
wilt thou go on a steed?

The hag: I would go, O fool-head
if no one were to see me.

O Sweeney, if I go,
may my leap be successful.

Sweeney: If thou shouldst come, O hag,
mayst thou not dismount full of sense!

The hag: In sooth, not just is what thou sayest,
thou son of Colman Cas;
is not my riding better
without falling back?

Sweeney: Just, in sooth, is what I say,
O hag without sense;
a demon is ruining thee,
thou hast ruined thyself.

The *Hag:*   Dost thou not deem my arts better,
thou noble, slender madman,
that I should be following thee
from the tops of the mountains?

Sweeney: A proud ivy-bush
which grows through a twisted tree—
if I were right on its summit,
I would fear to come out.

I flee before the skylarks—
'tis a stern, great race—
I leap over the stumps
on the tops of the mountains.

When the proud turtle-dove
rises for us,
quickly do I overtake it
since my feathers have grown.

The silly, foolish woodcock
when it rises for me
methinks 'tis a bitter foe,
the blackbird too that gives the cry of alarm.

Every time I would bound
till I was on the ground
so that I might see the little fox
below a-gnawing the bones.

Beyond every wolf among the ivy-trees
swiftly would he get the advantage of me,
so nimbly would I leap
till I was on the mountain-peak.

Little foxes yelping
to me and from me,
wolves at their rending,
I flee at their sound.

They have striven to reach me,
coming in their swift course,
so that I fled before them
to the tops of the mountains.

My transgression has come against me
whatsoever way I flee;
'tis manifest to me from the pity shown me
that I am a sheep without a fold.

The old tree of Cell Lughaidhe
wherein I sleep a sound sleep;
more delightful in the time of Congal
was the fair of plenteous Line.

There will come the starry frost
which will fall on every pool;
I am wretched, straying
exposed to it on the mountain-peak.

The herons a-calling
in chilly Glenn Aighle,
swift flocks of birds
coming and going.

I love not the merry prattle
that men and women make:
sweeter to me is the warbling
of the blackbirds in the quarter in which it is.

I love not the trumpeting
I hear at early morn:
sweeter to me the squeal
of the badgers in Benna Broc.

I love not the horn-blowing
so boldly I hear:
sweeter to me the belling of a stag
of twice twenty peaks.

There is the material of a plough-team
from glen to glen:
each stag at rest
on the summit of the peaks.

Though many are my stags
from glen to glen,
not often is a ploughman's hand
closing round their horns.

The stag of lofty Sliabh Eibhlinne,
the stag of sharp Sliabh Fuaid,
the stag of Ealla, the stag of Orrery,
the fierce stag of Loch Lein.

The stag of Seimhne, Larne's stag,
the stag of Line of the mantles,
the stag of Cooley, the stag of Conachail,
the stag of Bairenn of two peaks.

O mother of this herd,
thy coat has become grey,
there is no stag after thee
without two score antler-points.

Greater than the material for a little cloak
thy head has turned grey;
if I were on each little point,
there would be a pointlet on every point.

Thou stag that comest lowing
to me across the glen,
pleasant is the place for seats
on the top of thy antler-points.

I am Sweeney, a poor suppliant,
swiftly do I race across the glen;
that is not my lawful name,
rather is it Fer benn.

The springs I found best:
the well of Leithead Lan,
the well most beautiful and cool,
the fountain of Dun Mail.

Though many are my wanderings,
my raiment to-day is scanty;
I myself keep my watch
on the top of the mountains.

O tall, russet fern,
thy mantle has been made red;
there is no bed for an outlaw
in the branches of thy crests.

At ever-angelic Tech Moling,
at puissant Toidhen in the south,
'tis there my eternal rest-place will be,
I shall fall by a [spear]-point.

The curse of Ronan Finn
has thrown me in thy company,
O little stag, little bleating one,
O melodious little clamourer.

After that lay Sweeney came from Fiodh Gaibhle to Benn Boghaine, thence to Benn Faibhne, thence to Rath Murbuilg, but he found no refuge from the hag until he reached Dun Sobairce in Ulster. Sweeney leaped from the summit of the fort sheer down in front of the hag. She leaped quickly after him, but dropped on the cliff of Dun Sobairce, where she was broken to pieces, and fell into the sea. In that manner she found death in the wake of Sweeney.

12TH CENTURY.
Translator J. G. O'Keeffe.

PART III

The Bardic Tradition

COURT POETRY
TRANSLATED FROM THE GAELIC

Lamentation of Mac Liag
for Kincora[1]

Oh, WHERE, Kincora! is Brian the Great?
And where is the beauty that once was thine?
Oh, where are the princes and nobles that sate
At the feast in thy halls, and drank the red wine?
                Where, oh, Kincora?

---

[1] Mac Liag, the bard of Brian Boru, laments the killing of his patron
by the Vikings at the battle of Clontarf in 1014. Kincora was the
site of Brian's palace in Clare.

Oh, where, Kincora! are thy valorous lords?
Oh, whither, thou Hospitable! are they gone?
Oh, where are the Dalcassians of the Golden Swords?
And where are the warriors Brian led on?
                              Where, oh, Kincora?

And where is Murrough, the descendant of kings—
The defeater of a hundred—the daringly brave—
Who set but slight store by jewels and rings—
Who swam down the torrent and laughed at its wave?
                              Where, oh, Kincora?

And where is Donogh, King Brian's worthy son?
And where is Conaing, the Beautiful Chief?
And Kian, and Corc? Alas! they are gone—
They have left me this night alone with my grief,
                              Left me, Kincora!

And where are the chiefs with whom Brian went forth,
The ne'er vanquished son of Erin the Brave,
The great King of Onaght, renowned for his worth,
And the hosts of Baskinn, from the western wave?
                              Where, oh, Kincora?

Oh, where is Duvlann of the swift-footed Steeds?
And where is Kian, who was son of Molloy?
And where is King Lonergan, the fame of whose deeds
In the red battle-field no time can destroy?
                              Where, oh, Kincora?

And where is that youth of majestic height,
The faith-keeping Prince of the Scots?—Even he,
As wide as his fame was, as great as was his might,
Was tributary, oh, Kincora, to thee!
                Thee, oh, Kincora!

They are gone, those heroes of royal birth
Who plundered no churches, and broke no trust,
'Tis weary for me to be living on earth
When they, oh, Kincora, lie low in the dust!
                Low, oh, Kincora!

Oh, never again will Princes appear,
To rival the Dalcassians of the Cleaving Swords!
I can never dream of meeting afar or anear,
In the east or the west, such heroes and lords!
                Never, Kincora!

Oh, dear are the images my memory calls up
Of Brian Boru!—how he never would miss
To give me at the banquet the first bright cup!
Ah! why did he heap on me honour like this?
                Why, oh, Kincora?

I am Mac Liag, and my home is on the Lake;
Thither often, to that palace whose beauty is fled
Came Brian to ask me, and I went for his sake.
Oh, my grief! that I should live, and Brian be dead!
                Dead, oh, Kincora!

11TH CENTURY.
Translator James Clarence Mangan.

At Saint Patrick's Purgatory

BY Donnchadh mor O'Dala (d. 1244)

Pity me on my pilgrimage to Loch Derg!
O King of the churches and the bells—
Bewailing your sores and your wounds,
But not a tear can I squeeze from my eyes!

Not moisten an eye
After so much sin!
Pity me, O King! What shall I do
With a heart that seeks only its own ease?

Without sorrow or softening in my heart,
Bewailing my faults without repenting them!
Patrick the high priest never thought
That he would reach God in this way.

O lone son of Calpurn—since I name him—
O Virgin Mary, how sad is my lot!—
He was never seen as long as he was in this life
Without the track of tears from his eyes.

In a narrow, hard, stone-wall cell
I lie after all my sinful pride—
O woe, why cannot I weep a tear!—
And I buried alive in the grave.

On the day of Doom we shall weep heavily,
Both clergy and laity;
The tear that is not dropped in time,
None heeds in the world beyond.

I shall have you go naked, go unfed,
Body of mine, father of sin,
For if you are turned Hellwards
Little shall I reck your agony tonight.

O only begotten Son by whom all men were made,
Who shunned not the death by three wounds,
Pity me on my pilgrimage to Loch Derg
And I with a heart not softer than a stone!

Translator Sean O'Faolain.

The Dead at Clonmacnois

BY Angus O'Gillan

IN A quiet water'd land, a land of roses,
    Stands Saint Kieran's city fair:
And the warriors of Erin in their famous generations
    Slumber there.

There beneath the dewy hillside sleep the noblest
    Of the clan of Conn,
Each below his stone with name in branching Ogham
    And the sacred knot thereon.

There they laid to rest the seven Kings of Tara,
    There the sons of Cairbré sleep—
Battle-banners of the Gael, that in Kieran's plain of crosses
    Now their final hosting keep.

And in Clonmacnois they laid the men of Teffia,
   And right many a lord of Breagh;
Deep the sod above Clan Creidé and Clan Conaill,
   Kind in hall and fierce in fray.

Many and many a son of Conn, the Hundred-Fighter,
   In the red earth lies at rest;
Many a blue eye of Clan Colman the turf covers,
   Many a swan-white breast.

    14TH CENTURY.
    Translator T. W. Rolleston.

On the Breaking-Up of a School

BY Tadhg O'g O'Huiginn

Tonight the schools disperse,
Thereby arc beds left widowed,
The folk of each bed will shed tears
At parting.

Many lay down, how sad,
Last night, in the home where I dwelt,
Although this eve they are more likely
To watch than to lie down.

The glory of the home I dwelt in,
O God, I see naught
So inglorious today;
It is a sermon to one who could understand.

The men of art had ever
A tryst against All Hallowtide:
Were but one man living
Their departure would be no dispersal.

O ye who were in his dwelling
In quest of art and residence,
Well might ye loathe to hear
The utterance of the cuckoos.

When the school dispersed
Each man of art went to his own homeland:
None cometh since then from his father's house
In quest of art.

Long seemed to me until dispersal of the school
That I saw by Ferghal's side:
Longer than the dispersal of the school
Is it to have lost my teacher's kindness.

It were easier for them to separate
Than to seek a teacher in his stead:
It is a doom of captivity, O God, to his pupil
If he be with a strange teacher.

For thirty years
Or longer, I bear witness,
I was full of my breath from pride
Until anguish came to cool me.

My prowess in his banqueting hall
Has been punished by draughts of sorrow:
If I have lived riotously, O God,
The punishment is sorer.

For my training he would not have
Me one night away from him,
Till he loosed me against the birds
I was ever in one hut with O'Huiginn.

A reproach against me, to my hurt,
Made in secret to my ollave,[1]
Little profit was it to anyone who should utter it—
He would not endure a breath against me.

From childhood he would share with me
(God reward O'Huiginn therefor)
Every eager design that he formed
Until it was time for us to part.

The teaching that I give today
To his pupils after the poet's death,
It was Ferghal Ruadh who made it:
O Lord that it were like his!

Dear is the mystic hut of poesy,
Which I recognize after his loss:
O empty hut before me
Thou wast not wont to have a neighbour.

---

[1] A chief poet.

That Aine's son lives not
Has robbed poesy of her gaiety.
As a plank goes out of the side of a cask
The wall of learning has broken.

16TH CENTURY.
Translator Osborn Bergin.

The Student

The student's life is pleasant
    And pleasant is his labour,
Search all Ireland over,
    You'll find no better neighbour.

Nor lords nor petty princes
    Dispute the student's pleasure,
Nor chapter stints his purse
    Nor stewardship his leisure.

None orders early rising,
    Calf-rearing or cow-tending,
Nor nights of toilsome vigil,
    His time is his for spending.

He takes a hand at draughts
    And plucks a harp-string bravely,
And fills his nights with courting
    Some golden-haired light lady.

And when spring-time is come
The plough-shaft's there to follow—
    A fistful of goosequills
    And a straight deep furrow!

17TH CENTURY.
Translator Frank O'Connor.

Hugh Maguire

BY Eochy O'Hussey

Too cold this night for Hugh Maguire,
I tremble at the pounding rain;
    Alas that venomous cold.
    Is my companion's lot.

It brings an anguish to my heart
To see the fiery torrents fall;
    He and the spiky frost—
    A horror to the mind!

The floodgates of the heavens yawn
Above the bosom of the clouds;
    And every pool a sea,
    And murder in the air.

One thinks of the hare that haunts the wood,
And of the salmon in the bay,
    Even the wild bird, one grieves
    To think they are abroad.

Then one remembers Hugh Maguire
Abroad in a strange land tonight
  Under the lightning's glare
  And clouds with fury filled.

He in West Munster braves his doom,
And without shelter strides between
  The drenched and shivering grass
  And the impetuous sky.

Cold on that tender blushing cheek
The fury of the springtime gales
  That toss the stormy rays
  Of stars about his head.

I can scarce bear to conjure up
The contour of his body crushed
  This rough and gloomy night
  In its cold iron suit.

The gentle and war-mastering hand
To the slim shaft of his cold spear
  By icy weather pinned—
  Cold is the night for Hugh.

The low banks of the swollen streams
Are covered where the soldiers pass;
  The meadows stiff with ice,
  The horses cannot feed.

And yet as though to bring him warmth
And call the brightness to his face
   Each wall that he attacks
   Sinks in a wave of fire,

The fury of the fire dissolves
The frost that sheaths the tranquil eye,
   And from his wrists the flame
   Thaws manacles of ice.

   16TH CENTURY.
   Translator Frank O'Connor.

Civil Irish and Wild Irish

BY Laoiseach Mac an Bhaird

Man who follow English ways, who cut short your curling hair, O slender hand of my choice, you are unlike the good son of Donnchadh!

If you were he, you would not give up your long hair (the best adornment in all the land of Ireland) for an affected English fashion, and your head would not be tonsured.

You think a shock of yellow hair unfashionable; he hates both the wearing of love-locks and being shaven-headed in the English manner—how unlike are your ways!

Eóghan Bán, the darling of noble women, is a man who never loved English customs; he has not set his heart on English ways, he has chosen the wild life rather.

Your ideas are nothing to Eóghan *Bán;* he would give breeches away for a trifle, a man who asked no cloak but a rag, who had no desire for doublet and hose.

He would hate to have at his ankle a jewelled spur on a boot, or stockings in the English manner; he will allow no love-locks on him.

A blunt rapier which could not kill a fly, the son of Donnchadh does not think it handsome; nor the weight of an awl sticking out behind his rear as he goes to the hill of the assembly.

Little he cares for gold-embroidered cloaks, or for a high well-furnished ruff, or for a gold ring which would only be vexatious, or for a satin scarf down to his heels.

He does not set his heart on a feather bed, he would prefer to lie upon rushes; to the good son of Donnchadh a house of rough wattles is more comfortable than the battlements of a castle.

A troop of horse at the mouth of a pass, a wild fight, a ding-dong fray of footsoldiers, these are some of the delights of Donnchadh's son—and seeking contest with the foreigners.

You are unlike Eóghan *Bán;* men laugh at you as you put your foot on the mounting-block; it is a pity that you yourself don't see your errors, O man who follow English ways.

16TH CENTURY.
Translator Kenneth Jackson.

Maelmora MacSweeny

BY Tadhg Dall O'Huiginn (1550-1593)[1]

One night I came to Eas Caoille, till the Day of Doom I shall remember it; when the fortress itself shall have perished there shall still remain forever the events of that night, the doings of all who were present. The like of the men whom I found in the polished bright-hued castle, on the shapely benches of the crimson fortress, eye never saw before. But few remain of the beloved company whom I found in the bright castle, the death of the four that were within was a grief from which Banbha[2] did not look to recover.

I found Maelmora MacSweeny on the central bench of the graceful mansion, a man of generous and pleasant manner, favorite pupil of the schools of Conn's land.[3] Dear as life to me was the man I found in that domed castle with its ivory-hilted swords; as I have experienced twice its value of misery from the loss of it, the honor I received from him is the worse from its greatness. Both pupil and fosterer to the poets of Banbha throughout his days was the chess-king of the Finn, the goal of our emulation, our ready gift, storehouse of the hearts of the learned. Our healing herb, our sleep charm, our fruitful branch, our house of treasure; a piece of steel, yet one who never denied any man, most precious offspring of the Grecian Gaels.

---

[1] See Introduction, p. xxiv.

[2] A name for Ireland.

[3] Ireland in the second century (A.D.) was divided into two kingdoms, one ruled over by Eogan Mor, the other by Conn of the Hundred Battles. Henceforward the northern kingdom became known as Conn's Half (or Land) and the southern kingdom as Eogan's Half.

I found beside the son of Maelmurray[1] many men of letters worthy of recompense, while the choicest of every craft in the world were also reclining beside the chief of Derg. Till the day of his death the poets of the host of the House of Trim were ever with the chief of Conn's tribe in a gathering large enough for battle or assembly.

At that time in particular there sat by the warrior of Loch Key—well did their scholarship become them—three of the poets of Té's Hill. There was the poet of the Earl of the Burkes, and also by his soft bosom was one of whom the very mention was a surety, the poet of the famous race of Niall. There was the poet of the chieftain of the Moy, Mac William Burke of just awards—discouraging in sooth are the changes of the world, that not one of these remains is in itself a sermon. Brian O'Donnellan, kindly countenance, poet to the lion of Lough-rea; he with the schools as the moon above stars, peace to his gallant, noble form. Brian Macnamee, son of Angus, poet to the descendant of Nine-Hostaged Niall; a man whose attainment was the best of his time, he was fit to deliver wisdom's pledge. Conor, grandson of O'Huiginn, poet to the lord of Inishkea, almost equal to a prince was the poet, the head of his kindred in worth. The three poets that I found by the ruddy, fair-skinned hero—let a trio such as they be found in the land of Banbha!

With one accord they arise before me from beside the chieftain who was my chieftain; often I think of them in my heart, the utterances of the three drawing tears from my eyes. The soothing strains of harps, the sweetness of honey, the elation of ale—alas, that he of whom I had them no longer lives—these gave me pleasure.

For a while after my arrival they drank to me—gentlemen were their attendants—from cups of gold, from goblets of horn. When we had gone to our couches of rest to slumber, ere the coming of day, he who lay furthest from me would not admit that to be thus was not a sentence of bondage. I lay in

---

[1] I.e. MacSweeny, the host.

the midst of the four, the four forms that were most dear to me, the three comrades who have grieved my heart, and the champion of Magh Meann.

To the blossom of Tara and his three companions I relate a tale in return for reward; its dearness was a portent of fame for them, golden youth of the north. Four treasures endowed with virtue I take from them in payment for my story; that the like of the princely jewels may not be found—is not that enough to color one's tears? As the first award I was allowed I took the dappled steed from the hero of steed-abounding Slieve Gamph, him at whose death hospitality perished. The dappled steed that I took from Maelmora—woe is me that I took it— hardly is there its like in the world, a steed surpassing all the steeds of Bregian Banbha. From Brian son of Angus I took the choicest hound of Dá Thí's Plain; its excellence was such as to place it above all other hounds, it was one of the choice hounds of the world. It had been easier for Brian to renounce one by one all of the treasures of Ireland—wherefore should this not depress my spirit?—than his treasure of a noble hand- some hound.

From Brian son of Owen, ere the fair, rosy, kindly fellow slept, I got as a reward for my story a precious book, a brim- ming spring of the genuine stream of knowledge. The "Cattle- raids," "Wooings," "Destructions" of all the world were in the gift I received, with descriptions of the battles and ex- ploits thereof; it was the flower of the royal books of Ireland. Conor gave the magic harp, such a precious jewel as even a king would not bestow; long has that present been a sorrowful inheritance, it was no fitting gift from a poet. The harp of the poet of the Burkes will be ever an object of reverence; he from whom it was got is no more, but it remains in freshness to-day.

Alas for him by whom the givers of these were beloved, since it was destined that he should part from them; men never false in the house of election, men who loved to spread their fame. Alas for my beloved four, my bed-fellows, my confidants; four stems from a fruitful forest, trees fertile in gifts for us.

My reason wanders, restless is my mind after that shortlived company; alas for him who remains on earth without them, departing, they have left Brian's Banbha without fruits.

It is a heartbreak that the chief of the band which was within should be lacking to us; never before did poet lack the generous gift of his stout heart. May God requite Maelmora for the quantity of his wealth that I received; one who bestowed as much as any man gave, the benefactor of all. Suave in utterance, stern in resolve, ruthless in deeds, modest in speech; guardian of every man of his kindred, judge, soldier, poet, soothsayer. Treasure of contention of the race of Breóghan, winning of their game, defence of their pledge; satisfaction of the hearts of troublesome guests, love of melodious, merry, graceful women. Prudent preparation, generous disposition, a keeping of word, a breaking of peace; bright countenance from which the eyes could scarce wander, nursing knee of royal rule. Solving of problems, posing of counter-problems, Inisfail's[1] anvil of knowledge; hate of perpetual ease, love of conflict, surety for the peace and war of all. The son of Gormlaidh, a branch above the wood, keen in mind, gentle in response—where is his like for bestowing a troublesome award? Sternness and generosity he has in equal parts.

Though I have been in poverty since he fell, I should be above all the land of Fál in affluence if only Maelmora—limewhite skin, countenance of amber—remained. The remembrance of what I got from my friend will soon be but an omen of grief; I shall fear lest the greatness of my honor should come to me again in illusion.

Alas, not many of my comrades remain to me in their own shape; the world has cast me away, sending me travelling afar, in solitude. Pitiful it is to lack my three comrades, the race of Gormlaidh, from whom the day was short; Banbha, who looked for help from this clan, is now under a cloud of sorrow.

Translator Eleanor Knott.

---

[1] A name for Ireland (*Inis Fal*).

The First Vision

BY Tadhg Dall O'Huiginn

A Vision of a Queen of Fairyland
My soul to ravish came to me last night,
And never lady at my side did stand
To my undoing so unearthly bright.

Last night she came, a bright and lovely ghost,
And rose before me while I seemed to sleep,
And of that slumber where my soul was lost
My tongue shall tell while I my memory keep.

Fair was her face, her cheeks outblushed the rose;
There might you see the floods of crimson rise,
And dark unfaltering brows above disclose
The hyacinthine petals of her eyes.

Her pretty mouth more sweet than honeycomb
Would with red lips the budding rose excel,
And each soft whisper that from thence did come
Would charm the sick and make the dying well.

Between her lips like fallen rain of pearl
On scarlet cushions twain her teeth reposed;
How bright they shone, how sweetly spoke the girl;
Each languid word new loveliness disclosed.

Between her arms that taper to the hand
Are set twin glories, beautiful to see.
Two snowy mountains in her bosom stand,
Mid golden thickets of embroidery.

Gold-bordered slippers on her gentle feet
Do guard her steps wherever she may move;
You'd swear that maid so radiantly sweet
Had them a present from the God of Love.

Her purple mantle fringed with satin round,
Her golden shift with scarlet borders gay,
Her gilded bodice o'er her bosom bound
Did all her fairy loveliness display.

Then this fair lady spake in modest wise,
And gently did the amazéd dreamer greet,
And I when she had done did make replies
To that bright beauty with the visage sweet.

We spake awhile and then I made demand
That she should answer to my questioning:
"Fair lady, tell me of your native land!
Whence come you? From what country, or what king?"

'Run thro' two continents of earth or three!
'Tis easier so," said she to my appeal,
"But do not think to know my mystery,
For I have secrets I will ne'er reveal."

"I came to seek you: come away with me!"
Thus spake the lady, and her voice was low,
And in my ear she murmured secretly,
As softest notes from sweetest organs flow.

"I will not go!" I answered like a fool,
For love had brought me to distraction,
And as I spake that vision beautiful
Had vanished in the darkness and was gone.

And now my soul and body part in pain.
The queen with blushing cheek and brown-lashed eyes
Leaves me to pine and cometh not again,
Tho' she was kind and beautiful and wise.

To ruddy Connla long ago there came
A woman. Fodhla's[1] monarch to beguile,
And she I love is gentler, yet the same
As she that won his heart with many a wile.

A warrior father's noblest offspring he,
Brave Connla, son of Hundred-fighting Conn,
Thro' woman's guile he fled beyond the sea
And never vessel bore a braver one.

E'en such the woman who in mantle brown,
With branch of music from across the sea
Did visit Bran Mac Febal. ('Tis handed down,
A famous tale in Ireland's history.)[2]

The noblest sons of Desmond's land she bore
Across the sea, yea, even nine times nine,
Eighty with Bran to make the number more,
So by his flight perfecting her design.

----

[1] A name for Ireland.
[2] See page 131.

Connla deluded, Bran beguiled also,
By stranger woman ravished o'er the sea,
And I deceived by one I do not know!
Most strange of all the thing that's done to me!

The mound of Midhir with its rampart fair,
The fort of Sanbh, Abhartach's magic hill,
No lady in their castles can compare
With this sweet maid for whom I languish still.

Not in Emania of the apple-trees,
Nor halls of Aonghus of the golden sword,
The fairy dwells that hath such charms as these,
So soft a beauty or so kind a word.

But she is gone, and I would follow fast
To lands unknown, who languish in despair.
Would it were possible to find at last
That country and to dwell for ever there!

A little hour I loved her rosy cheek—
The ebb must follow ever on the flow—
The vision fled, the joy of love grew weak,
My spirit sank and I was left to woe.

Translator The Earl of Longford.

The Second Vision

BY Tadhg Dall O'Huiginn

Say, are you she that came to me last
Brought by enchantment in a vision?
My spirit ravished by the wondrous sight
Knows naught aright for deep distraction.

And if you be not she that came before
With slender body and soft fondling hand,
I'll ne'er believe that there are many more
So gently treading out of Fairyland.

Your kindling cheek, the azure of your eyes!
Could all the four great elements compose
Such coiling gold as o'er your shoulder lies,
A cheek so red, an eye to vie with those?

No tooth so white, no lip so crimson were,
No voice so soft to lull the brain to sleep,
No brow so dark as might with yours compare,
No wealth to match the treasure that you keep!

A throat more white than is the lily flower,
Long tapering hands, surpassing beautiful,
Soft flesh that robs the moonlight of its power,
And dims the foam and makes bright rivers dull.

White are your breasts as blossom, that do stand
High o'er the glorious slopes that gleam below,
Two gentle hills that rise from richest land,
Two wondrous mounds that Fairy people know.

Like flight of birds that sing not in the cold
About your body fall the rippling locks.
Oh, surely they are drenched in liquid gold,
As down they curve and glitter in their flocks!

Oh, trust me! You shall take no harm at all;
But tell if it was you that came last night,
To vex my heart, to trouble Inis Fail,[1]
Bright maid with eye so mild, with teeth so white!

Or was it you that came so long ago
To good King Arthur and his Table Round,
Sweet head whence radiant tresses softly flow?
For since that day no maid so fair was found.

Or was it you that came, for so 'twould seem,
Of old to Ughoine's son, the mighty Hugh,
From Slievenaman, of many a magic stream,
To Eire's people from the Fairy crew?

Or was it you, indeed I think 'twas you,
Who carried Murchadh across the sea,
The night you visited great Brian Boru,
Who lay encamped with all his soldiery?

---

[1] A name for Ireland.

Or was it you that came another day
The valiant Hound of Culann to beguile?
To lead the son of Deichtire astray
You left your bright and fruitful mound awhile.

Or was it you whose loveliness appealed,
O glorious vision with an angel's grace,
To Mahon O'Maille once on Banba's field,
Where many a war has marred the country's race.

Or was it you that came in days of old,
In ancient days when Conaire was King,
To craze the soul of warriors young and bold
At Tailteann Hill with valor mustering?

Or was it you, O maid of steadfast thought,
That bore young Bran away from Eire's strand?
The son of white-foot Febal once you brought
Across the Ocean to the Promised Land.

There came—Oh, were you there?—to Connacht's King
A glorious company of ladies fair,
On shores of Derg renowned, a wondrous thing,
As by the lake he lay. Oh, were you there?

Or was it you led Connla far away,
In spite of guarding spells of druidry,
From Fodhla's host, from cold, grey hills of Breagh,
O lovely face, not hateful unto me?

Or was it you that did myself beguile
A while ago, O vision of my joy.
And are you she that with her wizard wile
Doth still the men of Fodhla's land destroy?

Ah, yes! 'Tis she! I know that you must be
That very lady that before was here.
In leafy Banba there could never be
Another such; this beauty hath no peer.

O gentle maiden with the limbs of snow,
No fairy equals her I saw last night,
But you yourself. No magic castles show
By Boyne or waves of Cuan a form so bright.

For not the sea-washed mound of Assaroe,
Nor any fairy dwelling's warm recess,
Nor yet Rath Truim nor Youghal e'er did know
A maid of such unearthly loveliness.

For tho' last night I saw her beauty plain,
Another such I never shall discern
In dream or vision till she come again,
And all the wonder of that time return.

Twice hath she come. The maid with longing sore
Wasted my cheek and scarred my brow with care.
Twice hath she come and she will come once more.
And still I wait, for she is wondrous fair.

Translator The Earl of Longford

The Good Tradition

Ah! liberal-handed lady, though
Round Eire's shore the generous wave
Ebbs now, in thee 'tis still at flow;
No marvel that the bard's thy slave.

A lady passionate for song,
True friend of all the bardic kind,
Who cleaves to her can scarce go wrong;
Song to her loaned doth interest find.

The good tradition holds no more
Of open-handedness to art;
On later manners men set store
And close their purse-strings and their heart.

Now that the giving spirit's gone
And wealth and art are by the ears,
That poet's mad who labours on
And gives to song his wasted years.

In ancient Ulster as of old
Dwelt Liberality of right;
Now Ulster hearts are changed and cold,
From all that province she takes flight.

She's chased from Munster; Connacht too
Gives her no welcome as of yore;
The hapless hunger-stricken crew
Know Liberality no more.

She's known no more where the wide plain
Of Leinster spreads beneath the skies;
Unless another shape she's ta'en,
That hides her from the poet's eyes.

A mist has caught her from our sight,
A druid mist that hides her o'er;
Ask but a lodging for the night
And all men turn you from the door.

> 17TH CENTURY.
> Translator Robin Flower.

The Flight of the Earls[1]

This night sees Eire desolate,
Her chiefs are cast out of their state;
Her men, her maidens weep to see
Her desolate that should peopled be.

How desolate is Connla's plain,
Though aliens swarm in her domain;
Her rich bright soil had joy in these
That now are scattered overseas.

---

[1] Six years after their defeat at Kinsale in 1601, the earls of Tyrone and Tyrconnell fled to the continent with the surviving members of their clans. What remained of the Gaelic aristocracy was either destroyed or driven into exile during the Williamite War (1690-2).

Man after man, day after day
Her noblest princes pass away
And leave to all the rabble rest
A land dispeopled of her best.

O'Donnell goes. In that stern strait
Sore-stricken Ulster mourns her fate,
And all the northern shore makes moan
To hear that Aodh of Annagh's gone.

Men smile at childhood's play no more,
Music and song, their day is o'er;
At wine, at Mass the kingdom's heirs
Are seen no more; changed hearts are theirs.

They feast no more, they gamble not,
All goodly pastime is forgot,
They barter not, they race no steeds,
They take no joy in stirring deeds.

No praise in builded song expressed
They hear, no tales before they rest;
None care for books and none take glee
To hear the long-traced pedigree.

The packs are silent, there's no sound
Of the old strain on Bregian ground.
A foreign flood holds all the shore,
And the great wolf-dog barks no more.

Woe to the Gael in this sore plight!
Hence forth they shall not know delight.
No tidings now their woe relieves,
Too close the gnawing sorrow cleaves.

These the examples of their woe:
Israel in Egypt long ago,
Troy that the Greek hosts set on flame,
And Babylon that to ruin came.

Sundered from hope, what friendly hand
Can save the sea-surrounded land?
The clan of Conn no Moses see
To lead them from captivity.

Her chiefs are gone. There's none to bear
Her cross or lift her from despair;
The grieving lords take ship. With these
Our very souls pass overseas.

    17TH CENTURY.
    Translator Robin Flower.

Were Not the Gael Fallen

BY Peadar O'Mulconry

Were not the Gael fallen from their high estate
And Fola's warrior kings cast down by fate
And learning mocked in Eire's evil day,
I were no servant, Edmond, in thy pay.

Ye shall not stay my toil, once held divine,
Thou and thy fleering harlots at their wine,
Till all the brave are dead and out of reach
Eireamhon's people of the golden speech.

Edmond, I give good counsel. Heed it thou!
Leave mocking at my holy labours now,
Or such a rain of venomed shafts I'll send
That never a man shall save thee nor defend.

A tale I've heard that well might tame thy mood.
A gamesome chief of Gascony's best blood
Refused a poet once. The satire sped
And the man withered, strengthless, leprous, dead.

17TH CENTURY.
Translator Robin Flower.

Who Will Buy a Poem?

BY Mahon O'Heffernan

I ask, who will buy a poem? Its meaning is the true learning of sages. Would anyone take, does anyone want, a noble poem which would make him immortal?

Though this is a poem of close-knit lore, I have walked all Munster with it, every market-place from cross to cross— and it has brought me no profit from last year to the present.

Though a groat would be small payment, no man nor any woman offered it; not a man spoke of the reason, but neither Irish nor English heeded me.

An art like this is no profit to me, though it is hard that it should die out; it would be more dignified to go and make combs—why should anyone take up poetry?

Corc of Cashel lives no more, nor Cian, who did not hoard up cattle nor the price of them, men who were generous in rewarding poets—alas, it is good-bye to the race of Éibhear.

The prize for generosity was never taken from them, until Cobhthach died, and Tál; I spare to mention the many kindreds for whom I might have continued to make poetry.

I am like a trading ship that has lost its freight, after the Fitz-Geralds who won renown. I hear no offers—how that torments me! It is a vain matter about which I ask.

17TH CENTURY.
Translator Kenneth Jackson.

Geoffrey Keating[1] (c.1570-c.1650)
FROM *The History of Ireland*

How Emain Macha[2] *Got Its Name*

Now THE reason why it is called Eamhain Mhacha is this:
three kings out of Ulster held the sovereignty of Ireland,
namely, Aodh Ruadh son of Badharn, from whom is named
Eas Ruaidh, and Diothorba son of Deaman of Uisneach in
Meath, and Ciombaoth son of Fionntan from Fionnabhair;
and it was with this Ciombaoth that Ughaine Mor son of
Eochaidh Buadhach was brought up. And each of these kings
reigned seven years in succession, until each had held the
sovereignty of Ireland thrice. And the first of them to die was
Aodh Ruadh; and he left no issue but one daughter named
Macha. Macha demanded the sovereignty in her turn after her
father's death; and Diothorba and his children said that they
would not cede sovereignty to a woman; and a battle was fought
between themselves and Macha; and Macha triumphed over
them in that battle, and held the sovereignty of Ireland seven
years; and Diothorba died and left five sons, namely, Baoth,
Bedach, Bras, Uallach, and Borbchas. These demanded the
sovereignty of Ireland for themselves, as it was held by their
ancestors before them. Macha said she would only give them
battle for the sovereignty. A battle was fought between them,
and Macha defeated them. The children of Diothorba fled for
safety to dark and intricate woods; and Macha took Ciombaoth
son of Fionntan as her husband, and made him leader of her
warriors. and went herself in pursuit of the sons of Diothorba
in the guise of a leper, having rubbed her body with the dough
of rye, and found them in an intricate forest in Burenn, cooking a wild boar. The sons of Diothorba asked news of her, and
gave her a portion of the meat. She told them all the news she
had.

---

[1] See Introduction, p. xxv.
[2] The capital of ancient Ulster.

And then one of the men said that the leper had a beautiful eye, and that he desired to lie with her. Thereupon he and Macha retired into the recesses of the wood, and Macha bound this man and left him there, and returned to the rest. And they questioned her, "Where didst thou leave the man who went with thee?" said they. "I know not," said she; "but I think he feels ashamed to come into your presence after embracing a leper." "It is not a shame," said they, "since we will do the same thing." Thus she went into the wood with each of them in turn; and she bound them all, and so took them bound together before the men of Ulster at Eamhain; and she asked the Ulster nobles what she should do with them. They all said with one accord that they should be put to death. "That is not just," said Macha, "for that would be contrary to law; but let them be made slaves of, and let the task be imposed on them of building a fort for me which shall be the capital of the province for ever." Thereupon Macha undid the gold bodkin that was in the mantle on her breast, and with it measured the site of the fort which the sons of Diothorba were obliged to build. Now, the fort is called Eamhain, eo being a word for "a bodkin," while *muin* means "the neck," and hence the fort is called Eamhain that is, eo *mhuin*. Or, it is called Eamhain from Eamhain Mhacha, that is, the wife of Cronn son of Adhnaman. Now this woman was forced against her will to run with the horses of Conchubhar, king of Ulster; and she, though pregnant, outran them; and at the end of the race she gave birth to a son and a daughter; and she cursed the men of Ulster, whence they were visited with the pangs of labour; and these pangs continued to afflict them during nine reigns, that is, from Conchubhar to the reign of Mal son of Rochruidhe. . . .

Loingseach's Horse Ears

We read of Labhraidh Loingseach[1] that his ears were like those of a horse; and hence he used to kill on the spot everyone who cut his hair, lest he or anyone else might be aware of this blemish. Now he was wont to have his hair cropped every year, that is, to have cut off the part of his hair that grew below his ears. It was necessary to cast lots to determine who should crop the king each year, since it was his wont to put to death everyone who cropped him. Now it happened that the lot fell on the only son of a widow who approached the close of her life, and who lived near the king's stronghold. And when she heard that the lot had fallen on her son, she came and besought the king not to put her only son to death, seeing he was her sole offspring. The king promised her that he would not put her son to death, provided he kept secret what he should see, and made it known to no one till death. And when the youth had cropped the king, the burden of that secret so oppressed his body that he was obliged to lie in the bed of sickness, and that no medicine availed him. When he had lain long in a wasting condition, a skilful druid came to visit him, and told his mother that the cause of his sickness was the burden of a secret, and that he would not be well till he revealed his secret to some thing; and he directed him, since he was bound not to tell his secret to a person, to go to a place where four roads met, and to turn to his right and to address the first tree he met, and to tell his secret to it. The first tree he met was a large willow, and he disclosed his secret to it. Thereupon the burden of pain that was on his body vanished; and he was healed instantly as he returned to his mother's house. Soon after this, however, it happened that Craiftine's harp got broken, and he went to seek the material for a harp, and came upon the very willow to which

---

[1] King of Leinster in the third century B.C.

the widow's son had revealed the secret, and from it he took the material for his harp; and when the harp was made and set to tune, as Craiftine played upon it all who listened imagined that it sang, "Da o phill ar Labhraidh Lorc," that is, Labraidh Loingseach, meaning, "Two horse's ears on Labhraidh Lorc"; and as often as he played on that harp, it was understood to sing the same thing. And when the king heard this story, he repented of having put so many people to death to conceal that deformity of his, and openly exhibited his ears to the household, and never afterwards concealed them. I think this part of the story is a romantic tale rather than history. . . .

The Death of Curaoi

There were three orders of champions in Ireland at the same time; and there lived neither before their time nor ever since a body of the sons of Milidh who were bigger, stronger, braver, more skilled, more intrepid on the field of battle, and in exercises of valour and bravery than they; for the Fian of Leinster were not to be compared with them. The first order of these were the champions of the Craobh Ruadh under Conchubhar; the second order the Gamhanruidh of Iorras Domhnonn under Oilill Fionn; and the third order clanna Deaghaidh under Curaoi son of Daire in west Munster.

It was thus that the death of Curaoi came about. The champions of the Craobh Ruadh went to pillage an island in the ocean near Alba[1] called Manainn, where there was much gold and silver and wealth of various kinds, and many precious valuables besides; and the lord of the island had a comely, marriageable daughter who surpassed the women of her time in form and beauty. Her name was Blanaid. And when Curaoi heard that the champions were setting out on that expedition, he put on a disguise by magic, and went with the party; and

---

[1] Scotland.

when they were about to plunder the island in the guise of jugglers, they apprehended great difficulty in seizing on the dun which was in the island in which was Blanaid, and all the precious valuables of the island, both on account of its strength and of the great skill in magic of those who were defending it. Then Curaoi, who was disguised as a man with a grey cloak, said that if he got his choice of the valuables in the dun he would capture it for them. Cuchulainn promised him this; and thereupon they attacked the dun with the man in the grey cloak at their head. He stopped the magic wheel that was in motion at the door of the fortress, and enabled all to enter; and they plundered the dun, and took from it Blanaid and all the precious valuables it contained. They thence set out for Ireland and reached Eamhain; and as they were dividing the valuables, the man in the grey cloak asked for the valuable he should choose as was promised to him. "Thou shalt have it," said Cuchulainn. "Well, then," said he, "Blanaid is my choice of the valuables." "Thou mayst have thy choice of the other valuables excepting only Blanaid." "I will not accept any but her," said the man of the grey coat. Thereupon Curaoi sought an opportunity of carrying off Blanaid, and, seizing her unperceived, he bore her off in an enchanted mask. When Cuchulainn noticed that the lady was missing, he concluded that it was Curaoi who carried her off, and he pursued them by direct route to Munster, and overtook them at Solchoid; and the champions grappled with one another and engaged in strong, valorous wrestling; and Cuchulainn was brought to the ground by Curaoi, who inflicted on him the binding of the five smalls, and left him there a bound captive, having cut off his hair with his sword; and, leaving Cuchulainn bound as we have said, he took Blanaid with him to west Munster. But after this Laogh son of Rian of Gabhra came and unbound Cuchulainn; and they proceeded thence to the north of Ulster, and settled down beside Beanna Boirche for a year without coming to a meeting of the men of Ulster until Cuchulainn's hair grew; and at the end of that year Cuchulainn happened to be on Beanna Boirche, and he saw a large flock of black birds coming southwards from the surface of the ocean; and when they reached land he pursued them, and slew with his sling, by the exercise called *taithbheim* or "return-stroke," a bird out of each county, till he killed the last black bird of them at Sruibh Broin in west Munster; and as he was returning eastwards, he found Blanaid alone beside the Fionnghlaise in Ciarraidhe, where Curaoi's dwelling-fortress stood at that time. A conversation then took place between them; and she made known to him that there was not on the face of the earth a man she loved more than him, and asked him to come on the following Samhain with a full host and carry her off by fraud or force; and that he might the more easily do this, she would bring about that Curaoi should at that time have but few warriors and attendants. Cuchulainn promised to come to fetch her at that time. Thereupon he bade her farewell, and proceeded to Ulster, and gave Conchubhar an account of the incident.

As to Blanaid, she told Curaoi that he ought to build a stone fortress for himself which would excel all the royal fortresses of Ireland, and that the way in which that could be done was to send the clanna Deaghaidh to collect and bring together all the large stones that were standing in Ireland for the purpose of making a stone fortress for himself. And Blanaid's object in this was that clanna Deaghaidh might be scattered through the distant regions of Ireland far from Curaoi where Cuchulainn should come to carry her off. Now when Cuchulainn heard that clanna Deaghaidh were thus dispersed throughout Ireland, he set out secretly from Ulster with an army, and no tidings are recorded of him till he reached the oak wood that lay beside Curaoi's fortress; and when he arrived there, he sent word privately to Blanaid that he was there with an army; and the sign she sent him was that she would steal Curaoi's sword, and would thereupon pour a vat of new milk that was in the lios into the stream which was flowing from the homestead through the wood in which Cuchulainn was. Not long after he was informed of this token he saw the stream become white from the milk; and with that they attacked the fortress and sprang upon Curaoi in the lios and slew him alone and unarmed as he was. And the river referred to was called Fionnghlaise, through its having become white from the milk.

Curaoi's poet, who was called Feircheirtne, went after Blanaid to Ulster in hope of getting an opportunity of slaying her to avenge Curaoi; and on reaching Ulster he found Conchubhar and Cuchulainn and Blanaid, with a large assembly round them, at Ceann Beara point; and when the poet saw Blanaid standing there on the brink of a precipice, he went towards her and twined his arms round her, and cast himself and herself suddenly down the precipice, and thus they were both killed. . . .

Mochua's Riches

Mochua and Columcille were contemporaries, and when Mochua or Mac Duach was a hermit in the desert the only cattle he had in the world were a cock and a mouse and a fly. The cock's service to him was to keep the matin time of midnight; and the mouse would let him sleep only five hours in the day-and-night, and when he desired to sleep longer, through being tired from making many crosses and genuflexions, the mouse would come and rub his ear, and thus waken him; and the service the fly did him was to keep walking on every line of the Psalter that he read, and when he rested from reciting his psalms the fly rested on the line he left off at till he resumed the reciting of his psalms. Soon after that these three precious ones died, and Mochua, after that event, wrote a letter to Columcille, who was in Iona, in Alba, and he complained of the death of his flock. Columcille wrote to him, and said thus: "O brother," said he, "thou must not be surprised at the death of the flock that thou hast lost, for misfortune exists only where there is wealth." From this banter of these real saints I gather that they set no store on worldly possessions, unlike many persons of the present time. . . .

St. Columkille

Columcille came to Ireland having a cerecloth over his eyes, so that he might not see the soil of Ireland. For he was forbidden to look at the soil of Ireland from the time that Molaise imposed as penance on him to go to Alba and not to see the land of Ireland till death, and it was for this reason that he kept the cerecloth over his eyes while he was in Ireland until his return to Alba; and it is to relate Columcille's fulfilment of this penance that Molaise composed this stanza:

> Though Colum came from the east
> In a bark across the great sea,
> He saw nothing in noble Ireland
> On his coming to the convention.

Now the reason why Molaise imposed on Columcille the penance of going to Alba was that Columcille caused three battles to be fought in Ireland, to wit, the Battle of Cuil Dreimhne, the Battle of Cuil Rathan, and the Battle of Cuil Feadha. The cause of the Battle of Cuil Dreimhne, according to the old book called Uidhir Chiarain, was this: Diarmaid, son of Fearghus Ceirrbheoil, king of Ireland, held a Feis of Tara, and a nobleman was slain at that feis by Cuarnan, son of Aodh, son of Eochaidh Tiormcharna; and the reason why Diarmaid slew this Cuarnan was that he had slain the nobleman at the feis in violation of the law and sanctuary of the feis. And before Cuarnan was slain he put himself under the protection of the two sons of Mac Earca, to wit, Fearghus and Domhnall, and they put him under the protection of Columcille, and Diarmaid slew him in violation of Columcille's protection for having transgressed the law of Tara, and the result of this was that Columcille assembled clanna Neill of the north (on account of his own protection and that of the chil-

dren of Mac Earca having been violated), and the Battle of
Cuil Dreimhne was fought against Diarmaid and the men of
Connaught, and they were defeated through the prayer of
Columcille.

The Black Book of Molaga gives another reason why the
Battle of Cuil Dreimhne was fought, to wit, through the unjust judgment Diarmaid gave against Columcille, when he
secretly copied the Gospel from Fionntain's book, and Fionntain claimed for his own the copy which was written from his
own book. Accordingly, both sides chose Diarmaid as a judge
between them; and the judgment Diarmaid gave was that to
every cow belonged her calf and that to every book belonged a
copy of it; and that was the second reason why the Battle of
Cuil Dreimhne was fought.

The reason why Columcille caused the battle of Cuil Rathan
to be fought against the Dal nAruidhe and the Ultonians was
because a contention had arisen between Columcille and
Comghall, when the Dal nAruidhe showed themselves partial
in the contention.

The reason why Columcille had caused the Battle of Cuil
Feadha to be fought against Colman, son of Diarmaid, was
to avenge the affront given him in the murder of Baodan, son
of Ninnidh, king of Ireland, at Leim an Eich by Coman, son
of Colman, in violation of Colum's protection.

Now Colum, with his holy clerics, proceeded from Alba
to Ireland, as we have said, and when he was approaching the
convention the queen, Aodh's wife, told her son, Conall, not to
show any reverence to the heron-cleric or to his company. And
when Colum was informed of this before he arrived at the place
he said: "It is my will that the queen and her handmaid, in the
shape of two herons, be over that ford below until Doom." Here
is a proof from the Amhra repeating the words of Colum in this
stanza:

> Let her become a heron,
> Said the cleric in a great rage,
> And let her handmaid exactly be
> A heron in her company.

And the reason why he ordered that the handmaid become a heron together with the queen was that it was she who came with a message from the queen to Conall, telling him not to show any reverence to the heron-cleric or to his company. And I hear from many people that ever since two herons are usually seen on the ford which is beside Drom Ceat.

As to Columcille, when he arrived at the convention the party of Conall, son of Aodh, son of Ainmire, was the nearest to him in the assembly, and when Conall saw the clerics he incited the rabble of his party against them, thrice nine their number, and they pelted them with clods of clay, and they bruised and hurt the clerics. And Colum asked who were thus beating them. Colum was told that it was Conall, son of Aodh, who was inciting them to do this deed, and he ordered that thrice nine bells be rung on the spot against Conall, whom he cursed and deprived of royalty, of authority, of senses, of memory, of his understanding. And from these bells that were rung against him he is called Conall Clogach.

After this Colum went to the party of Domhnall, son of Aodh, and Domhnall went to meet him and bade him welcome, and kissed his cheek and seated him in his own place. Colum gave his blessing to Domhnall, son of Aodh, and prayed God that he might attain the sovereignty of Ireland; and it happened ultimately that he held the sovereignty of Ireland for thirteen years before he died.

Colum, accompanied by Domhnall, proceeded thence to the king's party, and when he had come into the king's presence the latter welcomed him—the king dreaded him greatly on account of what he had done to Conall, to the queen, to her handmaid, as we have said. "My welcome is compliance with my wish," said Colum. "It shall be granted thee," said the king. "Then," said Colum, "what I wish is this: I make three requests of thee, namely, to keep the filés whom thou art banishing from Ireland, and to free Scannlan Mor, son of Ceannfaolaidh, king of Osruighe, from the bondage in which thou keepest him, and not to go to impose a tribute on the Dal Riada in Alba." "I do not wish to keep the filés," said the

king, "so unjust are their demands and so numerous are they.
For there are usually thirty in the train of an ollamh, and
fifteen in that of an anroth, and so on for the other grades of
the filé down to the lowest." Each of them used to have a
separate train of attendants according to his degree, so that
nearly the third of the men of Ireland followed the bardic
profession.

Columcille said to the king that it was right to set aside
many of the filés, as they were so numerous. But he advised him
to maintain a filé as his own chief ollamh, after the example of
the kings who went before him, and that each provincial king
should have an ollamh, and, moreover, that each lord of a
cantred or district in Ireland should have an ollamh, and
Columcille proposed this plan and Aodh assented to it; and
it was to celebrate this benefit which Columcille conferred on
the filés that Maolsuthain composed this stanza:

> The filés were saved by this means
> Through Colum of the fair law;
> A filé for each district is no heavy charge.
> It is what Colum ordained.

From this regulation, which was made by Aodh, son of
Ainmire, and Columcille, if followed that the king of Ireland
and every provincial king and every lord of a cantred had a
special ollamh, and that each of these ollamhs had free land
from his own lord, and, moreover, the lands and worldly possessions of each of these ollamhs enjoyed general exemption
and sanctuary from the men of Ireland. It was also ordained
that a common estate should be set apart for the ollamhs where
they could give public instruction after the manner of a University, such as Raith Cheannait and Masruidhe Mhuighe
Sleacht, in Breithfne, where they gave free instruction in the
sciences to the men of Ireland, as many as desired to become
learned in seanchus and in the other sciences that were in
vogue in Ireland at that time.

The ardollamh of Ireland at that time was Eochaidh Eigeas,
son of Oilill, son of Earc, and it was he who was called Dallan
Forgaill, and he sent out ollamhs and set them over the prov-

inces of Ireland, namely, Aodh Eigeas over the district of
Breagh and over Meath, Urmhaol chief eigeas over the two
provinces of Munster, Sanchan, son of Cuairfheartach, over
the province of Connaught, and Fear Firb, son of Muiread-
hach, son of Mongan, in the ollamhship of Ulster; and, moreover, an ollamh in every cantred in Ireland under these high
ollamhs, and they were to have free land from their territorial
chiefs, as well as sanctuary, as we have said; and each of them
was to get certain rewards for their poems and compositions.

The second request Colum asked of Aodh was to set
Scannlan Mor, king of Osruighe, free, and let him go to his
own country. This the king refused. "I shall not press it
further," said Colum, "if it be God's will may Scannlan untie
my thongs or take off my shoes to-night when I am at matins."

"The third request I make of thee," said Columcille, "is
to grant a respite to the Dal Raida and not to go to Alba to
plunder them with a view of laying a tribute on them, for you
have a right only to a head-rent from them and a levy of forces
on land and sea." "I shall not grant them respite, but shall pay
them a visit," said Aodh. "Then," said Colum, "they will have
a respite from thee for ever," and so it was.

Thereupon Columcille, with his clerics, took leave of the
king and of the convention, and the Book of Glendalough
states that Aodhan, son of Gabhran, son of Domhanghurt,
king of Alba, was at that convention, and that he took his
leave of the king and of the assembly along with Columcille
The same book says that the convention of Drom Ceat sat for a
year and a month instituting laws and regulating tributes and
forming friendly alliances between the men of Ireland. . . .

Brian Boru[1]

When Brian Boraimhe was residing at Ceann Choradh without strife or discord he besought the king of Leinster, Maolmordha, son of Murchadh, to send him three masts of excellent
wood from Fiodh Gaibhle. The king of Leinster had the masts
cut down and went with them himself to Ceann Choradh
where Brian then was; and he ordered the Ui Failghe to carry
one of the masts and the Ui Faolain another and the Ui
Muireadhaigh the third, and a war of words arose between
them as they were going up Sliabh an Bhogaigh; and thereupon
the king of Leinster himself put his shoulder under the mast
assigned to the Ui Faolain, wearing a satin tunic which Brian
had given him sometime before, and which had gold borders to
it and a silver clasp. And so greatly did the king of Leinster
exert himself in bearing up the mast that the clasp of his tunic
snapped; and when they reached Ceann Choradh the king of
Leinster took off his tunic and gave it to his sister Gormfhlaith,
daughter of Murchadh (that is Brian's wife), to fix a clasp in it.
The queen took the tunic and cast it into the fire that was in
front of her, and proceeded to reproach her brother for being
in slavery of subjection to anyone on earth, "a thing," said
she, "which neither thy father nor thy grandfather brooked";
and she added, that Brian's son would make the same demand
of his son. Now Maolmordha kept in mind the queen's re-
marks; and the next day Murchadh, son of Brian, and Conaing,
son of Donn Cuan, happened to be playing chess, or according
to others it was the comhorba of Caoimhghin of Gleann da
Loch that was playing with Murchadh. Maolmordha, the king
of Leinster, set to instruct Murchadh, and taught him a move

---

[1] Patron of art, religion, and learning, Brian Boru was a Munster
chieftain who made himself High King of Ireland by extorting tribute
from all the other kings. He defeated the Danish king of Dublin at
Clontarf in 1014 but was himself killed as Keating describes.

which caused the game to go against him. "It was thou who gavest advice to the Lochlonnaigh which caused them to be defeated at the Battle of Gleann Mama," said Murchadh. "If I gave them advice which caused them to be defeated there," said Maolmordha, "I will give them another advice through which they will defeat thee in turn." "I defy thee to do so," said Murchadh.

Maolmordha was enraged at this and he went to his sleeping apartment, and could not be got to come to the drinking hall that night, and he took his departure early the next morning without bidding farewell to Brian.

Now when Brian heard that the king of Leinster left the mansion without bidding him farewell, he sent a page of his household to detain him that he might give him wages and gifts. The place at which the page overtook him was at the end of the plank bridge of Cill Dalua on the east side of the Sionainn, as he was mounting his steed, and he delivered to him the message Brian had sent him. Maolmordha, the king of Leinster, turned on the page and gave him three blows with the yew wand he held in his hand, so that he broke the bones of his skull, and it was in a litter that he was carried to Brian's house. The page's name was Cogaran and from him are the Ui Cogarain of Munster.

A party of the household of Ceann Choradh desired to pursue the king of Leinster and not to allow him to go to Leinster until he had submitted to Brian. Brian, however, said that it would not be permitted to practise treachery against him in his own house. "But," added he, "it is from the door-post of his own house that justice will be required of him."

Maolmordha, king of Leinster, went into his own country, and summoned and brought together to him the Leinster nobles, and told them that himself and all his province had been dishonoured and treated to abusive speech at Ceann Choradh. Accordingly what they agreed on was that they themselves and a Lochlonnach force should go against Brian, so that

the Battle of Cluain Tarbh was set on foot between them; and
since Brian had not left in Ireland as many of the Lochlonnaigh
as could fight a battle, having left only the party he suffered, on
the excuse of trading, to remain in Ath Cliath, in Loch Gar-
man, in Port Lairge, in Corcach and in Luimneach, for the
purpose of attracting commerce from other countries to Ireland, what the king of Leinster and the Lochlonnaigh decided
on was to send to the king of Lochloinn for a force with which
to meet Brian in battle on Magh nEalta at Cluain Tarbh. And
when the message reached the king of Lochloinn he sent his
two sons Carolus Cnutus and Andreas with a host of twelve
thousand Lochlonnaigh to help the king of Leinster to fight
the Battle of Cluain Tarbh, and when they landed at Ath
Cliath the king of Leinster sent word to Brian to give notice
that he would give him battle at Cluain Tarbh. . . .

And when they came together to one place on Magh nEalta
they prepared and arranged themselves for battle on either
side, the king of Leinster and the Lochlonnaigh on one side,
and two sons of the king of Lochloinn, to wit, Carolus Cnutus
and Andreas being their leaders; Brian with the nobles of
Munster, Connaught and Meath on the other side, with
Murchadh, son of Brian, as their leader. Maoilseachlainn, however, did not wish to help them.

The battle was bravely fought between them, and the
Lochlonnaigh and the Leinstermen were defeated; and the
two sons of the king of Lochloinn and the nobles of the fleet
who came with them fell there, together with six thousand and
seven hundred Lochlonnaigh. There also fell the men of Ath
Cliath and another company of the Lochlonnaigh of the fleet
about four thousand. In like manner fell the king of Leinster
and most of the nobles of Leinster together with three
thousand one hundred Leinstermen.

Now on the other side fell Murchadh, son of Brian, the heir
apparent to the throne of Ireland, and the majority of the
Munster and Connaught nobles around him together with
four thousand men. And a party of Lochlonnaigh who were

fleeing into the country from the slaughter came upon Brian's
tent, and some of them knew that it was Brian who was in it,
and Bruadar, their leader, who was of the party, went towards
Brian, and they slew him, but Brian's people slew Bruadar and
his people. . . .

Translator Patrick S. Dineen

PART IV

Modern Irish Poetry

TRANSLATIONS FROM THE GAELIC

Against Blame of Women

BY Gerald, Earl of Desmond (c. 1398)

Speak not ill of womankind,
    'Tis no wisdom if you do.
You that fault in women find,
    I would not be praised of you.

Sweetly speaking, witty, clear,
    Tribe most lovely to my mind,
Blame of such I hate to hear.
    Speak not ill of womankind.

Bloody treason, murderous act,
    Not by women were designed,
Bells o'erthrown nor churches sacked,
    Speak not ill of womankind.

Bishop, King upon his throne,
    Primate skilled to loose and bind,
Sprung of women every one!
    Speak not ill of womankind.

For a brave young fellow long
    Hearts of women oft have pined.
Who would dare their love to wrong?
    Speak not ill of womankind.

Paunchy greybeards never more
    Hope to please a woman's mind.
Poor young chieftains they adore!
    Speak not ill of womankind.

Translator The Earl of Longford.

Do Not Torment Me, Woman

Do not torment me, woman, for your honour's sake do not pursue me; whether my life be long or short do not torment me through all eternity.

I entreat a boon of you, O bright face and fair hair, do not torment me any more wherever I may be.

I have not spent night nor day, whether I have been here long or no, but that you have been beside me—slow-pacing foot and bowed head!

O cheek like embers, do not come in dreams to seek me in my sleep; and when I wake, stately and sweet one, come not to drive me to distraction.

Though it is hard for me to tell you, let me see you no more, do not destroy me; since I cannot escape from death, come not between me and the love of God.

You, my one love of all creation, tender sapling whom God has taught, woe to you who have so slain me, and I never slew any man.

Let not my misery be your gain, O gentle bough, with crystal eye; if you were witless as I am I would not slay you like this ever.

I know not what to do, your mouth like red berries has consumed me; my blessing on you, but get you aside, and do not drive me from the bosom of God.

Sweet-smelling mouth and skin like flowers, many a man comes courting you; O woman, love of my soul, do not pursue me of all men.

15TH-16TH CENTURY.
Translator Kenneth Jackson.

Reconciliation

Do not torment me, woman, let us set our minds at one; you to be my mate in Ireland, and let us put our arms around each other.

Set your strawberry-coloured mouth against my mouth, O skin like foam; stretch your lime-white rounded arm about me, in spite of all our discord.

Slender graceful girl, be no longer inconstant to me; admit me, soft slender one, to your bed, let us stretch our bodies side by side.

As I have given up, O smooth side, every woman in Ireland for your sake, do you give up every man for me, if it is possible to do so.

As I have given to your white teeth passion which is beyond reckoning, so you should give to me your love in the like measure.

     15TH-16TH CENTURY.
     Translator Kenneth Jackson.

He Praises Her Hair

Lady, the meshes of your coiling hair
    Hide like a mask my lovely one.
And thro' that veil I guess at things more rare
    Than Absalom, King David's son.

A flight of cuckoos bursting from a curl
    Do sing in every plaited tress,
Whose silent tune sets many hearts a-whirl,
    O'erborne with so much loveliness.

The drooping ringlets of your long bright hair
    Across your eyes their shadows fling,
Those eyes that flash and glow like crystal there,
    Or precious jewels in a ring.

Like some strange beauty from an unknown land
    In borrowed gems you ne'er were dressed.
I see no golden bracelets on your hand,
    A hundred rings upon your breast.

Round your smooth neck the wreathéd floods of gold
    Coil from your brows above,
And all your breast with jewelled chains enfold,
    A breast for men to love.

15TH-16TH CENTURY.
Translator The Earl of Longford.

No Sufferer for Her Love

They lie who say that love must be
A sickness and a misery;
He that ne'er loved woman knows
Never anything but woes.

I too love a woman; yet
My clear eyes are never wet;
Death has claimed me for his own,
Yet I live by love alone.

Clad in flesh and blood I move,
Though a swan-white maid I love;
Though I love, I eat and sleep,
Music's service still I keep.

I'm no reed in water swaying,
My free thought goes lightly playing;
I'm no lover chill through all
The piled cloaks of Donegal.

I'm a man like others still,
Fires burn me, waters chill;
If the young and strong must die,
Ne'er so doomed a man as I.

Rope will bind me, this know I,
Like a sponge my mouth's ne'er dry,
Softer is my flesh than stone,
I can't drink the sea alone.

Though love within my bones doth play,
I know the night is not the day,
Black's black, white's white, a boat's a boat
And not a stately ship afloat.

I never call a horse a crow,
The sea's no hill, that much I know,
Small is less than great, I feel,
And a fly smaller than a seal.

Though I love her more than all
The sun-riped maids of Donegal,
Yet, by all the gods above!
I'm no sufferer for her love.

15TH-16TH CENTURY.
Translator Robin Flower.

Of Women No More Evil

Of women no more evil will I say,
The lightsome loves that help my heart to live
—The sun sees nothing sweeter on his way—
They pledge their faith and break it. I forgive,
All I forgive and scandal them no more.
I am their servant. Let the witless jeer.
Though their slain loves are numbered by the score,
I love them living and their ghosts are dear.
The cunning wits are loud in their dispraise,
And yet I know not. If their breed should fail,
What comfort were in all the world's wide ways?
A flowerless earth, a sea without a sail.
If these were gone that make earth Heaven for men,
Love them or hate, 'twere little matter then.

> 15TH-16TH CENTURY.
> Translator Robin Flower.

He Praises His Wife When She Has Left Him

White hands of languorous grace,
Fair feet of stately pace
And snowy-shining knees—
My love was made of these.

Stars glimmered in her hair,
Slim was she, satin-fair;
The straight line of her brows
Shadowed her cheek's fresh rose.

What words can match her ways,
That beauty past all praise,
That courteous, stately air,
Winsome and shy and fair.

To have known all this and be
Tortured with memory—
Curse on this waking breath—
Makes me in love with death.

Better to sleep than see
This house now dark to me
A lonely shell in place
Of that unrivalled grace.

15TH-16TH CENTURY.
Translator Robin Flower.

Dark Rosaleen[1]

O, my Dark Rosaleen,
    Do not sigh, do not weep!
The priests are on the ocean green,
    They march along the Deep.
There's wine . . . from the royal Pope,
    Upon the ocean green;
And Spanish ale shall give you hope,
    My Dark Rosaleen!
    My own Rosaleen!
Shall glad your heart, shall give you hope,

---

[1] The author of "Dark Rosaleen" is unknown, but tradition has associated the poem with Hugh O'Donnell, Earl of Tyrconnell (c. 1572-1602), who depended on Papal and Spanish assistance to help him and Hugh O'Neill, Earl of Tyrone, repel the English at Kinsale in 1602. Rosaleen is Ireland.

Shall give you health, and help, and hope,
  My Dark Rosaleen!

Over hills, and through dales,
  Have I roamed for your sake;
All yesterday I sailed with sails
  On river and on lake.
The Erne . . . at its highest flood,
  I dashed across unseen,
For there was lightning in my blood,
  My Dark Rosaleen!
  My own Rosaleen!
Oh! there was lightning in my blood,
Red lightning lightened through my blood.
  My Dark Rosaleen!

All day long, in unrest,
  To and fro do I move.
The very soul within my breast
  Is wasted for you, love!
The heart . . . in my bosom faints
To think of you, my Queen,
My life of life, my saint of saints,
  My Dark Rosaleen!
  My own Rosaleen!
To hear your sweet and sad complaints,
My life, my love, my saint of saints,
  My Dark Rosaleen!

Woe and pain, pain and woe,
   Are my lot night and noon,
To see your bright face clouded so,
   Like to the mournful moon.
But yet . . . will I rear your throne
   Again in golden sheen;
'Tis you shall reign, shall reign alone,
   My Dark Rosaleen!
   My own Rosaleen!
'Tis you shall have the golden throne,
'Tis you shall reign, and reign alone,
   My Dark Rosaleen!

Over dews, over sands,
   Will I fly, for your weal;
Your holy delicate white hands
   Shall girdle me with steel
At home . . . in your emerald bowers,
   From morning's dawn till e'en,
You'll pray for me, my flower of flowers,
   My Dark Rosaleen!
   My fond Rosaleen!
You'll think of me through Daylight's hours,
My virgin flower, my flower of flowers,
   My Dark Rosaleen!

I could scale the blue air,
  I could plough the high hills,
Oh, I could kneel all night in prayer,
  To heal your many ills!
And one . . . beamy smile from you
  Would float like light between
My toils and me, my own, my true,
  My Dark Rosaleen!
  My fond Rosaleen!
Would give me life and soul anew,
A second life, a soul anew,
  My dark Rosaleen!

O! the Erne shall run red
  With redundance of blood,
The earth shall rock beneath our tread,
  And flames wrap hill and wood,
And gun-peal, and slogan cry,
  Wake many a glen serene.
Ere you shall fade, ere you shall die,
  My Dark Rosaleen!
  My own Rosaleen!
The Judgment Hour must first be nigh,
Ere you can fade, ere you can die,
  My Dark Rosaleen!

16TH CENTURY.
Translator James Clarence Mangan.

Death's Warning to Beauty

Lovely lady, rein thy will,
Let my words a warning be,
Bid thy longing heart be still.
Wed no man. Remember me.

If my counsel like thee not,
Winsome beauty, bright of blee,[1]
Thou knows't not what deeds I've wrought.
Wed no man. Remember me.

If thou knows't not they are clay:
That slim form eyes may not see,
That round breast silk hides away.
Wed no man. Remember me.

Keep my counsel lest thou slip.
If love or hate men offer thee,
Hide thy heart and hoard thy lip.
Wed no man. Remember me.

17TH CENTURY.
Translator Robin Flower.

---

[1] hue. NED.

He Charges Her To Lay Aside Her Weapons

BY Pierce Ferriter (c. 1653)

I charge you, lady young and fair,
  Straightway to lay your arms aside.
Lay by your armour, would you dare
  To spread the slaughter far and wide?

O lady, lay your armour by,
  Conceal your curling hair also,
For never was a man could fly
  The coils that o'er your bosom flow.

And if you answer, lady fair,
  That north or south you ne'er took life,
Your very eyes, your glance, your air
  Can murder without axe or knife.

And oh! If you but bare your knee,
  If you your soft hand's palm advance,
You'll slaughter many a company.
  What more is done with shield and lance?

Oh, hide your bosom limey white,
  Your naked side conceal from me.
Ah, show them not in all men's sight,
  Your breasts more bright than flowering tree.

And if in you there's shame or fear
  For all the murders you have done,
Let those bright eyes no more appear,
  Those shining teeth be seen of none.

Lady, we tremble far and near!
  Be with these conquests satisfied,
And lest I perish, lady dear,
  Oh, lay those arms of yours aside.

Translator The Earl of Longford.

The Harper

Master of discords John
    Makes harmony seem wrong;
His treble sings to his bass
    Like a sow consoling her young.

If he played with his shoulder blades
    He'd make a pleasanter tone;
He reaches out for a chord
    As a dog snaps at a bone.

Playing away to himself,
    Nobody knows what tune,
Even the man who made it
    Cannot recall his own.

A wonder, the way he works,
    He never keeps tune or time;
With skill and care he goes wrong,
    Mountains of error climb.

Give him the simplest catch
    And at once you're in at the kill;
He mangles it patiently
    Like an old loud derelict mill.

Copper scratched with a knife,
    Brass cut with a rasp,
His nails scrape at the strings
    Till all shudder and gasp.

God help you, gentle harp,
    Pounded and plagued bv his fist,
There isn't a chord in your breast
    Without a sprain or twist.

17TH CENTURY. Author unknown.
Translator Frank O'Connor.

The Woman of Three Cows

O Woman of Three Cows, agra! don't let your tongue thus
    rattle!
Oh, don't be saucy, don't be stiff, because you may have cattle.
I have seen—and, here's my hand to you, I only say what's
    true—
A many a one with twice your stock not half so proud as you.

Good luck to you, don't scorn the poor, and don't be their
    despiser;
For worldly wealth soon melts away, and cheats the very miser;
And death soon strips the proudest wreath from haughty
    human brows—
Then don't be stiff, and don't be proud, good Woman of Three
    Cows!

See where Mononia's heroes lie, proud Owen Mór's descend-
   ants.
'Tis they that won the glorious name, and had the grand
   attendants!
If they were forced to bow to Fate, as every mortal bows,
Can you be proud, can you be stiff, my Woman of Three Cows?

The brave sons of the Lord of Clare, they left the land to
   mourning;
Mavrone! for they were banished, with no hope of their returning.
Who knows in what abodes of want those youths were driven
   to house?
Yet you can give yourself these airs, O Woman of Three Cows

Oh, think of Donnell of the Ships, the Chief whom nothing
   daunted,
See how he fell in distant Spain unchronicled, unchanted!
He sleeps, the great O'Sullivan, where thunder cannot rouse—
Then ask yourself, should you be proud, good Woman of
   Three Cows?

O'Ruark, Maguire, those souls of fire, whose names are shrined
   in story—
Think how their high achievements once made Erin's greatest
   glory.
Yet now their bones lie mouldering under weeds and cypress
   boughs,
And so, for all your pride, will yours, O Woman of Three Cows.

The O'Carrolls, also, famed when fame was only for the
   boldest,
Rest in forgotten sepulchres with Erin's best and oldest;
Yet who so great as they of yore in battle or carouse?
Just think of that, and hide your head, good Woman of Three
   Cows.

Your neighbour's poor; and you, it seems, are big with vain
ideas,
Because, inagh,[1] you've got three cows—one more, I see, than
she has;
That tongue of yours wags more at times than charity allows;
But if you're strong, be merciful—great Woman of Three
Cows.

Avran[2]

Now, there you go! You still, of course, keep up your scornful
bearing,
And I'm too poor to hinder you; but, by the cloak I'm wearing,
If I had but four cows myself, even though you were my spouse,
I'd thwack you well to cure your pride, my Woman of Three
Cows!

17TH CENTURY.
Translator James Clarence Mangan.

The Reverie

BY Egan O'Rahilly (1670-1726)

ONE morning before Titan thought of stirring his feet
   I climbed alone to a hill where the air was kind,
And saw a throng of magical girls go by
   That had lived to the north in Croghan time out of mind.

All over the land from Galway to Cork of the ships,
   It seemed that a bright enchanted mist came down,
Acorns on oaks and clear cold honey on stones,
   Fruit upon every tree from root to crown.

---

[1] Forsooth.
[2] Summing Up.

They lit three candles that shone in the mist like stars
    On a high hilltop in Connello and then were gone,
But I followed through Thomond the track of the hooded
    queens
    And asked them the cause of the zeal of their office at
    dawn.

The tall queen, Eevul, so bright of countenance, said
    "The reason we light three candles on every strand
Is to guide the king that will come to us over the sea
    And make us happy and reign in a fortunate land."

And then, so suddenly did I start from my sleep,
    They seemed to be true, the words that had been so sweet—
It was just that my soul was sick and spent with grief
    One morning before Titan thought of stirring his feet.

    Translator Frank O'Connor.

The Geraldine's Daughter

BY Egan O'Rahilly

A beauty all stainless, a pearl of a maiden,
    Has plunged me in trouble, and wounded my heart.
With sorrow and gloom are my soul overladen;
    An anguish is there that will never depart.
I could voyage to Egypt across the deep water,
    Nor care about bidding dear Eire farewell,
So I only might gaze on the Geraldine's daughter,
    And sit by her side in some green, pleasant dell!

Her curling locks wave round her figure of lightness,
    All dazzling and long, like the purest of gold;
Her blue eyes resemble twin stars in their brightness,
    And her brow is like marble or wax to behold!
The radiance of heaven illumines her features
    Where the snows and the rose have erected their throne;
It would seem that the sun had forgotten all creatures,
    To shine on the Geraldine's daughter alone!

Her bosom is swan-white, her waist smooth and slender;
    Her speech is like music, so sweet and so fair;
The feelings that glow in her noble heart lend her
    A mien and a majesty lovely to see.
Her lips, red as berries, but riper than any,
    Would kiss away even a sorrow like mine!
No wonder such heroes and noblemen many
    Should cross the blue ocean to kneel at her shrine.

She is sprung from the Geraldine race, the great Grecians,
    Niece of Mileadh's sons of the Valorous Bands,
Those heroes, the seed of the olden Phenicians,
    Though now trodden down, without fame, without lands;
Of her ancestors flourished the Barrys and Powers,
    To the Lords of Bunratty she too is allied;
And not a proud noble near Cashel's high towers
    But is kin to this maiden—the Geraldine's Pride!

Of Saxon or Gael there are none to excel in
    Her wisdom, her features, her figure, this fair;
In all she surpasses the far-famous Helen,
    Whose beauty drove thousands to death and despair.
Whoe'er could but gaze on her aspect so noble
    Would feel from thenceforward all anguish depart,
Yet for me 'tis, alas! my worst woe and my trouble,
    That her image must always abide in my heart!

Translator James Clarence Mangan.

A Sleepless Night

BY Egan O'Rahilly

I have thought long this wild wet night that brought no rest
Though I have no gold to watch or horned kine or sheep,
A storm that made the wave cry out has stirred my breast—
Neither dogfish nor periwinkle was once my meat.

Ah, if the men that knew me were but here tonight
With their proud company that held me up secure,
Captains of Munster before their great defeat,
Not long would Corkaguiney see my children poor.

MacCarthy stern and fearless, that most upright man,
MacCarthy of the Lee whose hearth is dark and cold,
MacCarthy of Kanturk and all his kindred gone—
The heart within me breaks to think their tale is told.

The heart within my breast this night is wild with grief
Because of all the haughty men who ruled this place
From Cashel and through Thomond to the wave beneath
None lives, and where they lived lives now an alien race.

Ah, famous wave, you sang the livelong night below
And drove my senses crazy with your bellowing—
I swear if help could ever come to Ireland now
I'd strangle in your raucous throat that song you sing!

Translator Frank O'Connor.

A Grey Eye Weeping

BY Egan O'Rahilly.

That my old bitter heart was pierced in this black doom,
That foreign devils have made our land a tomb,
That the sun that was Munster's glory has gone down
Has made me a beggar before you, Valentine Brown.

That royal Cashel is bare of house and guest,
That Brian's turreted home is the otter's nest,
That the kings of the land have neither land nor crown
Has made me a beggar before you, Valentine Brown.

Garnish away in the west and her master banned,
Hamburg the refuge of him that has lost his land,
An old grey eye, weeping for lost renown,
Has made me a beggar before you, Valentine Brown.

Translator Frank O'Connor.

Egan O'Rahilly and the Minister

There was a splendid green-boughed tree of great value growing for many years close by a church which the wicked Crom-
well had plundered, above a spring overflowing with bright
cold water, in a field of green turf which a thieving minister
had extorted from an Irish gentleman; one who had been exiled

across the wild seas through treachery, and not through the
edge of the sword. This stinking lout of a damned minister
wanted to cut a long green bough of the tree to make household gear of it. None of the carpenters or workmen would
touch the beautiful bough, for its shade was most lovely,
sheltering them as they lamented brokenly and bitterly for the
bright champions who were stretched beneath the sod. "I will
cut it," said a bandy barelegged gallows-bird of a son of that
portly minister, "and get me an axe at once." The dull-witted
oaf went up into the tree like a scared cat fleeing a pack of
hounds, until he came upon two branches growing one across
the other. He tried to put them apart by the strength of his
arms, but they sprang from his hands in the twinkling of an
eye across each other again, and gripped his gullet, hanging him
high between air and Hell. It was then the accursed Sassenach
was wriggling his legs in the hangman's dance, and he standing
on nothing, and his black tongue out the length of a yard,
mocking at his father. The minister screamed and bawled like
a pig in a sack or a goose caught under a gate, and no wonder,
while the workmen were getting a ladder to cut him down.

Egan O'Rahilly from Sliabh Luachra of the Heroes was
there, watching the gallows-bird of the noose, and he recited
this verse:—

> Good is your fruit, tree;
> may the bounty of this your fruit be on every branch!
> Alas, that the trees of Ireland
> are not covered with your fruit every day!

"*What is the poor wild Irish devil saying?*"[1] said the minister.
"*He is lamenting your darling son,*"[1] said an idler who was beside him. "*Here is twopence for you to buy tobacco with,*"[1] said
the fat badger of a minister. "*Thankee,*[1] minister of the son of
curses," i.e. the Devil, said Egan; and he recited a verse:—

---

[1] In English.

Hurroo, minister who gave me your twopence
for lamenting your child!
May the fate of that child befall the rest of them
down to the last of them.

18TH CENTURY.
Translator Kenneth Jackson.

The Lament for Art O'Leary[1]

BY Eileen O'Leary

My love and my delight,
The day I saw you first
Beside the market-house
I had eyes for nothing else,
And love for none but you.

I left my father's house,
Fled far away with you,
And that was no bad choice,
You gave me everything.
Parlours whitened for me,
Rooms painted for me,
Ovens reddened for me,
Loaves baked for me,
Roast spitted for me,
Beds made for me,
I took my ease on flock
Until the milking time
And later if I pleased.

[1] See Introduction, p. xxvii.

My mind remembers
That bright spring day,
How your hat with its band
Of gold became you,
Your silver-hilted sword,
Your manly right hand,
Your horse on his mettle,
The foes around you
Cowed by your air;
For when you rode by
On your white-nosed mare
The English bowed
The head before you,
Not out of love for you
But only fear,
For, sweetheart of my soul,
The English killed you.

My love and my calf
Of the race of the earls of Antrim
And the Barrys of Eemokilly,
A sword became you,
A hat with a band,
A slender foreign shoe,
And a suit of yarn
Woven over the water.

My love and my darling,
When I go home
The little lad, Conor,
And Fiach the baby
Will ask me surely
Where I left their father;
I shall say with anguish
'Twas in Kilnamartyr.
They will call the father
That will never answer.

My love and my darling
That I never thought dead
Till your horse came to me
With bridle trailing,
All blood from forehead
To polished saddle
Where you should be,
Sitting or standing;
I gave one leap to the threshold,
A second to the gate,
A third upon her back.

I clapped my hands,
And off at a gallop,
I did not linger
Till I found you lying
By a little furze-bush
Without pope or bishop
Or priest or cleric
One prayer to whisper
But an old, old woman

And her cloak about you,
And your blood in torrents,
Art O'Leary,
I did not wipe it,
I dipped my hands in it.

My love and my delight,
Rise up now beside me,
And let me lead you home
Until I make a feast,
And I will roast your meat
And send for company
And call the harpers in,
And I will make your bed
Of soft and snowy sheets
And blankets dark and rough
To warm the beloved limbs
An autumn blast has chilled.

(*His sister*)

My little love, my calf,
This is the picture
That last night brought me,
In Cork all lonely
On my bed sleeping,
That the white courtyard
And the great mansion
That we two played in
As children had fallen;
Ballingeary withered,
And your hounds were silent,
Your birds were songless,
The time they found you
On the open mountain

Without priest or cleric
But an old, old woman
And her coat about you,
When the earth caught you,
Art O'Leary,
And your life's blood stiffened
The white shirt on you.

My love and my treasure,
Where is the woman
From Cork of the white sails
To the Bridge of Tomey
With her dowry gathered
And cows at pasture
Would sleep alone
The night they waked you?

(*His wife*)

My darling, do not believe
One word she is saying!
It is a falsehood
That I slept when others
Sat up and waked you—
'Twas no sleep that took me
But the children crying;
They would not rest
Without me beside them.

O people, do not believe
Any lying story!
There is no woman in Ireland
That had slept beside him
And borne him three children
But would cry out

After Art O'Leary
That lies dead before me
Since yesterday morning.

Grief on you, Morris!
Heart's blood and bowels' blood!
May your eyes go blind
And your knees be broken!
You killed my darling
And no man in Ireland
Will fire the shot at you.

Grief and destruction,
Morris, the traitor!
That brought death to my husband,
Father of three children,
Two on the hearth,
One in the womb
I shall not bring forth.

It is my sorrow
That I was not near
When they fired the shot
To catch it in my dress,
Or in my heart, what harm
If you but reached the hills,
Rider of the ready hands.

My love and my fortune,
'Tis an evil portion
To lay for a giant
A shroud and a coffin,
For a big-hearted hero
Who fished in the hill-streams
And drank in bright halls
With white-breasted women.

My comfort and my friend,
Master of the bright sword,
Rise, I say, from your sleep;
Yonder hangs your whip,
Your horse is at the door,
Follow the lane to the east
When every bush will bend
And every stream dry up
And man and woman bow
If things have manners yet
That have them not, I fear.

My love and my sweetness,
'Tis not the death of my people,
Donal Mor O'Connell,[1]
Conal[2] that died by drowning,
Nor the girl of six and twenty[3]
That went across the water
To be a king's companion,
'Tis not all these I speak of

And call on with voice broken,
But noble Art O'Leary,
Art of hair so golden,
Art of wit and courage,
Art the brown mare's master,
Swept last night to nothing,
Here in Carriganimma—
Perish it, name and people!

My love and my treasure,
Though I bring with me
No throng of mourners,

---

[1] Eileen O'Leary's father.
[2] Her brother.
[3] Her sister, who married an Irish officer ir
came an intimate of Empress Maria Theresa

'Tis no shame for me,
For my kinsmen are wrapped in
A sleep beyond waking,
In narrow coffins
Walled up in stone.

Though but for the smallpox
And the black death
And the spotted fever
That host of riders
With bridles shaking
Would rouse the echoes
Coming to the wakehouse,
Art of the white breast.

Could my calls but wake my kindred,
In Derrynane across the mountains
And Capling of the yellow apples
Many a proud and stately rider
Many a girl with spotless kerchief
Would be here before tomorrow,
Shedding tears about your body,
Art O'Leary once so merry.

My love and my secret,
Your corn is stacked,
Your cows are milking,
On me is the grief
There's no cure for in Munster.
Till Art O'Leary rise
This grief will never yield
That's bruising all my heart
Yet shut up fast in it,
As 'twere in a locked trunk
With the key gone astray
And rust grown on the wards.

My love and my calf,
Noble Art O'Leary,
Son of Conor, son of Cady,
Son of Louis O'Leary,
West of the Valley,
And east of Greenan
(Where berries grow thickly
And nuts crowd on branches
And apples in heaps fall
In their own season),
What wonder to any
If Iveleary lighted
And Ballingeary
And Gougane of the saints
For the smooth-palmed rider,
The unwearying huntsman
That I would see spurring
From Grenagh without halting
When quick hounds had faltered?
O rider of the bright eyes,
What happened you yesterday?
I thought in my heart
When I bought you your fine clothes
You were one the world could not slay.

'Tis known to Jesus Christ,
Nor cap upon my head,
Nor shift against my back,
Nor shoe upon my foot,
Nor gear in all my house,
Nor bridle for the mare
But I will spend at law,
And I'll go oversea
To plead before the king,
And if the king be deaf
I shall come back alone

To the black-blooded rogue
That killed my man on me.

O rider of the white palms,
Go in to Baldwin,
And face the schemer,
The bandy-legged monster—
May he rot and his children!
(Wishing no harm to Maire,
Yet of no love for her
But that my mother's body
Was a bed to her for three seasons
And to me beside her.)

Take my heart's love,
Dark women of the Mill,
For the sharp rhymes ye shed
On the rider of the brown mare.

But cease your weeping now,
Women of the soft, wet eyes
Till Art O'Leary drink
Ere he go to the dark school,[1]
Not to learn music or song
But to prop the earth and the stone.

Translator Frank O'Connor.

---

[1] I.e. before he is buried in Kilcrea Abbey.

Tara Is Grass

The world hath conquered, the wind hath scattered like dust
Alexander, Caesar, and all that shared their sway:
Tara is grass, and behold how Troy lieth low—
And even the English, perchance their hour will come.

18TH CENTURY.
Translator Padraic Pearse.

The Convict of Clonmel

How hard is my fortune,
    And vain my repining!
The strong rope of fate
    For this young neck is twining!
My strength is departed,
    My cheeks sunk and sallow,
While I languish in chains
    In the jail of Clonmala.

No boy of the village
    Was ever yet milder;
I'd play with a child
    And my sport would be wilder;
I'd dance without tiring
    From morning till even,
And the goal-ball I'd strike
    To the lightning of heaven.

At my bed-foot decaying,
　My hurl-bat is lying;
Through the boys of the village
　My goal-ball is flying;
My horse 'mong the neighbors
　Neglected may fallow,
While I pine in my chains
　In the jail of Clonmala.

Next Sunday the patron
　At home will be keeping,
And the young active hurlers
　The field will be sweeping;
With the dance of fair maidens
　The evening they'll hallow,
While this heart once so gay
　Shall be cold in Clonmala.

18TH CENTURY.
Translator J. J. Callanan.

The Midnight Court[1]

BY Brian Merriman (c. 1750-1805)

Twas my pleasure to walk in the river meadows
In the thick of the dew and the morning shadows,
At the edge of the woods in a deep defile,
At peace with myself in the first sunshine.
When I looked at Lough Graney my heart grew bright,
Ploughed lands and green in the morning light,
Mountains in ranks with crimson borders
Peering above their neighbours' shoulders.
The heart that never had known relief

---

[1] See Inroduction, p. xxvii.

In a lonesome old man distraught with grief
Without money or home or friends or ease
Would quicken to glimpse beyond the trees
The ducks sail by on a mistless bay
And a swan before them leads away,
A speckled trout that in their tracks
Splashed in the air with arching back,
The grey of the lake and the waves around
That foamed at its edge with a hollow sound.
Birds in the trees sang merry and loud,
A fawn flashed out of the shadowy wood,
Lowing horn and huntsman's cry,
Belling hounds and fox slipped by.

Yesterday morning the sky was clear,
The sun fell hot on river and mere,
Her horses fresh and with gamesome eye
Harnessed again to assail the sky;
The leaves were thick upon every bough
And ferns and grass as thick below,
Sheltering bowers of herbs and flowers
That would comfort a man in his dreariest hours.
A longing for sleep bore down my head,
And in the grass I scooped a bed
With a hollow behind to house my back,
A place for my head and my legs stretched slack.
What more could I ask? I covered my face
To keep off the flies as I slept for a space
But my mind in dream was filled with grief
And I tossed and groaned as I sought relief.

I had only dozed when I felt a shock
And all the landscape seemed to rock,
A north wind made my senses tingle
And thunder crackled along the shingle,

And as I looked up, as I thought, awake
I seemed to see at the edge of the lake
As ugly a brute as a man could see
In the shape of a woman approaching me,
For if I calculated right
She must have been twenty feet in height
With several yards of a hairy cloak
Trailing behind her in the muck.
I never beheld such a freak of nature;
She hadn't a single presentable feature,
And her grinning jaws with the fangs stuck out
Would be cause sufficient to start a rout,
And in a hand like a weaver's beam
She raised a staff that it might be seen
She was coming to me on a legal errand
For pinned to the staff was a bailiff's warrant.

And she cried in a voice with a brassy ring
"Get up out of this, you lazy thing!
That a man of your age can think 'tis fitting
To sleep in a ditch while the court is sitting!
An honester court than ever you knew
And far too good for the likes of you;
Justice and Mercy, hand in hand,
Sit in the courts of Fairyland.
Let Ireland think, when her troubles are ended
Of those by whom she was befriended.
In Moy Graney palace twelve days and nights
They've sat, discussing your wrongs and rights,
And it saddened the heart of the fairy king
And his lords and influential men
When they studied the cause of each disaster
That happened your people, man and master;
Old stock uprooted on every hand,
Without claim to their rent or laws or land;
The country waste and nothing behind

Where the flowers were plucked but the weeds and wild;
The best of your breed in foreign places,

And upstart rogues with impudent faces
Planning with all their guile and spleen
To pick the bones of the Irish clean.
But the worst of all these bad reports
Was that truth was darkened in their courts,
And nothing to back a poor man's case
But whispers, intrigue and the lust for place;
The lawyer's craft and the rich man's might,
Cozening, favour, greed and spite;
Maddened with jobs and bribes and malice,
Anarchy loose on cot and palace.

"Twas all discussed, and along with the rest
There were women in scores who came to attest
A plea that concerns yourself as well,
That the youth of the country's gone to hell,
And the population in decline
As only happened within your time;
Nothing but weeds for the want of tillage
Since famine and war have struck the village
And a flighty king and the emigration—
And what have you done to restore the nation?
Shame on you there without chick nor child
And women in thousands running wild;
The blossoming tree and the young green shoot,
The strap that would sleep with any old root,
The little white saint at the altar rail
And the proud cold girl like a ship in sail—
What matter to you if their beauty founder,
If belly and breast will never be rounder,
If ready and glad to be mother and wife
They drop, unplucked, from the boughs of life?
"And, having considered all reports,

'Twas agreed that in place of the English courts
They should select a judge by lot
Who would hold enquiry on the spot.
Then Eevul, Queen of the Grey Rock,
That rules all Munster, herd and flock,
Arose and offered to do her share
By putting an end to injustice there,
And the great council swore her in
To judge the women and the men,
To stand by the poor though all ignore them
And humble the pride of the rich before them,
Make might without right conceal its face
And use her might to give right its place.
Her favour money will not buy,
No lawyer will pull the truth awry;
The smartest perjurer will not dare
To make a show of falsehood there.
Her court is sitting today in Feakle,
So off with you now as quick as you're able.
Come on, I say, and give no back chat
Or I'll use my powers and knock you flat."
With the crook of her staff she hooked my cape
And away we went at a terrible rate
Off through the glens in one wild rush
Till we stood at Moinmoy by the ruined church.

Then I saw with an awesome feeling
A building ablaze from floor to ceiling,
Lighted within by guttering torches
Among massive walls and echoing arches,
And the Queen of the Fairies sat alone
At the end of the hall on a gilded throne,
And keeping back the thronged beholders
A great array of guns and soldiers.
I stared at it all, the lighted hall,

Crammed with faces from wall to wall,
And a young woman with downcast eye,
Attractive, good-looking and shy,
With long and sweeping golden locks
Who was standing alone in the witness box;
But the cut of her spoke of some disgrace,
I saw misfortune on her face;
Her tearful eyes were red and hot
And her passions bubbled as in a pot,
And whatever the devil it was provoked her
She was silent, all but the sobs that choked her.
You could see from the way the speaking failed her
That she'd sooner her death than the thing that ailed her.
But unable to express her meaning
She wrung her hands and continued her grieving,
And all we could do was stand and gaze
Till her sobs gave place to a broken phrase,
And little by little she mastered her sorrows,
And dried her eyes and spoke as follows—

"Yourself is the woman we're glad to see
Eevul, Queen of Carriglee,
Our moon at night, our morning light,
Our comfort in the teeth of spite,
Mistress of the host of delight,
Munster and Ireland stand in your sight.
My chief complaint and principal grief?
The thing that gives me no relief,
That sweeps me from harbour in my mind
And blows me like smoke upon every wind,
Is all the women whose charms miscarry
All over the land and who'll never marry;
Bitter old maids without house or home,
Put on one side through no fault of their own.
I know myself from the little I've seen

Enough and to spare of the sort I mean,
And to give an example, here am I
While the tide is flowing left high and dry.
Wouldn't you think I must be a fright
From the way I'm left at the start of life,
Heartsick, bitter, dour and wan,
Unable to sleep for the want of a man,
But how can I lie in a lukewarm bed
With all the thoughts that come into my head?
Indeed, 'tis time that somebody stated
The way that the women are situated,
For if men go on their path to destruction
There will nothing be left to us but abduction.
Their appetite wakes with age and blindness
When you'd let them cover you only from kindness
And offer it up for the wrongs you'd done
In hopes of reward in the life to come;
And if one of them weds in the heat of youth
When the first down is on his mouth
It isn't some woman of his own sort,
Well-shaped, well-mannered or well-taught,
Some mettlesome girl that studied behaviour,
To sit and stand and amuse a neighbour,
But some pious old prude or sour defamer
Who sweated the couple of pounds that shame her.
There you have it. It has me melted,
And makes me feel that the world's demented:
A county's choice for brains and muscle,
Fond of a lark and not scared of a tussle,
Decent and merry and sober and steady,
Good-looking, gamesome and rakish and ready,
A boy in the blush of his youthful vigour
With a gracious flush and a passable figure
Finds a fortune the best attraction
And sires himself off on some bitter extraction,
Some fretful old maid with her heels in the dung

And pious airs and venomous tongue,
Vicious and envious, nagging and whining,
Snoozing and snivelling, plotting, contriving—
Hell to her soul, an unmannerly sow
With a pair of bow legs and hair like tow
Went off this morning to the altar
And here am I still without hope of the halter!
Couldn't some man love me as well?
Amn't I plump and sound as a bell,
Lips for kissing and teeth for smiling,
Blossomy skin and forehead shining?
My eyes are blue and my hair is thick
And coils in streams about my neck—
A man that's looking for a wife,
Here's a face that will keep for life!
Hand and arm and neck and breast,
Each is better than the rest.
Look at my waist! My legs are long,
Limber as willows and light and strong,
There's bottom and belly that claim attention
And the best concealed that I needn't mention.
I'm the sort that a natural man desires,
Not a freak or a death-on-wires,
A sloven that comes to life in flashes,
A creature of moods with her heels in the ashes,
Or a sluggard stewing in her own grease,
But a good-looking girl that's bound to please.
If I were as slow as some I know,
To stand up for my rights and my dress show,
Some brainless, ill-bred country mope,
You could understand if I lost hope;
But ask the first you meet by chance,
Hurling match or race or dance,
Pattern or party, market or fair,
Whatever it was, was I not there?
And didn't I make a good impression,

Turning up in the height of fashion,
My hair was washed and combed and powdered,
My coif like snow and stiffly laundered;
I'd a little white hood with ribbons and ruff
On a spotty dress of the finest stuff
And facings to show off the line
Of a cardinal cloak the colour of wine,
A cambric apron filled with showers
Of fruit and birds and trees and flowers,
Neatly fitting, expensive shoes
And the highest of heels pegged up with screws,
Silken gloves and all in spangles
Of brooches, buckles, rings and bangles.
And you musn't imagine I've been shy,
The sort that slinks with a downcast eye,
Solitary, lonesome, cold and wild,
Like a mountainy girl or an only child.
I tossed my cap for the crowds of the races
And kept my head in the toughest places;
Amn't I always on the watch,
At bonfire, dance or hurling match
Or outside the chapel after Mass
To coax a smile from the fellows that pass?
But I'm wasting my time on a wild-goose chase,
And my spirit is gone—and that's my case!
After all my hopes and sulks and passions,
All my aping of styles and fashions,
All the times that my cards were spread
And my hands were read and my cups were read,
Every old rhyme, pisherogue and rune,
Crescent, full moon and harvest moon,
Whit and All Souls and the First of May,
I've nothing to show for all they say.
Every night as I went to bed
I'd a stocking of apples under my head,

I fasted three canonical hours
To try and come round the heavenly powers,
I washed my shift where the stream ran deep
To hear a lover's voice in sleep;
Often I swept the woodstack bare,
Burned bits of my frock, my nails, my hair,
Up the chimney stuck the flail,
Slept with a spade without avail;
Hid my wool in the limekiln late
And my distaff behind the churchyard gate;
Flax in the road to halt coach and carriage,
And haycocks stuffed with heads of cabbage,
And night and day on the proper occasions
Invoked Old Nick and all his legions,
But 'twas all no good and I'm broken-hearted
For here I am at the place I started,
And this is the cause of all my tears,
I am fast in the rope of the rushing years
With age and want in lessening span
And death at the end and no hopes of a man.
But whatever misfortunes God may send,
Spare me at least that lonesome end!
Do not leave me to cross alone
Without chick nor child when my beauty's gone
As an old maid counting the things I lack
The scowling thresholds that hurl me back.
God, by the lightning and the thunder,
The thought of it makes me ripe for murder.
Every idiot in the country
That marries a man has the right to insult me.
Sal has a slob with a well-stocked farm,
And Molly goes round on her husband's arm:
There's Min and Margery lepping with glee
And never done with their jokes at me.
And the bounce of Susie! and Kitty and Anne

Have children in droves and a proper man,
And all with their kind can mix and mingle
While I go savage and sour and single.

"Now I know in my heart that I've been too quiet
With the remedy there though I scorned to try it
In the matter of draughts and poisonous weeds
And medicine men and darksome deeds
That I know would fetch me a sweetheart plighted
Who'd love me, whether or not he liked it.
Oh, I see 'tis the thing that most prevails
And I'll give it a trial if all fruit fails—
A powerful aid to the making of splices
Is powdered herbs on apples in slices.
A woman I know had the neighbours hopping
When she caught the best match in the county napping,
And 'twas she who told me under a vow,
That from Shrove to All Souls, and she's married now,
She was eating hay as she said by the pail
With bog-roots burned and stuped in ale—
I've waited too long and was too resigned,
And nothing you say can change my mind;
I'll give you a chance to help me first
And I'm off after that to do my worst!"

Then up there jumps from a neighbouring chair
A little old man with a spiteful air,
Staggering legs and sobbing breath
And a look in his eye like poison and death,
And this apparition stumps up the hall
And says to the girl in the hearing of all—
"Damnation take you, you bastard's bitch,
Got by a tinkerman under a ditch,
No wonder the seasons are all upsot
Nor every beating Ireland got,
Decline in decency and manners,

And the cows gone dry and the price of bonhams!
Mavrone, what more can we expect
With Doll and Moll and the way they're decked?
You slut of ill-fame, allow your betters
To tell the court how you learned your letters!
Your seed and breed for all your brag
Were tramps to a man with rag and bag;
I knew your da and what passed for his wife
And he shouldered his traps to the end of his life,
Without knowledge nor niceness, wit nor favour,
An aimless lout without friend nor neighbour.
The breeches he wore were riddled with holes
And his boots without a tack of the soles.
Believe me, friends, if you sold at a fair,
Himself and his wife, his kids and gear,
When the costs were met, by the Holy Martyr,
You'd still go short for a glass of porter.
But the devil's child has the devil's cheek,
You that never owned cow nor sheep
With your buckles and brogues and rings to order—
You that were reared in the reek of solder!
However the rest of the world is cheated,
I knew you when you went half naked,
And I'd venture a guess that in what you lack
A shift would still astonish your back,
And shy as you seem, an inquisitive gent
Might study the same with your full consent.
Bosom and back are tightly laced
Or is it the stays that gives you the waist?
Oh, all can see the way you shine
But your looks are no concern of mine.
Now tell us the truth and don't be shy,
How long are you eating your dinner dry?
A meal of spuds without butter or milk
And the dirt in layers beneath your silk.
Bragging and gab becomes your like

But I know just where you sleep at night,
And blanket or quilt you never saw
But a strip of old mat and a bundle of straw
In a dirty hut without a seat
And the slime that slashes about your feet,
A carpet of weeds from door to wall
And the hens inscribing their tracks on all;
The rafters in with a broken back
And the brown rain lashing through every crack—
'Twas there you learned to look so fine;
But now, may we ask, how you came by the style?
We all admired the way you spoke—
But whisper, treasure, who paid for the cloak?
A sparrow with you would die of hunger—
And how did you come by all the grandeur,
All the tassels and all the lace?
Would you have us believe they were got in grace?
That frock made a hole in somebody's pocket,
And it wasn't yourself that paid for the jacket,
But leaving that and the rest aside,
Tell us, just how did the shoes arrive?

"Your worship, 'tis women's sinful pride
And that alone has the world destroyed!
Every young fellow that's ripe for marriage
Is hooked like this by some tricky baggage,
And no man is secure. For a friend of my own,
As nice a boy as ever I've known
That lives from me only a perch or two,
God help him, married misfortune too.
It breaks my heart to see her go by
With her saucy looks and her head held high,
Cows to pasture and fields of wheat,
And money to spare, and all deceit;
Well-fitted to rear a tinker's clan
She waggles her hips at every man;

With her brazen face and bullock's hide
And such airs and graces, and mad with pride.
And—that God may judge me!—only I hate
A scandalous tongue, I could relate
Things of that woman's previous state
As one with whom every man might mate
In any convenient field or gate
As the chance would come to him, early or late!
But now, of course, we must all forget
Her galloping days and the pace she set,
The race she ran in Ibrackane,
In Manishmore and Teermaclane,
With young and old of the meanest rabble
Of Ennis, Clareabbey and Quin astraddle;
Toughs from Tradree out on a fling
And Cratlee cutthroats sure to swing;
And still I'd say 'twas the neighbours' spite
And the girl did nothing but what was right,
But the devil take her and all she showed
I found her myself on the public road
On the naked earth with a bare backside
And a Garus turfcutter astride!
Is it any wonder my heart is failing
That I feel that the end of the world is nearing
When, ploughed and sown to all men's knowledge,
She can manage the child to arrive with marriage,
And even then, put to the pinch,
Begrudges Charity an inch,
For counting from the final prayer
With the candles quenched and the altar bare
To the day when her offspring takes the air
Is a full nine months with a week to spare?

"But you see the troubles a man takes on;
From the minute he marries his peace is gone,
Forever in fear of a neighbour's sneer,

And my own experience cost me dear.
I lived alone as happy as Larry,
Till I took it into my head to marry;
Tilling my fields with an easy mind
And going wherever I felt inclined,
Welcomed by all as a man of price,
Always ready with good advice;
The neighbours listened, they couldn't refuse
For I'd money and stock to uphold my views,
Everything came at my beck and call
Till a woman appeared and destroyed it all.
A beautiful girl with ripening bosom,
Cheeks as bright as apple blossom,
Hair that glimmered and foamed in the wind
And a face that blazed with the light behind,
A tinkling laugh and a modest carriage
And a twinkling eye that was ripe for marriage.
I goggled and gaped like one born mindless
Till I took her face for a form of kindness,
Though that wasn't quite what the Lord intended
For He marked me down like a man offended
For a vengeance that wouldn't be easy mended
With my folly exposed and my comfort ended.

"Now not to detain ye here all day,
I married the girl without more delay,
And I took my share in the fun that followed;
There was plenty for all and nothing borrowed.
Be fair to me now, there was no man slighted;
The beggarmen took the road delighted,
The clerk and the mummers were elevated
And the priest went home with his purse well weighted.
The lamps were lit; the guests arrived,
The supper was ready; the beer was plied;
The fiddles were flayed and the night advancing
The neighbours joined in the sport and dancing.

"A pity to God I didn't smother
When first I took the milk from my mother
Or any day I ever broke bread
Before I brought that woman to bed!
For though everyone talked of her carouses
As a scratching post of the publichouses
That as sure as ever the glasses would jingle,
Flattened herself to married and single.
Admitting no modesty to mention,
I never believed but 'twas all invention.
They added, in view of the life she led,
I might take to the roads and beg my bread;
But I took it for talk and hardly minded;
Sure a man like me could never be blinded!—
And I smiled and nodded and off I tripped
Till my wedding night when I saw her stripped,
And knew too late that the thing was no libel
Spread in the pub by some jealous rival—
By God, 'twas a fact, and well-supported
I was a father before I started!

"So there I was in the cold daylight
A family man after one short night,
The women around me, scolding, preaching,
The wife in bed and the baby screeching,
Stirring the milk while the kettle boiled,
Making a bottle to give the child.
All the old hags at the hob were cooing
As if they believed it was all my doing,
Flattery worse than ever you heard,
'Glory and praise to Our Blessed Lord,
Though he came in a hurry, the poor little creature,
He's the spit of his da in every feature.
Sal, will you look at the cut of that lip!
There's fingers for you! Feel his grip!
Would you measure the legs and the rolls of fat

Was there ever a seven-months' child like that?'
And they traced away with great preciseness
My matchless face in the baby's likeness;
The same snub nose and frolicsome air
And the way I laugh and the way I stare,
And they swore that never from head to toe
Was a child that resembled his father so.
But they wouldn't let me go near the wonder—
'Sure a draught would blow the poor child asunder!'
All of them out to blind me further—
'The least little breath would be noonday murder!'
Malice and lies, and I took the floor
Mad with rage and I cursed and swore,
And ordered them all to leave my sight,
They shrunk away with their faces white,
And they said as they handed me up the baby,
'Don't crush him now. Can't you handle him easy?
The least thing hurts them. Treat him kindly!
Some fall she got brought it on untimely.
Don't lift his head but leave him lying.
Poor innocent scrap, and to think he's dying!
If he lives at all till the end of day
Till the priest will come 'tis the most we'll pray!'

"I off with the rags and set him free
And studied him well as he lay on my knee,
That too, by God, was nothing but lies
For he staggered myself with his kicks and cries;
A pair of shoulders like my own,
Legs like puddings and hair full grown;
His ears stuck out and his nails were long,
His hands and wrists and elbows strong;
His eyes were bright, his nostrils wide,
And the knee-caps showing beneath his hide—
A champion, begod, a powerful whelp,
Hearty and healthy as myself.

"Young woman, I've made my case entire.
Justice is all that I require.
Once consider the terrible life
We lead from the minute we take a wife,
And you'll find and see that marriage must stop
And the men that's not married must be let off.
And child of grace, don't think of the race,
Plenty will follow to take our place;
There's ways and means to make lovers agree
Without making a show of men like me.
There's no excuse for all the exploiters,
Corner-boys, clerks, and priests and pipers,
Idle fellows that strip you naked
And the jars of malt and the beer that's wasted
When the Mother of God herself conceived,
Without asking the views of clerk or creed;
Healthy and happy, wholesome and sound
The come-by-twilight sort abound;
No one assumes but their lungs are ample
And their hearts as good as the best example.
When did nature display unkindness
To the bastard child in disease or blindness?
Are they not handsomer, better-bred
Than many that comes of a lawful bed?

"I needn't go far to look for proof
For I've always one beneath my roof—
Let him come here for all to view!
Look at him now! You'll see 'tis true.
Agreed, we don't know his father's name,
But his mother admires him just the same,
And if in all things else he shines
Who cares for his baptismal lines?
He isn't a dwarf or an old man's error,
A paralytic or walking terror,
He isn't a hunchback or a cripple,

But a lightsome, laughing, gay young divil.
'Tis easy to see he's no flash in the pan;
No sleepy, good-natured, respectable man
Without sinew or bone or belly or bust
Or venom or vice or love or lust,
Buckled and braced in every limb,
Spouted the seed that flowered in him;
For back and leg and chest and height
Prove him to all in the teeth of spite
A child begotten in fear and wonder
In the blood's millrace and the body's thunder.

"Down with marriage! 'Tis out of date,
It exhausts the stock and cripples the state.
The priest has failed with his whip and blinker
Now give a chance to Tom the Tinker,
And mix and mash in nature's can
The tinker and the gentleman;
Let lovers in every lane extended
Follow their whim as God intended,
And in their pleasure bring to birth
The morning glory of the earth;
The starry litter, girl and boy
That will see the world once more with joy.
Clouds will break and skies will brighten,
Mountains bloom and spirits lighten
And men and women praise your might,
You who restore the old delight."

The girl had listened without dissembling,
Then up she started, hot and trembling,
And she answered him with eyes alight
And a voice that shook with squalls of spite:
"By the Crown of the Rock, I thought in time
Of your age and folly and known decline
And the manners I owe to people and place

Or I'd paint my nails in your ugly face.
I'd scatter your guts and tan your hide
And ferry your soul to the other side
I'd honour you much if I gave the lie
To an impudent speech that needs no reply;
'Tis enough if I tell the sort of life
You led your unfortunate, decent wife.

"This girl was poor, she hadn't a home,
Hadn't a thing to call her own;
Drifting about, ignored, despised,
Doing odd jobs for other men's wives;
As if for drudgery created
Begging a crust from women she hated.
He pretended her troubles were over,
Married to him she'd live in clover;
The cows she milked would be her own,
The feather bed and the decent home;
The stack of turf, the lamp to light,
The sodded wall of a winter's night;
Flax and wool to weave and wind,
The womanly things for which she pined.
Even his friends couldn't have said
That his looks were such that she lost her head
How else would he come by such a wife
But that ease was the alms she asked of life?
What possible use could she have at night
For dourness, dropsy, bother and blight,
A basket of bones with thighs of lead,
Knees absconded from the dead,
Reddening shanks and temples whitening,
Looking like one that was struck by lightning?
Is there living a girl that could grow fat
Tied to a travelling corpse like that;
That twice a year wouldn't find a wish
To see what was she, flesh or fish,

But dragged the clothes about his head
Like a wintry wind to a woman in bed?

"Now was it too much to expect as right
A little attention once a night?
From all I know she was never accounted
A woman too modest to be mounted;
Gentle, good-humoured and God-fearing,
We need never suppose she denied her rearing.
Whatever the lengths his fancy ran
She wouldn't take fright from a mettlesome man,
And would sooner a boy would be aged a score
Than himself on the job for a week or more;
And dancing at night or Mass at morning,
Fiddle or flute or choir or organ,
She'd sooner the tune that boy would play
As midnight struck or at break of day.
Damn it, you know we're all the same,
A woman nine months in terror and pain,
The minute that Death has lost the game—
Good morrow, my love, and she's off again!
And then imagine what 'twas like
With a fellow like that in the bed at night
That never came close in a friendly way
From All Souls' Night to St. Brigid's Day!
You'd all agree 'twas a horrible fate—
Sixty winters on his pate;
An old dead tree with its timbers drained
And a twenty year old with her heart untamed
It wasn't her fault if things went wrong;
She closed her eyes and held her tongue;
She was no querulous, restless, bawling,
Rearing, leaping, pinching, scrawling,
Hussy from school who smooth and warm
Cushioned him like a sheaf of corn.
Line by line she bade him linger

With gummy lips and groping finger;
Gripping his thighs in a wild embrace,
Rubbing her brush from knee to waist,
Stripping him bare to the cold night air,
Everything that a woman would dare;
But she'd nothing to show for all her pain,
His bleary old eyes looked just the same;
And nothing I said could ever explain
All her misery and shame
Her knees in the air and the clothes beneath her,
Chattering teeth and limbs in fever,
As she sobbed and tossed through a joyless night
And gave it up with the morning light.

"I think you'll agree from the little I've said,
That a man like this must be off his head
To live like a monk to the end of his life,
Muddle his marriage and blame his wife.
The talk about women comes well from him
Without hope in body or help in limb;
If the creature that found him such a sell
Has a lover today, she deserves him well;
A benefit nature never denies
To anything born that swims or flies;
Tell me of one that ever went empty
And died of want in the middle of plenty.
In all the wonders west and east
Did anyone hear of a breed of beast
That turned away from fern and hay
To feed on briars and roots and clay?
You silly old fool, you can't reply
And give us at least one reason why
If your supper is there when you come home late,
You've such hullabaloo about the plate.
Will it lessen your store, will you sigh for more
If twenty millions used it before?

You must fancy women are all like you
If you think they'll go dry for a man or two;
You might as well drink the ocean up
Or empty the Shannon with a cup.
Sure, you must see that you're half insane!
Try cold compresses, avoid all strain,
And stop complaining of the neighbours,
If every man jack enjoyed her favours,
Men by the hundred under her shawl
Would take nothing from you in the heel of all.

"If your jealousy even was based on fact
In some hardy young whelp well used to the act,
Covetous, quarrelsome, keen on scoring,
Or some hairy old villain hardened with whoring;
A vigorous slasher, a rank outsider,
A jockey of note, or a gentleman rider,
But a man disposed in the wrong direction
With a poor mouth shown on a sham erection!

"But oye, my heart will grow grey hairs
Brooding forever on idle cares,
Has the Catholic Church a glimmer of sense
That the priests won't marry like anyone else?
Is it any wonder the way I am,
Out of my mind for the want of a man,
When there's men by the score with looks and leisure,
Walking the roads and scorning pleasure?
The full of a fair of primest beef,
Warranted to afford relief,
Cherry-red cheeks and bull-like voices,
And bellies dripping with fat in slices,
Backs erect and heavy hind quarters,
Hot-blooded men, the best of partners,
Freshness and charm, youth and good looks

And nothing to ease their mind but books!
The best fed men that travel the country,
Beef and mutton, game and poultry,
Whiskey and wine forever in stock,
Sides of bacon, beds of flock.
Mostly they're hardy under the hood,
And we know like ourselves that they're flesh and blood;
I wouldn't ask much of the old campaigners,
The good-for-nothings and born complainers,
But petticoat-tossers aloof and idle
And fillies gone wild for bit and bridle!

"Of course I admit that some more sprightly,
Would like to repent and I'd treat them lightly.
A pardon and a job for life
To every priest that takes a wife!
For many a good man's chance miscarries
If you scuttle the ship for the crooks it carries;
And though some as we know were always savage
Gnashing their teeth at the thought of marriage,
And, modest beyond the needs of merit,
Invoked hell-fire on girls of spirit,
Yet some that took to their pastoral labours
Made very good priests and the best of neighbours.
Many a girl filled byre and stall
And furnished her house through a clerical call.
Everyone's heard the priests extolled
For the lonesome women that they consoled;
People I've heard throughout the county
Have nothing but praise for the curate's bounty;
Or uphold the canon to lasting fame
For the children he reared in another man's name;
But I hate to think of their lonely lives,
The passions they waste on middle-aged wives,
While the women they'd choose if the choice were theirs

Go by the wall and comb grey hairs.
It passes the wit of mortal man
What Ireland has lost by this stupid ban.

"I leave it to you, O Nut of Knowledge,
The girls at home and the boys in college,
I'm blest if I can see the crime,
If they go courting in their prime,
But you that for learning have no rival,
Tell us the teachings of the Bible;
Where are we taught to pervert our senses
And make our natural needs offences?
Fly from lust, advised St. Paul,
He didn't mean men were to fly us all,
But to leave their father and friends behind
And stick to the girl that pleased their mind.
I'm at it again! I must keep my place;
It isn't for me to judge the case,
And you, a spirit born and queen,
Remember the texts and what they mean;
With apt quotations well supplied
From the prophets who took the woman's side,
And the words of Christ that were never belied,
Who chose for His Mother an earthly bride.

"But, oye, what use is pishrogue and spell,
To one like myself in the fires of hell?
What chance can there be for girls like me
With husbands for only one in three?
When there's famine abroad the need advises
To look out for yourself as the chance arises,
And since crops are thin and weeds are plenty
And the young without heart and Ireland empty,
And to fill it again is a hopeless job,
Get me some old fellow to sit by the hob,

Bind him in every way you can—
And leave it to me to make him a man."

Daylight crept in and the lights grew pale
And the girl sat down as she ended her tale;
The princess rose with her face aglow,
And her voice when she spoke was grave and low;
"Oyez," said the clerk, to quell the riot,
And wielded his mace till all sat quiet,
And then from her lips while the hall was hushed
Speech in a rainbow glory gushed.
"My child," she said, "I won't deny
That you've reason enough to scold and cry,
And as a woman, I can't but grieve
To see women like you and Moll and Maeve
With your dues diminished, your favours gone,
While none can enjoy a likely man
But misers sucking a lonely bone
Or hairy old harpies living alone.
I do enact according then
That all the young unmarried men
Shall be arrested by the guard,
Detained within the chapel yard,
Stripped and tied beside the gate,
While you decide upon their fate.
Those that you find whom the years have thwarted
With masculine parts that were never exerted,
To the palpable loss of some woman's employment,
The thrill of the milk and their own enjoyment,
Who having the chance of wife and home,
Took to the hills and lived alone,
Are only a burden on the earth,
So give it to them for all you're worth;
Roast or pickle them; some reflection
Will frame a suitable correction;

That you can fix at your own tribunal
And whatever you do will have my approval.
Fully grown men too old to function
You may punish without the least compunction,
Nothing you do can have consequences
To middle-aged men with failing senses,
And whatever is lost or whatever survives
We need never suppose will affect their wives,
Young men, of course, are another affair.
You may find them of use, so strike with care!

"There are poor men working in rain and sleet
Half out of their minds with the troubles they meet,
But men in name and in deed according,
They comfort their women by night and morning,
As their fathers did to console their mothers,
And these are the men I'd have for lovers.
In the matter of priests a change is due,
And I think I may say that it's coming too,
For any day now it may come to their knowledge
That the case has been judged by the cardinals' college,
And we'll hear no more of the ban on marriage
Before the priests go entirely savage;
And the cry of the blood in the body's fire
You can quicken or quell to your heart's desire,
But anyone else of woman born,
Flay him alive if he won't reform;
Abolish wherever my judgment reaches
The nancy boy and the flapper in breeches,
And when their rule is utterly ended
Give us the world that God intended.

"The rest of the work must only wait,
I'm due elsewhere and already late,
I have business there that I must attend
Though you and I are far from the end,

But I'll sit next month and God help the men
If they haven't improved their ways by then;
And mostly those who sin from pride
With women whose names they do not hide,
Who keep their tally of ruined lives
In whispers, nudges, winks and gibes.
Was ever vanity more misplaced
Than in married women and girls disgraced?
It isn't desire that gives the thrust,
The smoking blood and the ache of lust,
Weakness of love and the body's blindness,
But to punish the fools who show them kindness.
Thousands are born without a name
That braggarts may boast of their mothers' shame,
Men lost to nature through conceit,
And their manhood killed by their own deceit,
For 'tis sure, however, their wives may weep,
It's never because they go short of sleep."

I had listened to every word she uttered,
And then as she stopped my midriff fluttered,
I was took with a sort of sudden reeling
Till my feet seemed resting on the ceiling;
People and place went round and round,
And her words came back as a jumble of sound,
As the bailiff strode along the aisle,
And reached for me with an ugly smile;
She nipped my ear as if in sport
And dragged me out and up the court.
Then the girl who complained of the way she was slighted
Spotted my face and sprang up, delighted.
"Is it you?" says she. "Of all the old crocks,
I'm waiting for years to comb your locks;
You had your chance and missed your shot,
And devil's cure to you now you're caught!
Is there anyone here will speak in your favour,

Or would anyone think you worth the labour?
What little affair would you care to mention
Or whom have you honoured with your attention?
Though we'll all agree that the man's no beauty,
You must admit that he's fit for duty.
I know he's ill-made and as ugly as sin,
But isn't he sound in wind and limb?
I'd sooner him pale and not so plump,
But I've no objection to his hump.
It isn't a feature that intrudes,
Or one that especially goes with prudes;
You find bandy legs with a frolicsome figure
And arms like pegs on a man of vigour;
To be sure the wretch has some secret reason
That kept him single out of season.
As welcome at the country houses,
As at the villagers' carouses;
Called in wherever the fun was going,
And the fiddles being tuned and the whiskey flowing—
I'll never believe that there's truth in a name;
A wonder the Merrymans stand the shame!
The doggedest divil that tramps the hill
With the grey in his hair and a virgin still.
O leave me alone till I settle the savage,
You can spare your breath to cool your porridge
The truth of it's plain upon your forehead,
You're thirty at least and still unmarried!
Listen to me, O Fount of Luck,
This fellow's the worst that ever I struck,
The venom of years that I've locked inside
Won't let me rest till I tan his hide.
Can't you all help me? Catch him! Mind him!
Winnie, girl, run and get ropes to bind him!
Where are you, Annie, or are you blind?
Sally, tie up his hands behind!
Molly and Maeve, you fools, what ails you?

Isn't it soon the courage fails you?
Take the rope and give him a crack,
Earth it up in the small of his back.
That, young man, is the place to hurt you,
We'll teach you to respect your virtue,
Steady now, till we give you a sample—
Women alive, he's a grand example!
Hurry now and we'll nourish him well!
One good clout till we hear him yell!
And the more he yells the harder we'll strike
Till we teach his friends to be more polite.
No blesseder act restored the nation,
We must write the date as a famous occasion,
The First of January, Seventeen Eighty—"

And there I stood, half stripped, half crazy;
For nothing, I felt, could save my skin,
And she opened her book and immersed her pen,
And she wrote it down with careful art,
While the women sighed for the fun to start,
I shivered and gave myself a shake,
Opened my eyes and was wide awake.

Translator Frank O'Connor.

I Am Raftery

BY Anthony Raftery (c. 1784-1835)

I am Raftery the poet,
Full of hope and love,
My eyes without sight,
My mind without torment.

Going west on my journey
By the light of my heart,
Tired and weary
To the end of the road.

Behold me now
With my back to a wall,
Playing music
To empty pockets.

Translator James Stephens.

The County Mayo

BY Anthony Raftery

Now with the coming in of the spring the days will stretch a bit,
And after the Feast of Brigid I shall hoist my flag and go,
For since the thought got into my head I can neither stand
  nor sit
Until I find myself in the middle of the County of Mayo.

In Claremorris I would stop a night and sleep with decent men,
And then go on to Balla just beyond and drink galore,
And next to Kiltimagh for a visit of about a month, and then
I would only be a couple of miles away from Ballymore.

I say and swear my heart lifts up like the lifting of a tide,
Rising up like the rising wind till fog or mist must go,
When I remember Carra and Gallen close beside,
And the Gap of the Two Bushes, and the wide plains of Mayo.

To Killaden then, to the place where everything grows that is
  best,
There are raspberries there and strawberries there and all that
  is good for men;
And if I were only there in the middle of my folk my heart
  could rest,
For age itself would leave me there and I'd be young again.

  Translator James Stephens.

The Brow of Nephin

Did I stand on the bald top of Nefin
    And my hundred-times loved one with me,
We should nestle together as safe in
    Its shade as the birds on a tree.

From your lips such a music is shaken,
    When you speak it awakens my pain,
And my eyelids by sleep are forsaken,
    And I seek for my slumber in vain.

But were I on the fields of the ocean,
    I should sport on its infinite room,
I should plough through the billow's commotion
    Though my friends should look dark at my doom.

For the flower of all maidens of magic
    Is beside me where'er I may be,
Not a woman takes pity on me.
And my heart like a coal is extinguished,

How well for the birds in all weather,
    They rise up on high in the air
And then sleep upon one bough together
    Without sorrow or trouble or care;

But so it is not in this world
    For myself and my thousand times fair,
For away, far apart from each other,
    Each day rises barren and bare.

19TH CENTURY.
Translator Douglas Hyde.

My Grief on the Sea

My grief on the sea,
    How the waves of it roll!
For they heave between me
    And the love of my soul!

Abandoned, forsaken,
    To grief and to care,
Will the sea ever waken
    Relief from despair?

My grief and my trouble!
    Would he and I were
In the province of Leinster
    Or the county of Clare.

Were I and my darling—
    Oh, heart-bitter wound!—
On board of the ship
    For America bound.

On a green bed of rushes
    All last night I lay,
And I flung it abroad
    With the heat of the day.

And my love came behind me—
    He came from the South;
His breast to my bosom.
    His mouth to my mouth.

19TH CENTURY.
Translator Douglas Hyde.

Ringleted Youth of My Love

RINGLETED youth of my love,
    With thy locks bound loosely behind thee,
You passed by the road above,
    But you never came in to find me;
Where were the harm for you
    If you came for a little to see me;
Your kiss is a wakening dew
    Were I ever so ill or so dreamy.

If I had golden store
    I would make a nice little boreen
To lead straight up to his door,
    The door of the house of my storeen;
Hoping to God not to miss
    The sound of his footfall in it,
I have waited so long for his kiss
    That for days I have slept not a minute.

I thought, O my love! you were so—
    As the moon is, or sun on a fountain,
And I thought after that you were snow,
    The cold snow on top of the mountain;
And I thought after that you were more
    Like God's lamp shining to find me,
Or the bright star of knowledge before,
    And the star of knowledge behind me.

You promised me high-heeled shoes,
    And satin and silk, my storeen,
And to follow me, never to lose,
    Though the ocean were round us roaring,
Like a bush in a gap in a wall
    I am now left lonely without thee,
And this house, I grow dead of, is all
    That I see around or about me.

19TH CENTURY.
Translator Douglas Hyde.

I Shall Not Die For Thee

For thee I shall not die,
    Woman high of fame and name;
Foolish men thou mayest slay,
    I and they are not the same.

Why should I expire
    For the fire of any eye,
Slender waist or swan-like limb,
    Is't for them that I should die?

The round breasts, the fresh skin,
    Cheeks crimson, hair so long and rich;
Indeed, indeed, I shall not die,
    Please God, not I, for any such.

The golden hair, the forehead then,
    The chaste mien, the gracious ease,
The rounded heel, the languid tone,
    Fools alone find death from these.

Thy sharp wit, thy perfect calm,
   Thy thin palm like foam of sea;
Thy white neck, thy blue eye,
   I shall not die for thee.

Woman, graceful as the swan,
   A wise man did nurture me,
Little palm, white neck, bright eye,
   I shall not die for thee.

19TH CENTURY.
Translator Douglas Hyde.